BEYOND THE
BESTSELLER

BEYOND THE BESTSELLER

A LITERARY AGENT TAKES YOU INSIDE THE BOOK BUSINESS

RICHARD CURTIS

NAL BOOKS

NEW AMERICAN LIBRARY

A DIVISION OF PENGUIN BOOKS USA INC., NEW YORK
PUBLISHED IN CANADA BY
PENGUIN BOOKS CANADA LIMITED, MARKHAM, ONTARIO

Copyright © 1989 by Richard Curtis

All rights reserved. For information address New American Library.

Published simultaneously in Canada by Penguin Books Canada Limited.

Portions of this book have previously appeared as articles in *Locus* magazine.

 NAL BOOKS TRADEMARK REG. U.S. PAT. OFF. AND FOREIGN COUNTRIES
REGISTERED TRADEMARK—MARCA REGISTRADA
HECHO EN DRESDEN, TN, USA

SIGNET, SIGNET CLASSIC, MENTOR, ONYX, PLUME, MERIDIAN
and NAL BOOKS are published *in the United States* by New American Library,
a division of Penguin Books USA Inc.,
1633 Broadway, New York, New York 10019,
in Canada by Penguin Books Canada Limited,
2801 John Street, Markham, Ontario L3R 1B4

Library of Congress Cataloging-in-Publication Data

Curtis, Richard.
  Beyond the bestseller : a literary agent takes you inside the book
  business / by Richard Curtis.
    p.   cm.
    ISBN 0-453-00670-1
    1. Book industries and trade. 2. Publishers and publishing.
  3. Authors and publishers. 4. Literary agents. 5. Authorship.
  I. Title.
  Z278.C85   1989
  070.5'2—dc19   88-35322
                                                                      CIP

Designed by Mari De Mitchell

First Printing, May, 1989

    2   3   4   5   6   7   8   9

PRINTED IN THE UNITED STATES OF AMERICA

*This book is lovingly
dedicated to Leslie,
my wife and best friend*

Contents

Section One—Agents Demystified

Section Two—Breaking In

Section Three—Busting Out

Section Four—Sins of Commission

Section Five—Manners and Morals

Section Six—Publishing and Perishing

Section Seven—Let's Work It Out

Preface

This book was born out of my frustration with the fact that nobody seemed to be making sense out of the terrible upheavals taking place in the publishing industry over the last decade, or expressing alarm over the threat they posed to everyone associated with books. In the early 1980s, as I began to grasp the immensity and the implications of these changes, I proposed to write a monthly column for *Locus*, the leading trade publication catering to science fiction writers, publishers, and fans. Science fiction writers have always been among the most concerned members of the writing profession, and the most aggressive in the protection of authors' interests. I suspected that a series of articles written by an active literary agent examining and evaluating publishing practices would find a responsive audience. This turned out to be true.

The column, "Agent's Corner," first saw the light of day early in 1981, and out of the first two dozen or so pieces I developed my book, *How to Be Your Own Literary Agent*. Although the book contained a number of critical observations about the way things are done in the book trade, its purpose was largely instructional. I had realized that most authors were appallingly uninformed about the business side of writing. Despite many unhappy experiences they'd had in their dealings with publishers, they did not seem to realize that knowledge is the best armor, and my book set out to enlighten them about contracts, rights, royalty statements, and other fundamentals.

After publication of that book in 1983, I continued to produce my column but ventured to explore in it some provocative issues revolving around business ethics, authors' rights, and the future of the publishing and writing professions. How does the acquisition of one publisher by another ruin authors, paralyze editorial processes, and orphan books? Why is the publishing industry collapsing under the weight of an archaic merchandising system? Is unionization of authors a realistic possibility? Should publishers turn down books on moral grounds? Are editors necessary any longer? These are some of the major questions you will find discussed in the following pages.

Not all of the matters I wrote about were of such profound moment, however. I've continued to instruct and, on the principle that a drop of honey makes the medicine taste better, tried where appropriate to entertain. So you will also discover in this book my thoughts about such topics as: How should writers behave when they deal with editors? What are some of the things authors do that annoy their agents? Are there better and worse publication dates for your book? And—one of my favorites—should agents lend money to their clients? Though these questions are pretty basic, I am constantly amazed to discover that most writers I meet have seldom been given any guidance on them by their agents, editors, or writer friends.

The response to these articles has been inspiring. They seem to have had an impact not only on novice writers but on successful professionals as well, on my fellow literary agents, on publishing people at every level, and on members of other professions such as accountants and lawyers. Apparently, a great many people connected with this business are worried and disillusioned, and not a few are angry. I was particularly impressed by the supportive reactions of editors, who have begun to realize that they are becoming as alienated from the system as authors.

Having pinpointed some of the most pressing problems, I have not been content to lament the decline of our industry and let it go at that. I have instead attempted to prescribe specific and positive solutions. Some are simple and practical. Others are visionary, even revolutionary. If they stimulate a dialogue and produce some healthy changes, I shall be quite content. Some of the criticisms I leveled in my last book about the way publishers report royalties to authors raised the consciousness of a whole generation of writers about these procedures and led to improvement at a number of houses in the rendering of statements. So, change for the good is possible once everybody has enough information to work with.

The most important discovery I made as I assembled this manuscript is how strongly I feel that publishers and literary agents, in whom tremendous power is vested, have a social responsibility. The publishing and writing professions find themselves in, perhaps, the most precarious state of all time. Stupendous economic and technological forces have radically transformed both in recent times, and the emerging interrelationships among editors, authors, and agents are almost unrecognizable from what they were even a few short years ago. Authors, editors, and even whole publishing companies are being swept out of the business, and the stability of an industry that nurtured the development of America's greatest literary figures has been shattered. If anything stands out for me as I prepare this book for publication, it is the realization that we are in equal jeopardy from the volcanic changes that the publishing industry is undergoing. If we do not find a way to confront the perils courageously, we may one day find ourselves equal victims of a tragedy that will leave everyone connected with literature, including you the reader, irreversibly impoverished.

Richard Curtis
New York City
August 1988

Acknowledgments

Virtually all of the material in this book originally appeared in *Locus*, the trade publication of the science fiction world. Its publisher, Charles Brown, offered me carte blanche in the selection and treatment of my subjects, a rare commitment for which I am immeasurably grateful. Without the forum provided by Charlie, there would be no book here.

I wish to thank the executive staff of my publisher, New American Library, for its sensitivity and responsiveness. In particular, Elaine Koster, Robert Diforio, Alan Kaufman, Arnold Dolin, and Judith Richard have been most supportive. Though they may not always endorse my views, their tolerance in permitting me to express them has been tremendously gratifying.

My editor, John Silbersack, offered splendid guidance in the organization and refinement of the text and was most patient with me on the occasions when I behaved like an author. And I thank him for reminding me that editors have to eat, too.

My copy editor, Willa Speiser, performed an exemplary rendering of her craft, and I hereby exempt her from any criticism of her colleagues to be found in the text.

Above all, I thank my wife, Leslie, who among her countless other virtues is an inspiring editor and shrewd critic. Her influence is palpable on every page of this work.

And now for a word about sex.

Though I've tried wherever possible to refer to persons of both sexes as "he and she," the English language has yet to create a graceful solution to this frustrating problem. It is particularly galling for people in the publishing business, an industry as sensitive to feminist sensibilities as any in the world and one whose work and executive forces are at least fifty percent female. The best I can do is to rely, as I did in my previous book, on the publishing tradition in which, on most contracts, the masculine pronoun signifies writers of either sex. But I don't like it, and I apologize to any reader who may take offense.

Section One

Agents Demystified

CHAPTER 1

Clout

Whenever authors gather to discuss the merits of their agents (it may legitimately be wondered whether they ever discuss anything else), the word "clout" inevitably enters the conversation. Clout is the measure of an agent's influence over publishers, and though it is by no means the sole criterion by which agents are judged, it is certainly the ultimate one. What is clout? How do agents wield it? And is it everything we crack it up to be?

The definition of clout has two important components. The first is access: the enclouted agent is intimate with the most powerful men and women in the publishing industry. "They put me through to the head of the company whenever I call," an agent might boast. Or, "I can have your manuscript on the editor-in-chief's desk tomorrow morning."

The second component is power, the capability to effect, yea to coerce, positive decisions. The agent with clout does not merely have access to the honchos (and honchas) of certain publishing companies, he has the ability to make them say yes, and to say yes when they would have said no to some other agent.

Unquestionably, clout exists in our business as it does in any other, and there are indeed agents who can make publishers jump every time they call them on the phone, or render a positive verdict when they were originally inclined to render a negative one. At the same time, there are many erroneous impressions about clout stemming from the widely held belief that power in publishing is concentrated in the hands of an elite

3

circle of men and women, a belief promoted by the press, which tends to quote the same people every time it does a story on industry trends. Let's look a little closer at these impressions.

1. *Agents with clout know the top people in the business.* It is not that hard to meet and know, or at least claim to know, the top people in publishing. For one thing, ours is an extremely small industry consisting, according to my short list of key contacts, of no more than two or three hundred men and women with acquisition authority in the trade book field, a number sufficiently small so that in the course of a season of publishing parties, lunch and drink dates, and office visits, any agent could meet 75 percent of them.

Of course, it is one thing to be acquainted with these folks and quite another to truly know them as one knows friends or family. Among that two or three hundred I mentioned, I doubt if I know more than half a dozen in a way that goes beyond the superficial. More pertinent is whether an agent *should* be too tight with the people he does business with. If my own experience is indicative, I would say there are few true friendships between agents and publishers for the simple reason that business all too often gets in the way of consistently close friendship. A time inevitably comes when one or the other must get hard-nosed about something, and few friendships survive the test of a knock-down drag-out negotiation, for it's impossible to dig in and take a hard stand when you're afraid of hurting the other guy's feelings. Bear in mind also that as genuinely warmly as agent and publisher may feel toward each other, the former is responsible to his clients, the latter to his company, and the pressures exerted on them are immensely daunting to friendship. The most one can hope for, I think, is solid mutual respect.

As for an agent's boasts of his ability to get an author's manuscript promptly on a publisher's desk, it's hard not to laugh, for if you could see some publishers' desks you would wonder why anyone would want to add to the mountainous chaos to be found there. I know of one editor whose office is so cluttered with unread manuscripts that his staff calls it the Bermuda Triangle. A story is told that one day an agent received a manuscript that this editor had finally gotten around to reading and rejecting. The agent dropped him a line thanking him for at last returning the script, but pointed out that the book had been sold to another publisher, published, gone on and off the best-seller list, and been remaindered.

The truth is that most heads of publishing companies have too much administrative work to read manuscripts or even, for that matter, read all the books their firms are publishing. I would guess that more than half the time, when an agent submits a manuscript to the head of the company, that person is going to turn it over to an editor or reader and ask for a report. Unless the report is a rave, this executive will take the reader's word about the merits of the work. And again one has to ask, is going to the head of the company necessarily the wise thing to do? This tactic can backfire for an agent, for if the publisher thinks the manuscript is a stinker, he may be less inclined the next time to spend a valuable evening reading that agent's submission. An agent's credibility is his stock in trade, and once lost it's extremely hard to retrieve. Best to go through channels 99 percent of the time, and to be damned sure about the one time in a hundred you attack at the top.

One more myth about accessibility. It's commonly believed that clout among agents is the power not to return phone calls. Although executives in all industries have their phone calls screened by subordinates, I know of few agents who are not available to the lowliest of editors or to any professional author desirous of speaking to them.

2. *Agents with clout can make publishers buy things they wouldn't ordinarily buy.* The judicious use of a close association with a publisher can made a difference in certain cases, particularly when a close decision teeters on the fulcrum of the key man's or woman's opinion. On such an occasion the agent may call in a favor, or beg one, or utilize any of his countless wiles ranging from bluster to blarney in order to elicit a yes decision. But because of the democratic process by which most decisions are reached by publishing companies today, few chief executives are going to make it a practice to overrule their editorial boards. The agent who tries to force positive decisions too often will eventually antagonize even his closest buddies in the business.

But I'm not sure that making the head of a company buy books is the best use for such personages, for, as I say, they are not as influential editorially as they are in other areas of the publishing process. The higher in a company that an editor rises the less he is involved in editorial matters and the more in administrative ones. The editor-in-chief, publisher, and other titled executives are the principal transmitters of corporate policy. Such matters as advertising and promotional budgets, payout schedules, royalty scales, and reserves against returns are controlled by those persons, and if there is any flexibility on policies in such areas, it's to be found in their offices. And it's there that the agent is best advised to use his clout, except that clout is a terribly brutish word for a process that calls for the utmost finesse and diplomatic skill.

Because publishing in the last three decades has become highly conglomeratized and bureaucratized, decisions that used to be made by just one person who was accountable to nobody are now made by committee. Consensus is achieved by the input not merely of editors but of financial, legal, production, marketing, advertising, design, art, promotional, publicity, and advertising specialists. These individuals form a dismaying picket of decision-makers, each a potential nay-sayer. The agent's task thus becomes far more challenging than it used to be: It is no longer a matter of bullying, coaxing, or charming one person but of manipulating an entire system. Naturally, an agent can't approach the art director, head of subsidiary rights, in-house counsel, marketing director, vice-president in charge of publicity, and the half dozen editors who sit at a publisher's weekly convocations, whenever he tries to sell the company a book. But he might speak to one or two key board members whose reluctance to vote yes may be jeopardizing a deal or other important decision. The full measure of the agent's tact must be used here, for if he blunders the reaction may be likened to what happens when one inserts one's arm into a hornet's nest. Only at the utmost risk do you play office politics with somebody else's office.

One of the advantages a literary agent has over the unagented author is that the agent is usually familiar with the dynamics of each publishing house and is able to adapt his methods to the style and structure and personality of each company. He knows all about their organizational structure and power hierarchy, their policies, their negotiating strategies, knows all about the friendships and rivalries that form the corporate profile. To know how a company reaches its decisions is to know how to influence those decisions.

One may learn for instance who sits on the editorial board and how much weight is attached to the contribution of each member. If one member carries an undue amount of power, the agent might acquaint himself with him or her so that when an important decision is to be reached by the board sometime in the future, the agent might contact and seek that person's help.

There are other techniques for influencing decisions from without, ranging from relatively harmless ones such as cultivating and flattering secretaries (of either sex, I hasten to add) to the extremely dangerous one of going over the head of the person you're dealing with. For the agent who does not understand the company dynamic, who misjudges it, or who overplays the game, serious and possibly permanent damage may be rendered to his relations with that publisher. Some firms are so rigidly structured that any attempt to tamper with the system will create terrible turmoil.

Some years ago I was negotiating a contract with an editor who was obdurate in her espousal of company policy on certain terms, terms I knew could be relaxed if only she would speak to her boss. But I couldn't get her to speak to her boss. Luckily for me, or so I thought, I was having lunch with the man that week, and so I asked him if he wouldn't mind saying a word or two to his young editor. He said he'd think about it, but I thought I detected a cloud crossing his face. The next day the young editor phoned me. "I understand you've been trying to get my boss to pressure me," she said indignantly. "Well, he's referred the matter back to me and the answer is still no, and please don't do that again." The organization had closed ranks around its own, and my ploy had flopped.

In another instance, the editor of a terrific book that had just been published complained to me that his boss wasn't getting behind it, and alas this editor had no influence over her. I said, "Do you think If I wrote her a letter she might be more responsive to your suggestions?" He beamed. It sounded like a great idea. So I wrote his boss a letter that started, "Once a year I presume to tell a publisher how to run his business, and this is that once a year." I went on to praise the book fulsomely, to beg her to throw her influence behind it, and I even enclosed rave reviews on the chance she'd been too busy to see them.

The result? I got a call a few days later from the editor. He'd been called on his boss's carpet and chewed out within an inch of his job for promoting this bit of chicanery.

3. *Agents with clout get higher prices.* There is a good deal of truth to this but not necessarily for the reasons you think. High prices are a function of boldness; you get big money only if you ask big money. Agents with reputations for landing huge deals earn their celebrity by seeking prices that other agents would hesitate to demand, and by risking everything by refusing to back down. But it takes two to make a deal, and if publishers accept an agent's demands, it's because the profit-and-loss statements they've drawn up before negotiations commence indicate that they can make a profit even if they meet the agent's outrageous terms. If a publisher takes a bath the fault rests with the executives who wanted the book so badly they were willing to delude themselves about its prospects in order to acquire it. Of course, one thing that agents with clout do best is foster such delusions by reassuring publishers that they will earn back all that money. But seldom can an agent charm a publisher into overpaying again and again, for at a certain point along the chain of failures, people start getting fired.

I do know of one agent who used to move an author from one publisher to another, getting high prices for him by inflating the previous publisher's sales figures but giving the new publisher so little time to make a decision that it was impossible to check the numbers furnished by the agent. Thus did this nomadic author wander from publisher to publisher, trailing clouds of hype, until his agent's reputation caught up with him. Today such a tactic would be extremely hard to bring off, because publishers have much better access to each other's sales figures and demand verification before committing themselves to a deal.

Don't forget, too, that agents usually publicize the huge prices they get (and often puff up the modest ones), which attracts big-name authors and celebrities who command high prices too. Eventually the agent's "stable" is packed with thoroughbreds, and the cycle of high prices becomes self-perpetuating.

One last myth about clout that deserves to be punctured: It is seldom exercised by means of a raised voice. The image of a cigar-chomping agent-bully browbeating an editor into submission is not one with which I'm familiar except in movies. Almost all of the agents I know ply their trade in conversational tones, even when the going gets rough. One of the most clout-laden ones I know seldom raises his voice above a whisper, but heaven help the publisher who does not detect the apocalyptic undertones in his voice when he murmurs, "Are you sure that's your final offer?"

I believe the reason he doesn't have to shout is that he's realized that in the last analysis, true clout resides not in good agents but in good authors.

There are hundreds of literary agents plying their trade in New York, California, and many locations between coasts, and I'd guess that you've never heard of most of them. They don't get their names and faces in the trade papers every week like some agents we all know. Yet almost all of them make a living, and some make very good livings indeed, simply because they know that a good book is the master key to most editorial doors. So perhaps you should ask not what your agent can do for you, but what—by way of a good book—you can do for your agent.

CHAPTER 2

All Agencies Great and Small

I'm not sure that authors understand the structures of literary agencies much better than they understand those of publishing companies. For those of you who are shopping for an agent or thinking of switching agencies, or who are simply interested in organizational dynamics, it might be interesting to compare agencies of different sizes and structures and to discuss the advantages and disadvantages of each type.

I am keenly aware, as I marshal my thoughts, of how completely dependent on personalities is the quality of service offered by the various kinds of agencies. On every level, from the one-celled organism known as the sole practitioner to the highly complex bicoastal giants like William Morris, you can find many marvelous agents. And many considerably less than marvelous.

First, but not least, is the one-man or one-woman agency. And when I say *one* man or woman I don't mean one man or woman plus a secretary, for, as we shall soon see, the presence of a second person can radically alter an agent's style, service, and clout. Most such agents start out either as editors of publishing companies or as staff members of large agencies; a few join our profession from the legal and other related fields. To agenting they bring their special knowledge and experience and those are always big pluses for prospective clients. They can also be handicaps, however. The lawyer who becomes a literary agent will soon discover that publishing law is so vastly different in theory and practice from any other kind of law as to render his training and experience virtually useless. Agents who leave big agencies to set up their own don't always make good agents, as they may be unused to operating outside the context of a supporting organization. Editors who become agents may know a great deal about publishing procedures, but that knowledge doesn't necessarily make them good deal-makers. I remember getting a distress call from a former paperback editor who had started her agency about a year before. "Can I ask you a dumb question?" she said.

"Sure."

"Where do these publishers get the nerve to sit on money for so long?"

I gritted my teeth. "I could strangle you. A year ago when you worked for a publisher yourself, you had every excuse in the book for sitting on money. I remember you even telling me the treasurer had been bitten by a *dog*! So, nobody should know the answer to your question better than you. If you want to know how to *get* the money, you can treat me to a very long lunch."

The sole practitioner must do everything by and for himself, and from an author's viewpoint there are many desirable aspects of such a setup. Chief among them is accessibility. Phone answering machines or services notwithstanding, you know that when you call your agent, you will get him or her. That means you can maximize your input, communications, and control, which is great unless your input, communications, and control happen to be lousy. Remember that you hired an agent in the first place because you need someone who understands the publishing business better than you, someone who is more experienced and skillful in negotiations, is more objective, and remains calm when push comes to shove. If you take advantage of your agent's accessibility, then all you are doing is manipulating him like a puppet, programming into him the very same emotional shortcomings that you most desperately need to be defended from.

For the sole practitioner, the credit for success belongs exclusively to him or her, and deservedly so. But so, deservedly, does the blame for mistakes. Because there is no insulation between author and agent, both positive and negative emotions tend to run stronger than they might if the author were not so intimate with everything having to do with the handling of his business. Indeed, the author represented by a sole practitioner is all too often quite intimate with the business of his agent's other clients, too, and among the emotions that run strongly in these cases, therefore, is jealousy.

In short, you cannot ask for more personalized service than you get when you engage a one-man or one-woman agency, and if the relationship is solid and harmonious it can be like owning a custom-made automobile. But custom-made automobiles tend to react oversensitively to every bump in the road. And their owners tend to tinker with them.

From the viewpoint of one who has been a sole practitioner, the biggest disadvantage is that the one-person company cannot utilize what businesspeople refer to as a "devil," someone to blame.

It is essential for the new agent to cultivate and ingratiate himself with the influential editors in the business. Needless to say, this agent will be loath to alienate those editors by being overly tough and demanding in negotiations. If an agent starting out in business gets a reputation for being unreasonable, he may lose business. He can of course blame his intransigence on his clients, but in most cases the editors will know it's not the author who's the troublemaker, but his agent. Besides, one of the things authors hire agents for is to take the fire for hard decisions in order to allow clients to maintain pleasant working relationships with editors. If only there were someone working for your agent with whom he could play Good Guy-Bad Guy, he could have some leeway when it comes to playing hardball. His associate might sometimes serve as the devil, taking tough positions in negotiations. Then, just when it looked as if a deal was going to fall through, his boss would intervene and offer a compromise that mitigated his employee's inflexibility. In other cases the assistant could be the good guy who wishes he could be more lenient but, well, his boss is a tough bird who simply will not yield.

This may be the commonest game played by businessmen and women, but it requires two to each side, and the sole practitioner is one shy of that minimum. Exposed as he or she is, the one-man or one-woman agent must, almost by defini-tion, be a courageous individual.

With the introduction of a second person into the agency—even a secretary with no discretionary power—the dynamics of the firm usually alter sharply. The agent can if he chooses make himself less accessible, a state that is often tactically desirable. He at last has somebody to blame, perhaps not for negotiating and other serious mistakes, but at least for some of the clerical screwups that bedevil all business enterprises. On the other hand, the operation of the business should become more effi-cient, a fair tradeoff for the agent's withdrawal from the firing line. If the employee is anything more than a warm body occupying a desk, he or she can create some important oppor-tunities for strategic games, can serve as a reader rendering a second viewpoint on the salability of manuscripts or as a sound-ing board for marketing, negotiating, and other decisions. And if that person is interested in and good at certain specialized tasks—handling movie, television, magazine, or foreign rights, for example—or has a good grasp of certain markets that the boss has no interest in or feel for, or if he or she is good at handling certain clients—then you have the makings of a potent team and the foundation for a successful agency.

From that point on it becomes a matter of adding new staff members and deploying them according to the organization that best suits the agent's style—a style that may transmute as the agent gains experience. As a rule, the smaller the agency the less specialized are the tasks performed by its staff: Everybody, in other words, handles everything. As the firm grows, a struc-ture usually emerges along lines of staff specialization. One structure might be described as vertical, with the agent at the pinnacle handling the clients, supported by a staff that services the clients' properties but does not necessarily have contact with the clients themselves. One staff member might handle foreign rights, another movie, another serial, another book-keeping, another filing, and so on.

The advantage of vertical system, generally, is excellent service, for every aspect of the client's needs, every facet of the property, will be taken care of by a specialist. The disadvantage is that the client list must be kept relatively small—no larger than the capacity of the head of the company to handle his clients' work and needs comfortably. Another disadvantage is the vulnerability of the agency in the event of the death or disability of its owner, for there will be no one with deep experience at handling clients to take his or her place. If the agent should go out of town for an extended trip or vacation, the agency may be reduced to a maintenance capacity and not be capable of dealing forcefully with the sorts of emergencies that always seem to attack writers the moment their agents board an airplane.

As an agent becomes successful he will be solicited by many authors seeking representation. Many are excellent writers with good track records who need the guidance and assistance of a good agency. A combination of profit motive and compassion will compel the agent to offer representation to them. But—how can he fit them into his stable without curtailing the time, attention, and service he is now able to lavish on the rest of his clients?

Some agents resist this temptation, harden their hearts, and shut their doors to newcomers. Others resort to hiring employees to handle the overflow of clients. An agency engaging a roster of agents might be described as horizontal, and obviously there is no limit to the number of clients such a firm can take on, for as soon as it reaches capacity it can always add a new agent to take on the excess. The boss will still be the boss, and there will still be a staff of specialists to handle subsidiary rights and clerical and administrative functions. But on the middle level will be these other agents, replicating what their boss does. They may be generalists, handling the gamut of literature from genre to mainstream, or they may deal in such specialties as juveniles, nonfiction, or science fiction. I would say that most middle-sized and large agencies fit this horizontal pattern; in fact, it's hard to imagine how an agency can become large unless it does expand horizontally.

From the writer's viewpoint, an agency of this type is attractive for several reasons. First, it enables him to locate within the organization the individual agent best suited to his work and style. Second, if the organization is well run, he will enjoy the benefit of a team approach under the supervision of the principal agent. And third, if one's agent is out of town or on vacation, or is so thoughtless as to die, there is a good likelihood that he will find a replacement in the ranks of the other agents at the same firm. In other words, the bumpy ups and downs you often experience with a one-person agency will be absorbed by a larger organization, and that is a secure feeling. But there's also a catch.

Most clients of middle-sized and large agencies are content to be represented by an agent who is not the head man or woman, as long as there is a sense that the chief is at least overseeing the work of the subordinate agents and making sure that all of the agency's authors are being properly serviced. Inherent in the very nature of large organizations, however, is a degree of insulation between the head of the company and the activities of those clients he or she does not directly represent. If an author begins to feel that the agent handling his work is not doing an adequate job, he may conclude that the head of the company has more important concerns than the scribblings of a fifteen-thousand-dollar-a-year midlist writer. Thus is created what might be described as the "A List–B List Syndrome," meaning that the agency has two client lists: the Grade A clients handled by the boss, and the Grade B ones handled by the secondary agents. When that sort of suspicion begins to gnaw at a client, he may eventually decide he must either move up or move out and seek an agency where he will receive more personal attention from the top agent.

It is therefore incumbent on the heads of agencies to make sure that the subordinate agents keep in very close touch with him and with each other. At many agencies, that is precisely what happens. In others, the boss has administrative and client demands that make supervision of the other agents' activities difficult. Now, it can certainly be assumed that some of those agents are ambitious, and so an atmosphere is created in which a subordinate agent, operating with little supervision, begins to wonder just what he needs a boss for anyway. He may be making a good salary and even collecting commissions, but as so much of the revenue he generates must go to paying overhead and a profit to the firm he works for, as surely as the sun will rise tomorrow will the idea occur to him that he could do better on his own. For many of his clients, the notion of joining this agent when he starts his own agency is extremely appealing, for in a stroke those clients will be transformed from B Listers to A Listers. Things don't always turn out as satisfyingly as that fantasy, though, for the agent may discover that he does not, on his own, enjoy the same influence he did when he was a member of a large and influential organization. It is extremely hard and perhaps impossible for the client of a larger agency to sort out just what is the true source of his agent's power and success. Does the person handling you consult with the head of the company or is he handling your account strictly on his own? Is his effectiveness due in good measure to the influence, reputation, and support of his organization, or are these incidental to his performance? Some authors discover the answers to these questions by leaving; others, by staying on.

At the summit are the giant agencies, representing many illustrious authors, extremely well connected in the movie and television area, and moving tremendous amounts of properties, rights, and money. These firms are often broken down into departments, and you the author will be handled by someone in the literary department. These departments usually have senior and junior staff members and operate as potent fiefdoms in a great bicoastal kingdom. Because the overhead of these firms is stupendous, the clients they take on must be pretty heavy hitters and often are authors whose work is highly adaptable to film and television. The disadvantage is the intimidating vastness of such organizations.

Somewhere in all this is a place for you, and in few businesses is it more true that what's great for one person may be awful for another. I doubt if many authors retain one agent for the span of their entire career. Indeed, for the sake of an author's personal growth, having the same agent from cradle to grave may be a very poor idea.

At least, that's what I tell myself whenever I lose a client.

CHAPTER 3

Rivals

At a gathering of literary agents, one of my friends told me about a particularly difficult author who had asked him to represent her. He had turned her down. She had then asked him if he would be good enough to suggest another agent who might want to take her on. When he told me the name of the agent he'd referred her to, I blinked. "Why'd you do that? You hate that agent!"

"Oh," he smiled, "I only refer authors to agents I hate."

This remark raises some questions about the relations among literary agents. Are they friendly with each other? Are they mutually suspicious or hostile? Do they steal authors from each other at every opportunity? Do they cooperate with one another? Do they have a code of behavior? Are they too competitive to act collectively?

To the extent that the book publishing business is a pie to be sliced into just so many pieces, and the number of profitable authors is a finite one, I suppose it can be argued that agents are rivals. Yet I don't think most agents feel that way. Unlike some other businesses we can think of, where the survival of one firm is achieved only at the expense of another, there appears to be enough business in the publishing field to enable all literary agents who stay in the game long enough and run their businesses prudently to earn a living and to be gracious toward each other while doing so. Though we have seen bad times in our industry, they have never been so bad that there was not a publisher somewhere buying books. Nor has the pool of potential clients ever shrunk to the degree that a resourceful agent could not find authors to make money with. In short, I don't believe agents lose too much sleep worrying that the supply of or the demand for their products and services is going to dry up.

What agents do worry about is maximizing the earning power of their clients, helping their authors realize the full measure of their talents and exploiting every bit of financial potential in their work: to put it plainly, to make them rich and famous. Obviously, the agent whose clients become rich and famous will become rich and famous too. And, just as obviously, a dissatisfied author will eventually seek new representation.

And it is here that agents sometimes start throwing elbows.

Authors don't live in caves. They talk to each other, belong to writers groups, attend conventions, visit their publishers. If they are unhappy with their agents they will ask fellow writers or editors to recommend other agents, and they will get in touch with them. Now, there is nothing among agents like the formalized codes of ethics to be found in the medical and legal professions, but if there is one point of honor among literary agents, it rests on the question of soliciting each other's clients. Essentially, the formulation is, if the author is determined to leave his current agent, he is fair game. But if he's not certain, if he's sort of thinking out loud, just window-shopping as it were, the agent of the second part is obliged to display restraint in his efforts to woo the author away from the agent of the first part. Oh, he may sing the virtues of his agency, but must at the same time make it clear that only after the author has expressly notified his other agent that he is leaving him may one proffer representation.

Antagonism between agents flares up over the interpretation of just how loudly, sweetly, and aggressively an agent sings his firm's praises to the interested author. You might think of it as the Smoking Gun theory of client-stealing: If the author walks in the door of another agency in a state of uncertainty but walks out clutching a signed agreement with his new agent, it can be inferred that something considerably more than a soft sell occurred behind that door. At least, most of the time such an inference is justified. But not always. Many an author not comfortable with his agent has visited another agency and, with little persuasion, realized from a brief chat and a look around and a sniff of the atmosphere that he has been much more than not comfortable with his agent; he has actually been quite miserable with his old agent but could not admit it until that moment.

However that may be so, the author's old agent is going to strongly suspect that the other agent gave a snow job to his former client. Because I treasure the friendships of (most of) my colleagues, I call them when I become the beneficiary of a former client of theirs, to reassure them that I did not actively solicit that client, and to pave the way for cooperation on old business concerning that author. And I have always appreciated it when my colleagues did the same for me. In some cases, when the parting is friendly and by mutual consent, agents will refer authors to other agents—and I don't mean agents they hate.

Most agents have had the experience of having their colleagues refer clients to them. In many cases this is intended, and should be regarded by the recipient of the referral, as a genuine favor. Some agents have become too successful and busy to handle authors who are still struggling to find their stride, and they generously offer such promising writers to fellow agents whose stables still have some unoccupied stalls. Or an agent may confess that he does not have a good "feel" for a genre or writing style but knows of a colleague who specializes in science fiction or juveniles or avant-garde literature.

In point of fact, agents work with each other to a much greater degree than they work against each other. I do know of a few suspicious, curmudgeonly types who jealously guard their flocks as if their colleagues were wolves poised to pounce on helpless clients and carry them off to their lairs. And I suppose there is in all of us a certain degree of what the Germans call *Schadenfreude*, which might be defined as pleasure in a friend's misfortunes. But on the whole, agents enjoy each other's company, help each other, are anxious to remain on one another's good side, and to a degree act collectively on matters that affect their community of interest.

Agents call each other frequently seeking advice on all manner of problems: Who do you know at Random House? How do you phrase your option clause? Who's buying westerns? How did you conduct that auction? How did you get that terrific price? What should I do about this problem client?

On occasion, agents cooperate on deals. For instance, if an author leaving Agent A wishes Agent B to handle subsidiary rights to his old books—a situation fraught with the potential for contention—the two agents might work things out so that they split a commission. Agent A will be satisfied because he doesn't have to do all that much work to earn his share of the commission, and Agent B will be satisfied because he didn't have to sell the books originally.

In other cases, such as collaborations, there may be two agents for two authors and the agents work out the division of labor and commissions. I may have a client with a fantastic story to tell who can't write, but I don't represent quite the right author to team up with him. And my buddy Agent X may have just the right author. After exploring the questions of our clients' compatibility and the division of work and money, Agent X and I discuss just how we're going to cooperate. Am I going to be the principal agent in making a deal with the publisher? If so, am I to take my commission off the top—off the total advance, that is—or do I take my commission only on that portion of the advance allocated to my client? Who is going to handle the subsidiary rights, Agent X or my agency? You can see that unless there is a solid friendship and abundant goodwill between agents, there is going to be friction, and in potentially fatal doses. Many a lucrative deal has gone down the tubes because two agents couldn't reach agreement on such matters. An editor recently told me about a meeting in her office of two agent heavyweights, one whose client possessed the essential source material for a book, the other representing a star author whose byline and talent guaranteed a best-seller. The discussions went swimmingly until the question of commissions was raised. "Since I brought this project to the publisher and made the deal," said the first agent, "I expect to get my commission off the top. You can take your commission out of your client's share, net after I have taken my commission."

"Uh-uh," said the second agent. "My client is critical to the success of this book. I want a commission off the top too."

The first agent glared at him for a moment, then rose and went to the phone on the editor's desk.

"Who are you calling?" the editor asked.

"My driver," said the agent. And that was the end of that.

CHAPTER 4

What I Have Done for You Lately

One day, I got a phone call from an agitated editor. His voice was trembling and he could scarcely contain his emotion. The emotion was fear.

It seems that a hotheaded client of mine had gotten so upset over some editorial work done on his book that he'd threatened in a loud voice, during a visit to the editor's office, to pulp his face. Some of his colleagues had interceded and ushered the distraught author out of the building. Of course, beating up your editor is a time-honored writer's fantasy, but my client had taken it further than most authors do. Pulping an editor's face is a serious breach of etiquette. "What can I do to help?" I offered.

"Restrain him," the editor said.

"You mean, physically?"

"Yes, if need be."

I could not suppress an ill-timed laugh.

"What the hell is so funny?" he demanded.

"Well," I said, "I've done everything else, I might as well be a bodyguard for an editor, too."

After settling the dispute by eliciting promises of good behavior from my client and assurances of more thoughtful blue-pencilling from the editor, I reflected on some of the unusual things that agents are called upon to do in the course of their careers. I am often asked to speak to groups of aspiring writers and to explain just what literary agents do. I wonder how the audience would react if I told them that among other things, literary agents babysit for their clients' kids, paint their clients'

22

houses, and bail their clients out of jail. They even fall in love with their clients and marry them. In fact, I have done all these things and more.

A brochure issued by one literary agents' organization describes some functions that authors should not expect their agents to perform. Most of my colleagues would lose half their clients overnight if they took these guidelines seriously, however. For instance, the brochure advises that you shouldn't expect your agent to edit your book. But most agents I know would consider themselves remiss if they did not do some light, and sometimes heavy, editing to improve a book's chances of acceptance, help the author modify a manuscript for magazine serialization, or simply make it the best book it can be.

Here are some other things the brochure mentions:

• *The agent cannot solve authors' personal problems.* As a writer myself, and a friend or agent of many writers, I can testify how tightly interconnected the personal, financial, and creative elements of an author's life are. Trouble in one area almost invariably indicates trouble in the others. The agent who turns his back on an author's personal problems may well be diminishing that author's earning power. So for reasons of self-interest if not compassion, an agent may find himself playing psychiatrist to a client, sticking his nose into an author's marital disputes or taking a depressed author to a baseball game.

• *The agent cannot lend authors money.* Ha! In this age of glacial cash flow, agents are being asked more and more frequently to play banker. I'm not sure authors always appreciate that the agent who advances them money lends it interest-free, or that the agent's total advances to clients at any given time may come to tens of thousands of dollars. But I don't know too many agents who can gaze unflinchingly into the eyes of a desperate client and say, "If you need a loan, go to a bank."

• *The agent cannot be available outside office hours except by appointment.* Many business and personal crises arise for authors at times that, inconveniently, do not correspond to regular business hours. Book negotiations can carry over into the evening, and global time differentials put Hollywood three hours behind New York, and New York at least five hours behind Europe. An agent's day is not the same as a civil servant's.

Many of my clients have my home phone number. I only ask them to use it sparingly.

• *The agent cannot be a press agent, social secretary, or travel agent.* A lot of agents I know take on these functions to supplement the author's or publisher's efforts. Literary agenting is a service business, and anything within reason that an agent can do to free a client from care should be given thoughtful consideration. Rare is the agent who has not driven clients to the airport or booked them into hotels, arranged business or social appointments, or helped them secure tickets to a hot Broadway show.

Sometimes, though, our dedication to clients takes us very far afield indeed. For instance, although I have negotiated countless book deals for my clients, I suspect I'm the only literary agent who ever conducted an auction for a prosthetic leg. It happened that a client of mine, an author of books chronicling his sailing adventures, developed a circulation problem a few years ago and had to have his leg amputated above the knee. An artificial leg was made for him that was fine for most people, but after brooding on his fate for a year he decided he must go down to the sea again. Indeed, he determined to circumnavigate the globe in a sailboat. A conventional prosthetic leg would not do for ocean sailing, however. The salt air and water would corrode ordinary metal, and slippery decks require a strong-gripping rubber tip. The price quoted by one manufacturing firm for this made-to-order limb seemed too high to us, so we shopped a deal elsewhere and, using experience so hard-won in such battle theaters as Pocket Books, Bantam, and Dell, I got the price down to one that my client could afford.

Like my colleagues I have a large quiverful of sales techniques ranging from sweet talk to harangues. But I wonder how many agents have donned costumes and performed burlesque routines to sell books? It happened. Some clients of mine had written a satire of the best-selling book *The One Minute Manager*. Theirs was called *The One Minute Relationship*, demonstrating how you could meet, fall in love, marry, and divorce within sixty seconds of the first heartthrob. It was to be published by Pinnacle, but about a week before Pinnacle's sales conference, the editor-in-chief called me. "I'm thinking of something different for presenting this book to the sales staff. Could your clients cook up a cute skit?"

I promised to see what I could do and called my clients. They came to my home and we brainstormed a skit over take-out Chinese food. The shtick we came up with featured an Indian swami who has developed the One Minute Technique. He has to wear a white robe and a turban with a jewel in it. The "jewel" in this case was a thick slice of kosher salami and we called it the Star of Deli. My clients and I fell on the floor laughing. Then they suggested that since I had the robe, the turban, and the salami, and did a passing fair imitation of a Hindu fakir, I should perform the starring role in front of the Pinnacle salespeople. It took several bottles of Chinese beer to make me agree, but at length I went along, reasoning that these days, whatever it takes to sell books is okay by me. The skit went over well, climaxed of course by my gleefully stuffing the Star of Deli into my mouth. Pinnacle loved it so much they took our show on the road, videotaping our performance and featuring it at the American Booksellers Association convention.

Agents are not the tight-lipped stiffs that some have made us out to be. Like Shylock, we bleed if you prick us and laugh if you tickle us. I have cried with and for my authors when misfortune (and I'm not talking about disappointing royalty statements) strikes, and rejoiced with them at their weddings and the births of their children.

I have also had some great laughs, not a few at the expense of clients and colleagues, for I am an inveterate practical joker. On one occasion, I was sitting across the desk from a publisher discussing a deal. As I'd forgotten to bring my notepad I borrowed hers and wrote her offer down on it. The offer was lower than I'd hoped. I said I'd think about it and I went back to my office. There, I discovered I'd taken her notepad. I conjured up some wickedly mischievous things I could do with these fifty sheets of her personalized memo paper, but ultimately decided the best thing to do was to mail it back to her, and I did. But not before writing, on the top sheet, "We will meet Curtis's terms if we have to."

It didn't work.

One joke that did I pulled off about ten years ago. A client and good friend bought himself a telephone answering machine, and was so anxious about missing important calls that whenever he was away for any length of time he called home every fifteen minutes to get his messages by means of a remote control signal. He worried that machine to death. If he returned to find no messages, he would examine the phone and the answering machine for malfunctions.

One day, I decided to indulge his worst paranoid fantasy, and left the following message on his answering machine: ". . . Studios. If you don't return my call by five P.M. we will assume you're not interested and we will withdraw our offer." The poor fellow spent an hour phoning movie studio executives on both coasts explaining that his phone machine had malfunctioned in the middle of a message, and asking if they happened to be the people who left an offer on his machine that day.

Most people do not think of literary agents as leading adventurous lives, and that is largely true. Most of the time our conduct is as tightly circumscribed as that of business people in any other profession. Our greatest thrill is grappling in close combat with an editor during a six-figure negotiation, or stalking a check through the treacherous thickets of a publisher's bookkeeping system. Accounts of such adventures make for exciting listening only if you happen to be another literary agent, but somehow they don't carry the same weight as the tales of mountainous seas and mutinous tribes, challenging mountains and charging rhinos, that you can routinely hear at any meeting of the Explorers Club.

Nevertheless, because our profession brings us into contact with unusual characters, we do occasionally find ourselves carried far from the stereotypical role of submitting manuscripts in the morning, collecting checks in the afternoon, and going to lunch for three hours in between.

In 1966 I was in London setting up the English office of Scott Meredith's literary agency. Novelist Evan Hunter and his wife were passing through London on their way to the Cotswolds, and we spent a delightful afternoon dining al fresco at my boss's expense. I bade them good-bye and wished them a pleasant journey, and figured that was that. About a week later, however, I got a call from Evan in Southampton. They were about to embark on a ship for America when his wife realized she had left her jewelry in a safe in the Ligon Arms Hotel in the Cotswold town of Broadway. "I'm going to ask an important favor of you," Evan said. "I want you to take a train out there and get the jewels back. Bring them to London and we'll arrange for them to be shipped home."

At that time I was in my twenties and, beyond getting stuck in an elevator for two hours and having my tonsils taken out, I had never been at hazard in many Real Life Situations. This sounded like an opportunity to experience the kind of peril that confronted the Burtons, Spekes, and Hilarys through whom I'd lived vicariously.

"They're not just going to hand the jewels over to me," I protested.

"Of course not," said Evan. "There'll be a password."

"A password?"

"When you get to the hotel, go to the desk and tell the lady you're there to recover our jewelry. Then say the password."

A password! This was a scheme worthy of Evan Hunter, who under the penname of Ed McBain had created my favorite police procedural series, "The 87th Precinct." "And what is the password?" I asked.

There was a long pause and I sensed that Evan was looking furtively around for eavesdroppers. He uttered a phrase in a *voce* so *sotto* I had to ask him to say it again. " 'Phoenix Rising'," he said. "Repeat it."

" 'Phoenix Rising,' " I said. "Heavy!"

That afternoon I caught a British Railways train to Evesham, the station closest to Broadway. The taxi driver I hired to take me to Broadway looked like Central Casting's notion of a Dickensian cutpurse, including addressing me as "Guv'nor." When he asked me, just being friendly, my business in Broadway, I told him, "Just touring." He arched an eyebrow. I wore a three-piece English-cut suit and a tense smile and didn't look remotely like a tourist. I looked like a man trying not to look like a man who was soon to bear tens of thousands of dollars' worth of jewelry on his person.

The Ligon Arms Hotel had been built in an era when

Englishmen were four feet tall, as I quickly discovered when I grazed my skull on a lintel. I wobbled to the desk and found a diminutive woman peering at me who looked as if she would crumble into powder if I spoke too loudly. I cleared my throat and murmured, "Phoenix Rising."

She gazed owlishly at me and my heart sank. Something had gone wrong. Evan had not told her the password. He had told her the wrong password. She had not heard it correctly. She had stolen the jewels.

"Phoenix Rising. Phoenix Rising," she muttered, searching at least ninety years of memory for an association with this mysterious phrase. Then the light of recognition kindled in her eyes. Her hand leaped to her mouth. "*Phoenix Rising!* You're Phoenix Rising! EVERYONE, IT'S PHOENIX RISING! HE'S HERE, HE'S HERE!" Whereupon bellhops, maids, cooks, and guests poured into the lobby to see The Bearer of the Password. I doubt if anything quite like this had happened here since the Norman Invasion.

We crowded around the safe as the jewels, rolled in a pocketed length of embroidered velvet, were set before me. Delicately, my friend untied a drawstring, making certain not to touch the jewelry itself. I stared at a handsome collection of baubles. There was a hurried conference when we realized I had no inventory of what was supposed to be there, and I was required to sign a receipt itemizing each piece. The staff gathered at the entrance to bid adieu to Alias Phoenix Rising. "Quick tour, Guv'nor," my driver observed as I stepped back into the taxi. "Saw what I came to see," I replied tersely, clutching the pouch in a death grip.

Obviously, these days authors don't merely ask their agents what they've done for them lately, but rather, what *else* they've done for them lately, and I guess just about anything goes.

CHAPTER 5

Building Careers

As you can see, a literary agent's life involves far more than reading, lunching, and deal-making. His or her services embrace the literary, legal, financial, social, political, psychological, and even the spiritual, and the jobs we are obliged to tackle run the gamut from typewriter repair to espionage. But because our business is a day-to-day, book-to-book affair, we tend to lose perspective. With our preoccupation with advances and royalties, payout schedules and discounts, with movie rights and foreign rights and serial rights and merchandise rights, with option clauses and agency clauses and acceptability clauses and termination clauses, it is all too easy for us to forget that our primary goal is to build careers, to take writers of raw talents, modest accomplishments, and unimpressive incomes and render them prosperous, successful, and fulfilled.

This endeavor demands the application of all the skill and experience we command, plus something else: vision. Vision in this context may be defined as an agent's ideal of the best work an author is capable of achieving, matched to the best job his publishers can perform. An agent's vision should illuminate the author's path, oftentimes far into his future if not for his entire career.

In order for our vision to be fulfilled, three conditions must be met. First, we have to learn and understand what the author's own vision is. Second, we have to align his vision with our perception of his talent: Do we believe he has what it takes to realize his dream? And finally, we have to help the author

29

fashion his work to suit the demands and expectations of the marketplace.

I cannot overstate how much easier said than done the process of building an author's career is. Human nature being what it is, the forces militating against success are heartbreakingly formidable. The agent's vision and the author's vision may be at serious odds with one another, or at odds with the publisher's. The author's talent or stamina or financial resources may simply not be up to the task he has cut out for himself. His publisher may not like or understand his work. His audience may reject it. Every imaginable contingency may beset an author along life's path: death and disability, divorce and disaster—the same ones that beset everybody else, plus a few that are indigenous to creative people. The attrition rate for authors and their dreams is extremely high, and the odds against talent flourishing under perfect conditions are prohibitive. With so much at stake, it should come as no surprise that agents approach the building of their clients' careers with the utmost solemnity.

Let me try to elaborate on the elements that go into this task.

First and foremost is The Dream. Every author I have ever known has had it, and despite the infinite differences among authors, The Dream seems to be pretty much the same for all of them. It can be expressed as something like this:

> I have great books in me, but I can't afford
> to take time off to write them, so I will
> write whatever I have to in order to earn
> enough money to buy that time. Then, one day . . .

For most creative people, time is the medium in which masterpieces are created, but it must be paid for in hard cash. Since most writers do not have the cash, everything they produce is, in their eyes, a compromise.

Literary agents are usually sensitive enough to understand both The Dream and The Compromise, and their charge is to help their clients achieve the former and come to grips with the latter. Translating this into everyday terms, it means that we help writers earn a good living and put money away for retirement. The difference between the writer and everyone else, however, is that instead of taking his retirement savings and traveling to the Far East with it or buying a Florida condo near a golf course, the writer hopes to spend it on time to write the books he has longed to write all his life.

When a writer becomes my client I sit down with him or her to explore immediate and long-term goals. I ask writers how much it costs to live comfortably, how much they earn per book, and how long it takes them to write. It should then be a matter of simple arithmetic to determine what I must do to keep their careers on a steady keel: simply divide their yearly nut by the number of books they are capable of producing annually. This gives me the amount of money they must earn (after commission, I hasten to remind them) per book to make a living.

Unfortunately, life is not a matter of simple arithmetic. Even in the unlikely event that the author lives within his means and nothing untoward befalls him and his family, there is no room in the above equation for profit, and *The Dream requires an author to earn a profit.* Otherwise, how will he be able to afford The Era of No Compromise?

Now, books that earn a profit for authors are not easily come by (not, at any rate, as easily come by as books that earn a profit for publishers). Good luck and good agenting may sometimes make one happen, but it is unwise for an author to depend on either. This means the author has to make it happen on his own—by writing a breakout book. But how can he do that if he can't buy the time?

Even if you are blessed with an unexpected windfall, there is no guarantee that you will achieve your dream, thanks to Fehrenbach's Law. T. R. Fehrenbach, the brilliant Texas historian, once wrote to me that "Expenses rise to meet the cost of every sellout." In other words, the profit that authors make does not necessarily go into the fund marked, "This Time I'm *Really* Going to Write That Book." More likely, it will go toward something that is easier to grasp, like a new Pontiac Firebird, a twenty-one-inch Sony Trinitron, or a two-week vacation on Lake George.

The truth is that writers are no better equipped to fulfill their dreams than other middle-class people are, because compromise is an easy habit to get into when it is rewarded with comforts and luxuries. Austerity, integrity, sacrifice, relentless determination, and other virtues associated with uncompromising artistic endeavor are seldom a match for a brand-new living room suite or wall-to-wall carpeting for the master bedroom. So the dream gets postponed a bit longer, and a bit longer after that, until perhaps that terrible day comes when the dream deferred pops, in Langston Hughes's phrase, "like a raisin in the sun." Death and disability, divorce and disaster are not the only terrible things that can befall an author, or even the worst things. Giving up his dream is the worst thing, and that is truly tragic. I believe it's an agent's sacred duty to keep this from happening, to keep the flame of hope burning in the author's breast, to encourage him in every way possible to seize the moment when an opportunity to reach for greatness presents itself.

Most authors' dreams usually take a concrete form, a particular book or series of books. In some cases, these are an extension of what the author now writes for a living but on a grander scale. In others, the projected works are radical departures. Whatever the case may be, here again the agent can be immensely useful. First, in helping the author to articulate his Grand Design, to elicit from him the theme and story line, the setting and time span, the characters, the relationships, the conflicts, the pace. In his dialogue with the author, an agent may find himself transcending the role of sounding board and becoming almost a collaborator.

More important, I think, the agent must make a judgment as to whether the author's talents are up to these ambitious projects. They are not always, by any means. Authors are no more objective about their strengths and weaknesses than anyone else, and when their self-perceptions are deficient, it is vital for their agents to shed light on those blind spots.

Let me give you a few instances. I represent an author of historical novels of tremendous beauty and power. And it happens that the farther back in history she goes, the more evocative her books become. By the same token, the closer to modern times she gets, the more unbelievable her characters become.

Language that is lilting in the mouths of her ancient characters becomes pompous and wooden in the mouths of characters closer to our own time. If this author told me that it was her dream to write a contemporary novel I would strenuously object, for my assessment of her talent is that her strength, indeed her heart, would not be in it.

Another author I know has a wonderful sense of humor, but almost none of it showed up in her first novel. When I pointed this out to her she was at first somewhat insulted, for she felt that humor was inconsonant with important literature. But progressively she allowed it to suffuse her books, until most recently she brought forth a genuinely hilarious one that may be destined for the best-seller list.

Things don't always work out so happily. Often, an author becomes so successful writing a certain kind of book that his publisher and his readership resist his attempts to try something new and different. Many a good author has been broken on that rack. The pressure to keep a successful writer in his place can be intense, and an agent must mercilessly examine his own motivations to make sure he is not abetting these efforts to imprison his client in a gilded dungeon. Given the fact that the commissions on such writers are often juicy, this is no small task.

The third way that agents help authors build their careers is to match their "product"—an unpleasant but useful word—to the demands of the marketplace. In other words, to make it commercial. It is not enough for a writer to fulfill his dream if his dream happens to be to write perfect imitations of Virgil, parodies of Thackeray, or metaphysical poetry. The agent must therefore be as intimate with publishing and reading trends as he is with the soul of his author, and to make sure the author's work plays into those trends.

The problem doesn't always lie with the author. Some publishers are simply better at publishing certain types of books than others, and an author's development may eventually reach the point where his publisher simply can no longer accommodate it. Then it may be time to move the author to a house that understands his needs and his work and offers an environment in which these can be nurtured properly. It is not always greed that motivates agents to switch authors to new publishers. Most of the time, yes, but not always.

If all goes well—and we have seen how seldom it does—you will gradually, or perhaps suddenly, move on to a new and lofty plateau, maybe even onto the very summit itself. Hand clasped in your agent's, you will breathe the heady, rarefied atmosphere of success. You will have fulfilled your dream, your talent will now be a splendidly fashioned tool, and you will be published by a publisher that knows how to realize every dollar of commercial value from your masterpieces for your mutual enrichment. Only one thing remains to be done to place the capstone on your sublime triumph.

Why, drop your agent, of course.

Section Two

❋ ❋

Breaking In

CHAPTER 6

Sometimes a Great Notion

Most publishing people can relate to the following scenario:

You are attending a party and are introduced to another guest. "So, what line of business are you in?" the guest asks, a respected opening social gambit.

"I'm in the publishing business," you reply. "I work with authors."

"Hey, that's great. You must lead a really interesting life." He then goes on to explain that he is a postal clerk, a fabric salesman, a dishwasher repairman, a sanitation worker. Your companion suddenly brightens. "Hey, you may be just the guy I've been looking for!" He then takes you by the arm and furtively escorts you to an isolated corner of the room. Your stomach begins to sink, because you know what's coming.

His eyes dart suspiciously from guest to guest as he takes you by the lapels and puts his mouth close to your ear. "You got any writers looking for a *great* idea? *Because I've got one!* I would write it myself, but I don't have the time or the talent. But if you got somebody, I'll go in with him, fifty-fifty."

You look past him, seeking your host to rescue you, but it is hopeless. The fellow has an iron grip on your lapels. "Okay, I'll tell you the idea if you swear not to tell another soul."

"Stack of Bibles," you say, raising your palm to the sky.

He leans even closer. "Okay. What it is, is . . ."

What it is, is usually awful. But even if it isn't, the truth is that I cannot help him. For how can I explain to him that the last thing that professional writers need is ideas, that most of the writers I know have enough ideas to last them a lifetime?

37

They may need time, yes. They may need money. They may need peace and quiet. They certainly need love. But the one thing they have more than enough of is ideas.

Most people who have never seriously attempted to write books subscribe to what might be termed the Big Bang theory of inspiration. They perceive artistic ideas to be stupendous epiphanies that are visited once in a lifetime on a chosen few, like Moses receiving the Ten Commandments from God.

There is no denying that many sublime works of art, music, and literature are born that way. Most of us take ideas for granted, and why shouldn't we? We have dozens of them every day, and seldom do they seem to be of such moment that we pause in wonder to contemplate their splendor. Only when we examine books, pictures, and other artistic endeavors closely do we think about the intellectual processes that gave birth to them, and if these works are truly great, we may well be reminded that the generating of ideas is a phenomenon worthy of genuine reverence. By what mysterious mechanism they originate is surely as unknowable as how life itself was first created. Indeed, as the word "inspiration" literally means the entering of spirit into that which was hitherto lifeless, it could well be said that at no time are humans closer to divine than when they are inspired with noble ideas.

But ask a professional writer about ideas and he may well respond as inarticulately as my friend at the party. In all likelihood, he'll ask, "Which ideas?," because he's got a million of them, and his biggest problem is choosing one. His next biggest problem is finding the time and money to develop it. For this kind of writer, the real inspiration comes when he is writing. It magically flows from a remote region of his unconscious into his fingertips and seems almost unfailingly to illuminate every character description, every plot twist, every metaphor, perhaps every sentence. Big Bang? No, the image of a water tap is probably more apposite. Turn it on for an hour or two and out comes a daily ration of good, maybe great work. I hesitate to say "inspired" because most professional writers are too modest and self-critical to call it that. But the creative process by which literature—even popular literature—is produced may legitimately be described as miraculous.

It usually starts with the question, What If? It may be a grandiose What If, the kind that science fiction writers commonly ask: What if humans invented a way to travel to the moon? To travel faster than the speed of light? To travel forward or backward in time? To enter another's mind? To live in another galaxy? To fly like a bird or swim like a fish? It may be a more commonplace speculation about human nature: What if the children of two feuding families fell in love with each other? What if a man who committed the perfect crime couldn't live with his conscience? What if a white boy befriended a runaway black slave?

The ideas for literature literally are to be found in every imaginable place. Henry James, discussing Turgenev in James's preface to *Portrait of a Lady,* said, "As for the origin of one's wind-blown germs themselves, who shall say, as you ask, where *they* come from . . ? Isn't it all we can say that they come from every quarter of heaven, that they are *there* at almost every turn of the road? They accumulate, and we are always picking them over, selecting among them." James was perhaps the consummate writer on the subject of artistic inspiration, and in the prefaces to his collected novels and tales he describes the infinite ways in which an artist who is open to impressions can find his themes, plots, and people. A snatch of conversation, a glance between dinner companions, an inconsequential *objet* in an antique store, a string of paste jewels around a beautiful woman's neck, a glimpse of a man mourning over a gravestone, a stroll through an empty house. But for James, these were but the starting places for his superb tales. It was in the elaboration of his "wind-blown germs," in the development of his ideas, that the artistic challenge was to be found.

At first glance, most people would say that literary agents operate far from this ethereal realm of ideas. After all, we make our livings appraising the value of the commodities known as books, and helping the producers of those commodities to turn them into hard cash. But look again. Unlike rug dealers, car salesmen, or bond brokers, the merchandise we traffic in is intellectual. Our stock in trade is ideas, ideas that have been smelted and fashioned by authors into the precious metal called literature. A manuscript may be no more than a pound or two of paper, but when an agent pitches that book at an editor, it isn't the value of the paper he's describing. It's the value of the idea.

A critical aspect of a literary agent's job, then, is midwifing authors' ideas. Although the process may seem as casual as a dormitory bull-session, it may well have profound consequences, for the fate of a writer's career is intimately bound up in such questions as, Which idea is appropriate to a novel and which to a short story? Which idea should I work on now and which should I tackle later? Which idea do I feel passionately about and which lukewarm? Which idea have I fully realized in my mind, and which is only half-baked?

As I talk with an author about ideas, I ask myself some very pragmatic questions. How do those ideas fit in with the author's career goals and financial circumstances? He may have a magnificent vision that takes my breath away, but—where is he going to find the forty thousand dollars he needs to write that book under the tranquil conditions he requires, particularly since he is currently getting five thousand dollars a book! Or he may have a brilliant scheme for a sword-and-sorcery trilogy, but I'm worrying whether there will still be a strong market for it when he turns his book in. He may have an awe-inspiring idea for a sweeping historical novel, but while he's telling it to me I'm asking myself how his publisher is going to hold the book's list price down to $16.95.

Another thing I look and listen for is energy. An author may well have dozens of ideas for books, but he does not hold them all equally dear. When writers relate their ideas to me, do their eyes kindle with fire and their voices resonate with passion? Do they gesture frenetically with their hands or seem to lapse into a sort of trance? Do they speak in a singsong tone, as if it's all the same to them which book they write and which one they abandon?

The agent who encourages an author to develop the wrong idea, or who doesn't help him realize an idea fully, or who doesn't take into account that idea's appropriateness for its intended market, or doesn't consider an idea in the context of an author's talent and skill, or doesn't calculate the time and money that the author will require to fulfill his idea—that agent may inflict serious harm on his client's career. It's a very big responsibility, and my fellow agents and I worry about it *a lot*.

Once we are satisfied that we have the right idea, and that we have it where we want it, we must help the author develop it into an outline form that is useful both as a scenario for the writer to follow and as a sales instrument we can pitch to publishers. As you'll see in the next chapter, the two functions can differ vastly. The key difference is that in the latter, the idea is presented with as much intensity as author and agent can possibly endow it with. We try to boil a book's complexity down to its very essence, and to articulate that essence with words that stimulate associations in editor's minds with such abstractions as beauty, as well as with less abstract values like profit. We strive (and sometimes slave) to make every word of description pique an editor's imagination.

Obviously, many and perhaps most books are more complex than any one-line summary can possibly convey. And many of them are not half as good. One agent friend of mine is fond of saying that his idea of a book is usually a lot better than the book itself. "I don't sell the book, I sell my idea of the book," he says.

The process doesn't stop with the agent's pitch to the editor. It continues down the line as the editor tries to conceptualize the book for his or her colleagues. The publisher's sales force must in turn transmit the idea to the bookstore buyer, and the store's sales staff must get the message across to its customers. And because no one in this chain of people has a great deal of time (including the customer), the idea must be expressed in the pithiest possible way, otherwise attention may wander and the sale will be lost. So we all practice refining our descriptions of books into concepts that are so concentrated and potent they are practically radioactive. And we use a wide variety of audio and visual aids to get the idea across; good titles and subtitles, eye-catching covers, arresting dust-jacket blurbs, intriguing advertising copy, plugs by celebrities.

What concerns me is that the publishing business is becoming entirely too idea-driven. In our frenzy to encapsulate ideas so that we can sell them to each other effectively, we may well be forgetting that it is not the idea that excites us when we read a book, not the idea that makes us laugh or cry or stay up to the small hours turning pages raptly while our hearts thunder with the thrill and suspense and tragedy and comedy of it. It's the way the author realizes that idea and evokes it in our own imaginations. To put it succinctly, it's good writing. But there is a tendency today to presell great ideas, then develop them in predictably formulaic plots and package them for an audience that has been conditioned for formulas by television. What would poor Henry James think!

CHAPTER 7

Outlines

Many excellent works are available about how to write, but there is one category of writing that even topflight professionals struggle with, and that's outlines. I have not seen outlines covered adequately in the how-to literature I've read, probably because most writers who write about writing have never seriously examined why we need outlines. If you think we need them only to help us write books, you're probably doing something wrong.

Too many writers dismiss outlines as unworthy of serious attention, or not essential to the practice of their trade. "I'm a good writer, but a lousy outliner," I frequently hear, and the statement often sounds like a boast. "What does it matter?" goes another typical remark. "My finished books don't resemble my outlines anyway, so why bother?" Still others say, "The outline is in my head, and as long as my books turn out well, why should I have to outline them on paper?"

These scoffers have failed to understand the critical truth about outline writing: Publishers are less interested in what's going into your book than they are in what's going onto your cover.

From what I know about publishing history, the use of outlines to sell books to publishers is a relatively recent phenomenon. Before World War II, it was de rigueur for authors to submit completed manuscripts to their publishers. Even established authors wrote their books before seeking contracts with their regular publishers. Oh, they might consult with them in the formative stages, but it was pretty much taken for granted

43

that the author knew what he was doing and where he was going with his book, and that editors served to help shape or tidy up the finished product. The purpose of outlines was, as you might expect, to help authors conceptualize and develop their books. It didn't matter if the outlines were long or short, well written or scribbled, highly compressed or elaborate (my friend Henry James composed forty-thousand-word summaries of his later novels): An outline was a working sketch for the sole use of the author. It was not designed for display, particularly to publishers.

After World War II, the nature of publishing changed dramatically, affecting not only what kinds of books were written but how they got sold. Not the least of the transformations was that of the outline from writing tool to selling tool.

A critical reason for this metamorphosis was that the decision-making process at publishing companies had begun to alter. Previously the functions of publisher and editor had been closely allied; indeed, they were often vested in one and the same individual. But now, with the emergence of publishing as big business, with the acquisition of publishing companies by conglomerates or their absorption into immense entertainment complexes, a schism was created between the editorial and the business functions. Tremendous tensions were created as publishers demanded better justification for the purchasing of books. Profit-and-loss statements and market projections had to be drawn up before submissions were accepted. Editorial and publishing committees replaced the judgments of individual editors whose rationales for acquisition were often no more than intuition, enthusiasm, or personal pleasure.

In order to crack this growingly formidable system, authors were required to produce detailed and polished presentations that answered not merely the question "What is it about?" but such questions as "How does it differ from similar books?," "What is the target market and how large is it?," and "Can a publisher make a profit on it?" It no longer mattered if an individual editor was wild about a book or a proposed book, because he was no longer the only person making the decision. Indeed, many of the people now making the decision might not have read the work at all, and not a few of them weren't particularly interested in books except in terms of their bottom-line value as merchandise: how to "package" them, how to position advertising and promotion for them, how to price them, how to "move" them. Some writers realized that in order to satisfy this growing cadre of specialists, they'd have to learn a kind of writing very far from the sort of thing they'd been doing until then, not synopses but sales pitches cunningly contrived to subdue the anxieties of publishing personnel ranging from art director to head of sales to subsidiary rights director to publicity chief to vice-president in charge of marketing to—oh yes, I almost forgot: to editor.

If you piled all the outlines I have read in my lifetime on top of each other, they would reach the summit of Kanchenjunga. So I can say with some authority that few writers have grasped this crucial distinction between outlines designed to guide oneself through the complex terrain of plot and character and those written to turn on the staff of a publishing company. All too often I see chapter-by-chapter outlines of fifty or a hundred pages describing every twist of story and every nuance of character development, outlines that are 95 percent longer than most editors have the time or inclination to read, and that are deficient in many elements that are tempting to potential buyers. Such outlines should go back where they belong: beside the author's typewriter, helping him construct his book. But they don't belong on an editor's desk.

Let's look at the components of a solid outline. Naturally, we have to divide proposals into two categories: those for nonfiction books and those for novels.

Nonfiction books are both easier to outline and easier to sell from outline. A nonfiction work lends itself to easy encapsulation because its subject is finite and usually defines itself. A war, a biography, a history of a period, a murder case, seventeenth-century Dutch art, Greek cooking, traveling through Japan—all are limited by the factual information available, at which point it becomes a matter of selection and arrangement of that information. It is relatively easy to convey in an outline an author's familiarity with his subject, his enthusiasm for it, his authority, the uniqueness of the proposed work, its organization, and so forth. It is even possible to convey in an outline how good a writer the author is. A good nonfiction outline is a pleasure from the viewpoint of publishers. It takes five minutes to read, requires little imagination to grasp, and enables an editor (or anyone else at a publishing company) to make his mind up quickly and decisively. It is hard for most writers to visualize the joy it gives an editor to be able to reach a clean, fast decision, and this factor may have contributed in no small measure to the increased predilection for nonfiction at most trade publishing companies over the last few years.

A solid nonfiction outline should follow these basic precepts:

• *Establish your authority*. At the very outset you must show the publisher your credentials. It has become extremely difficult to sell proposals by writers who do not have a Ph.D. or M.D. after their names or cannot otherwise demonstrate long and vast experience in the field in which they are writing. As you might do with any other resume, if you have great bona fides, pile them on; if you don't, then stress the next best thing, to wit: "Although I am not an M.D. I have written about medical subjects for leading national magazines for the last twenty years." And if you cannot even boast that much, I strongly advise you to write a large piece of the book so that your authority and familiarity with your subject shine through by virtue of the writing itself.

• *Present your thesis dramatically*. The best outlines read like the best short stories, and like great stories should have a beginning, a middle, and an end. In enunciating the subject, you should present a disturbing problem that cries out for resolution: "The teenage suicide rate has tripled in the last ten years"; "As the First Continental Congress convened, the American colonies seemed very far indeed from the unification we take for granted today"; "Although there are many books available on Jewish cooking, to date there is no comprehensive work on cheese blintzes."

You now have the editor worried: How did the teenage suicide rate get to be so bad, what is the profile of a potential teen suicide, what can parents do about it? Here is where you display your intimacy with your subject, for as these questions occur to the editor considering your presentation, one by one your outline answers them satisfyingly and if possible entertainingly.

Like a good short story, your outline should rise to a satisfying climax, and here is where your writing skills must be displayed in all their splendor, for editors know that an author's interest and energy tend to flag in the final stages of a book and they want to see whether you can sustain the same level of intensity in the finale as you did in the opening stages of the work. You should therefore describe in vivid detail the culmination of your book. Whatever it was that originally inspired you to write it must be communicated here, and whether you're writing a biography, history, medical self-help, or even a blintz cookbook, you must demonstrate in these final passages of your synopsis your intense absorption in your material. Depict in full dress that final battle, that cure, that turning point in the life of your biographical subject. Let your editor know you're in love with this idea and will live in a constant state of torment until you have got it out of your system.

• *Furnish a table of contents.* Each chapter of your proposed book should be summarized in a short paragraph. Although a table of contents would appear to go over the same ground as your synopsis, it actually serves a different purpose. A synopsis is a narrative summarizing the topic and exhibiting the author's grasp of his material and writing skill. A table of contents demonstrates the author's organizational abilities and conveys the "feel" of the final book. It may seem redundant, but editors demand it. Don't leave home without one.

• *Anticipate a publishing committee's questions.* However masterfully you have synopsized your book, some important questions will probably linger in the editor's mind, and others will be raised by noneditorial staff members of the publishing committee. What competitive books exist or are in the works? What is the potential audience, and how can a publisher be sure that that audience will buy the book? Could a Big Name be induced to write an introduction or endorsement? Can you state with assurance that this organization or that society will approve the book, recommend it to members, purchase a minimum number of copies?

It is unfortunate that authors must do the sort of research

that is the rightful province of publishers, but because publishing people have so little time and money to spare for market surveys, library searches, legal investigations, profit-and-loss evaluations, and the like, any author who does the publisher's homework for him will definitely raise his chances of landing a sale. So go the extra mile. You've always said you could do a better job than a publisher: Here's your chance to prove it.

The outlining of fiction is an entirely different ball game. None of the criteria that enable editors to make quick and easy decisions about nonfiction book proposals applies to fiction outlines, for almost everything is subjective. Although it is even more important for a novel outline than it is for a nonfiction book outline to read like an enthralling short story, even wonderful novel outlines don't necessarily demonstrate convincingly that the writer is a good storyteller, has fine descriptive abilities, is capable of capturing subtleties of emotion, or knows how to build character and relationships. And paradoxically, any attempt to portray such elements in an outline often results in a long and tedious one that is excruciatingly dull. Furthermore, nothing in an outline can demonstrate whether the author can go the distance or will falter or lose energy or inspiration during the writing of the novel. It is far more common for novelists to slump in the midst of a book than for nonfiction writers, whose inspiration derives from already existing material rather than from anything they have to create. And while editors who have the novelist's track record to go by can say, "See? He finished six novels, what makes you think he isn't going to finish his seventh?" a novel proposal must be judged by a lot of noneditorial people at a publishing company. Many of them are a little suspicious of, or even downright hostile to, the creative process, and therefore skeptical that a novelist will be able to stay the course. What is worse, they can relate many unfortunate experiences bearing their skepticism out. Resistance to fiction outlines runs extremely high at most publishers, and that's why one finds prodigious piles of them on so many editors' desks.

There are important exceptions, of course. The well-established novelist can land a contract on the basis of an outline, and often a brief one. And writers doing novels in a series, or proposing books for a particular line, will of course have to do outlines. But authors who have no solid fiction track record are going to get nowhere in their quest to raise funds to complete their books. Or if they do, miraculously, get an offer, it will undoubtedly be a stingy one, because the publisher is being asked to invest his risk capital, and the costs of risk capital are extremely high.

I therefore advise anyone in that position to write a long, boring, detailed outline of his novel-to-be, take it to his typewriter, and sit down and write the novel. Not a third; not a half; *all* of it. Shift the risk from the publisher to yourself—because it means shifting the rewards as well. Give an agent a finished novel that he likes and watch him do his thing: He can auction it, set a tight deadline for decisions, get a high price, break the author out.

What's that you say? You can't afford to write that novel on speculation? I'm afraid you'll have to do what the novelists of yore did: They begged, borrowed, stole, got day jobs, or married into money. One of my colleagues, a very tough lady agent with a tongue like a trash can, was once visited by an author who presented her with a portion and outline of a novel. She read it that night and next day summoned him to her office. "It's great," she declared. "It's brilliant."

The author was thrilled. "So?"

"So? Whaddya mean, so?"

"I mean, what happens now? Are you going to hold an auction or what? Are you going to seek a high floor or solicit a preemptive . . ."

"Hold on. I said it's brilliant, I didn't say I could sell it. For me to sell it, you have to finish it."

The author turned pale and began to sputter. "But . . . but . . . how am I going to support myself while I'm finishing it?"

"Drive a f*****g taxi," she said.

He drove a f*****g taxi and returned, eight months later, with a great novel, which she sold for a lot of money and which established him as a leading commercial novelist.

Applications for chauffeurs' licenses are now being accepted.

CHAPTER 8

Hardcover vs.
Softcover vs. Hard-Soft

I take considerable pride in my belief that my advice helps writers clarify their understanding of the workings of the publishing industry. It even helps me. The acts of focusing on the subject at hand, of researching and composing and exploring a viewpoint, have enabled me to grasp some things that I seldom have time to reflect about in the daily hurly-burly of running a business. I'm afraid, however, that the topic of this chapter is so complex and subtle that I wonder how much light I will be able to shed on it. And that's the question of what makes some novelists better suited to being published in hardcover and others to paperback?

I must confess at the outset that I'm far from certain I know the answer. My only consolation is that publishers often don't know it either. For every book they cite that must, incontrovertibly, be published in hardcover, I can name a similar one that enjoyed immense success as a paperback original. And for every piece of "trash" that, indisputably, was meant to be published originally in paperback, I can name an even trashier book that rode the crest of the best-seller list for twenty or thirty weeks.

At this time a number of trends are evident. The first is that the distinctions between what is appropriately hardcover and appropriately paperback have crumbled, and cross-pollination, as healthy in literature as it is in nature, is becoming commonplace. Literature that was once restricted to the paperback side of the street has crossed over to hardcover, is enjoyed by a more affluent and cultivated segment of our society, and appears with growing frequency on hardcover best-seller lists. It's even studied in college courses. Who would have imagined, a few decades ago, that science fiction, western, and romance novels would one day move hundreds of thousands and even millions of hardcover copies?

Meanwhile, "serious" authors, literary writers who might have recoiled at the notion of initial publication in mass market or trade paperback, now appear in that format willingly and even happily, enriching both themselves and their readers in the process. Although original publication of serious literature in original paperback is by no means unprecedented in American publishing history (there have actually been three of four "paperback revolutions"), and is commonplace in Europe, hardcover snobbery has only recently begun to crumble beneath the economic pressures that make hardcover publication prohibitive.

The prejudice against paperback originals still strongly persists, however, and by no means merely among elitist literati; it is extant in the minds of publishing and movie people, the reading public at large, and indeed, in the minds of many writers themselves. It is a formidable prejudice and, like most prejudices, is backed by enough truth to make me feel that it will not be dislodged for a long, long time to come. Maybe we haven't looked it squarely enough in the eye. I have a few ideas. But first, a brief historical disquisition that I hope you will find pertinent.

In the dawn of the paperback revolution at the end of World War II, the distinctions between hardcover and paperback were pretty simple. Paperbacks fell roughly into three categories: the classics, reprints of hardcover best-sellers, and paperback originals aimed largely at male audiences: westerns, space operas, lusty thrillers, soft porn, and the like. But as publishing entered the 1960s, major changes were brewing. The most significant was the intense competition among paperback publishers for reprint rights to best-sellers. These publishers, after spending and spending and overspending, realized they needed more money and clout to survive in this auction-dominated jungle. They therefore resorted to a number of strategies: They merged with, acquired, or were acquired by hardcover publishers to create hard-soft combines; they sold out to conglomerates and entertainment complexes in order to lay their hands on big capital for the acquisition of best-sellers; and they intensified the development of original paperback fiction, particularly that aimed at the women's market—gothics, historical romances, and contemporary romances.

The third strategy is most relevant to this discussion. In the mid-sixties, original paperbacks became a powerful tool used by paperback companies to offset the spiraling costs of reprint acquisitions. Why, the reasoning went, should we invest half a million dollars or more to buy and publish the reprint of a best-seller when we can hire an author for ten-thousand dollars to write a book almost as good, spend fifty-thousand dollars to promote and advertise it, and sell almost as many copies?

This philosophy took firmer and firmer grip in the paperback industry, and over a decade came to dominate it. Many hardcover publishers failed to perceive what was happening, however. Continued heavy bidding for reprint rights to their best-sellers lulled them into thinking that no fundamental change had taken place in the way the game was played. But at the turn of the 1980s the bubble burst, and, accelerated by an overall economic recession, prices for reprint rights plummeted. Hardcover houses that had paid high prices for big-name authors and potential best-sellers found themselves high and dry without paperback support. The original had become the principal stock in trade of the paperback industry.

The yanking of the paperback rug from under the feet of the hardcover industry forced hardcover publishers to become extremely discriminating about what they acquired. The word was, if it can't make it on its own in hardcover, don't acquire it. A great many authors who'd been breezing along with midlist books now found themselves without hardcover publishers, or with hardcover publishers pressing them to accept cutbacks in terms. Not a few of these authors dropped out. Some of them tried harder and wrote blockbusters. A great many of them, however, lined up outside the doors of paperback houses and asked if there was any work for them. There was. Whatever else had happened to the paperback industry, it was still populated by folks who preferred good writing to bad. But, ironically, the entry into paperback originals of all those terrific writers depressed the prices paid for originals. The old hands, feeling themselves shouldered out of the business, accepted lower terms for their work just to hang on; the new hands, seeking reentry into publication at whatever price it took—well, they accepted whatever price it took.

In the meantime, something else of great significance was occurring: Both hardcover and paperback houses were discovering the joys of male genre book publishing. During the seventies, male fiction had become a well-kept secret harbored by small paperback houses like Ace, Pinnacle, Zebra, Tower, and Manor. Suddenly the big paperback houses, making tons of money on women's historical and contemporary romance, realized that men liked to read too. They geared up in a big way for male genre books, and at long last those books were restored to a place of profit and prominence. Among the many other benefits of this renascence was the driving out of business of some schlocky paperback outfits, and the raising of quality among the survivors. Indeed, the quality, as well as the quantity, of genre books became so high that it attracted the attention of hardcover publishers, who reasoned that if five hundred thousand or a million people bought an author's paperback originals, surely a few tens of thousands of them at the very least would buy the same books in hardcover. This reasoning proved correct. Writers who were selling big in paperback were moved up into hardcover. A great many of them thrived. Today, the hardcover best-seller lists are chock-full of successful graduates of the paperback original school, with genre stuff like westerns, romances, science fiction and fantasy, and action-adventure making appearances there in unprecedented numbers.

For those of you who have not followed my drift, let me now draw you to it: The overall quality of popular literature is genuinely higher than it was twenty, ten, or even five years ago. After the Great Shakeout, the standards of acceptability among both hardcover and paperback publishers rose steeply, and because marginal publishers got driven out, the markets for marginal authors have all but disappeared. In the good old days of the sixties and seventies an agent could always find a quickie paperback assignment, a sex novel or a movie tie-in, to offer to a desperate client, or could sell something out of that author's trunk to some end-of-the-line paperback house. Those days are gone. The remaining paperback publishers are leaner, and if they also seem meaner, some of that may be attributed to authors, agents, and hardcover publishers having been spoiled by the extravagance of a decade ago, when even indifferent first novels were getting banged down for twenty or thirty thousand dollars on the reprint auction block. The rest is attributable to the fact that today's market belongs to the buyer. The message to today's professional writer is crystal clear: Be tough or be gone.

This raising of the stakes is reflected most vividly in hardcover. The principal reason is that most hardcover fiction is review-dependent. Hardcover books that get panned are, with one notable exception I will mention in a moment, going to lose money for their publishers, whereas paperback originals get scant review attention, and if that attention is negative the effect on sales in seldom fatal. We are seeing a little more attention paid by reviewers to paperback originals, and a few originals have experienced remarkable flights with the help of well-timed and well-placed favorable reviews. These, I am convinced, are only exceptions that prove the rule.

Here, then, we come to the crux: The single most important difference between hardcover and paperback publication is review coverage. But not, as most people think, because it satisfies author vanity or helps to sell books. As I see it, the true importance of reviews is that they *legitimize* books. A reviewed book, for most of us, is a "real" book, and that's why hardcover books are considered more "real" than paperbacks. Although we can all think of exceptions, in great measure a book brought out in hardcover is likelier to be seriously considered by magazine editors, foreign book publishers, and most particularly by movie people, than the same book published originally in paperback.

There is, as I indicated, one exception. When best-selling paperback writers advance into hardcover, their sales will usually not become much more dependent on reviews than they were when their books came out in paperback. That is because these authors bring with them a ready-made audience, one that has never been susceptible to reviews. Fans of paperback authors usually don't ask if the new book is any good, they just ask when does it go on sale, and this passionate loyalty follows the author into hardcover. If the hardcover happens to get good notices, that's great, for it will bring new fans into the fold. But that substantial hardcore audience will not be affected. Promotion, at this level, is far more effective than reviews in moving books.

If, in your efforts to figure out what's a hardcover and what's a paperback, you've also wondered what kind of book is more appropriate for hard-soft publication, it's the kind I have just described. Hard-soft combines were created to accommodate both the hardcover publisher's desire to have a guaranteed paperback reprint when he acquired a big book and the paperback publisher's desire to buy reprint rights to best-sellers for less than astronomical advances. But hard-soft deals also accommodate major authors. First, they give them the huge advances they demand, something few hardcover publishers can afford without paperback backup. And second, by allowing them to retain 100 percent of both hardcover and paperback royalties, hard-soft neutralizes the resentment best-selling authors begin to feel when they see their hardcover publishers keeping 50 percent of the money collected from licensing reprint rights to outside paperback houses.

Assembling all these factors, the answer to our original question would seem to be that very little fiction is too good to be published originally in paperback. Rather than try to force your way into hardcover before it is timely to do so, I would recommend that you think paperback for just about everything you turn out, and let the hardcover market discover you in its own time.

If I were plotting the ideal career of a talented new author, I would establish him in paperback in whatever genre he produces best, for genre books offer the most opportunities for writers to break into the business. He will develop his craftsmanship and make a living, too—earn while he learns. I would advise him not to be ashamed to be a paperback writer; it has become a respectable profession populated by many fine writers and interesting people. Don't worry about reviews; there won't be that many and you will therefore be allowed to build up your confidence without being unduly influenced by public opinion.

Stay in paperback as long as possible, establishing an audience, winning the respect of editors at your own and other publishing companies, and making money not just for yourself but for your publisher. In due time, natural processes (and, I would hope, a smart agent) will lead you into hardcover publication. You may write that long-awaited breakout novel, or you may simply be recognized for a consistent and excellent body of work. Don't try to do anything differently once the question of hardcover is raised. Hardcover publication does not mean you now have to become a better writer; more likely it means that professionals in the publishing industry think that you *are* a better writer. In due time, thanks to review coverage and promotion, your books will sell to movies and television, to magazines, and to foreign publishers. Book club and reprint rights to your books will start to reach spectacular proportions. That will be the time for you to switch to a hard-soft publisher if you're not there already. Then your biggest problem will be income taxes.

CHAPTER 9

A Modest Wager

I have a standing bet with many publishers, backed by one thousand dollars payable to the charity of their choice. The bet is that a professional author can write a book faster than a publisher can write a check. And I hereby reaffirm the bet publicly.

So far nobody has taken me up on this wager, and I doubt if anybody will. But if someone wants to—well, just make your check payable to the Special Olympics, sucker.

There is no gimmick here. At least a dozen professional writers on my client list are capable of turning out a novel in two to four weeks, even less if their publisher is desperate. But I know of scarcely any major publisher capable of routinely preparing contracts or, once contracts have been signed, cutting a check in that period of time. Unless it's an emergency, in which case it takes about three weeks longer.

I don't believe my clients are unique in this respect. Many agents handle or know of authors capable of turning out genre fiction, male adventure, westerns, romances, and the like, within weeks. In fact, many writers would go under if they were not capable of producing at least a book a month.

But—are the books good? What is the relationship between the quality of a book and the time it takes to produce it? I'll be exploring these questions in a moment. But I'm not quite through with publishers.

The contracts and accounting departments of most publishing companies are extremely burdened with work and, under the best of circumstances, move with maddening bureaucratic casualness. Absent, it seems (to authors and agents), is the sense that the papers being shuffled have any bearing on the basic needs, the food and clothing and rent and car payments and college tuitions, of the human beings "hereinafter referred to as Authors." One agent, in a frothing fit of frustration, likened the process to the admitting office of a hospital emergency room, where the life fluids of victims trickle out of their bodies while the admitting clerk takes down their address, Social Security number, and mother's maiden name. I don't know if I would go that far, though I do remember a case of one crazed client who informed his editor he had just had his cat destroyed because an unconscionably late contract and check had made it impossible for him to pay for the poor creature's medical treatments. But I might, if I were of a cynical turn of mind, be tempted to suggest that the torpid pace of the contracts and accounting departments of some publishing companies is yet another example of how publishers cling to money as long as possible at the expense of authors. Luckily, I am not of a cynical turn of mind.

In fact, one's heart might almost go out to the gallant minions of the contracts and accounting departments. Anyone who has actually seen them in action, or inaction, must appreciate that the choreography of procedures for drafting a contract and drawing a check is highly complex in even the most efficiently run publishing houses. Once an editor has concluded negotiations with an agent or author, he or she draws up a contract request enumerating all of the deal points plus any variations in the boilerplate language that the author or agent may have requested. This contract request joins the many others awaiting action by the contracts department. The terms in the contract request are then transferred onto contract forms.

These forms must now be reviewed, sometimes by the original editor, sometimes by department heads, sometimes by the chief executive of the company, sometimes by all of them. The contracts are then submitted to author or agent, and if, heaven forbid, there should be but one or two minor items to be negotiated or renegotiated that the editor or contracts person does not have sole authority to decide, approval of those changes must be secured from someone at the company who *is* in authority. I have seen a contract held up for a month because I requested upping the number of free authors' copies from ten to twenty, or extending the delivery date by one month. Some contract department heads are fanatical about initialing alterations, requiring weeks of additional back-and-forthing. Some agents have become quite masterful at forging their clients' initials on contracts, and though this is a potentially dangerous practice, it seems like the only practical tactic to counter massive delay. One of my colleagues grinningly boasts, "If I spent a day in jail for every set of initials I've forged, you'd never see me again."

Once the contracts have been signed by the author, the machinery for procuring the check begins to grind. The contracts department issues a voucher instructing the accounting department to draw the check due on signing the contracts. Such vouchers must in the normal course of things be reviewed by the comptroller or some other executive in charge of financial affairs. Once the check is drawn, it will be examined by that executive and possibly by the publisher before it is signed by one or both of these officers. Needless to say, it is not as if these folks have nothing else to do.

If, therefore, you wonder why a publishing company can't just type up a contract the way you might scribble a thank-you note, and dash off a check the way you dash one off to pay your landlord, now you know, and perhaps you'll feel a bit more compassion for the clerical staffs of publishers.

I do. But my bet still stands.

Despite this lengthy digression and a muffled tone of querulousness, this chapter is not about how slow publishers are. It's about how fast writers are.

Outsiders—by which I mean people with little firsthand experience of the creative and technical aspects of writing—have difficulty making peace with the idea that any kind of book, let alone a good one, can be turned out in thirty days or less. *The New York Times*, in an article published on September 5, 1984, reported the Seventh International Three-Day Novel Writing Contest, sponsored by Pulp Press Books. Some four hundred entrants started their novels at midnight on Friday, August 31, and had to complete them seventy-two hours later at the end of the Labor Day weekend.

I for one am not impressed. I know of several professional writers who wrote full-length novels over a weekend, not because they wanted to but because they had to in order to accommodate publishers in a jam. A tightly scheduled manuscript had not been delivered on time, covers were printed, rack space reserved, the printer's time booked. "Can do," these heroes quietly said, and on Monday morning, looking somewhat like Gabriela Schiess-Andersen staggering into Olympic Stadium in the 1984 Women's Marathon, they showed up at their publisher's door with a manuscript.

Ah, you murmur, but were they *good* manuscripts?

This annoying question arises again and again whenever prolific writers are mentioned. It's easy to understand how the public at large would classify such feats as belonging to that end of the spectrum of human accomplishment reserved for flagpole sitting and marathon dancing. It's harder to understand why many editors feel that way too. But a large number have the attitude that the quality of literature rises in direct proportion to the time required to produce it. Publishers, even those who publish lines of genre fiction that call for short and rigid deadlines, are quite suspicious of prolific authors. They can't believe a book written that fast can be that good.

One of my clients works for three different publishers under three different names, and none knows about the others. In fact, each believes the author is working exclusively for him. Every three months he turns in a book for each, and each is very happy with it. Why? Because they believe it takes him three months to write his books. Actually it takes him one month. If I told that to his publishers, they would stop buying his work because they would feel he's rushing.

Facility among genre writers is suspect enough; among more serious writers it may be fatal to their careers. I know of one writer of popular history and biography who suffers from a cruel paradox. He has had a total of sixty books published, mostly in hardcover, on an astonishing range of subjects. He has been able to write so fast because he is a brilliant scholar with a highly retentive memory, which enables him to turn out a solid and entertaining nonfiction book in one draft. The acquisition of a word processor has almost doubled his speed.

You would think that publishers would be pounding his do<
down. Sadly, the opposite is true. Publishers examining |
lengthy track record have characterized him as a "hardcov
hack" and, convinced he would treat his subjects superficiall
turn him down for prospective projects. On some occasior
publishers engaged him to write bigger, more scholarly books
but paid him advances so low he was unable to undertake the
research and travel that would enable him to treat his subject in
depth. Thus he was forced to turn in work that confirmed his
reputation for superficiality. His editors' prophecies became
self-fulfilling.

I have always felt that in order to qualify to practice their
profession, editors should be required to write a novel. They
would then undoubtedly discover that many of the skills they
now consider dismayingly hard are actually quite easy, while
many they regard as a cinch are inordinately difficult. One
thing they would appreciate, I'm certain, is that an experienced
professional writer working an eight-hour day and typing at
average speed can produce five-thousand words daily in clean
first draft without pushing. That's a finished book in twelve to
fifteen working days.

But—one draft? How can a writer produce "first draft-final
draft"?

One reason is that he has no choice. The author who writes a
good book in one draft will earn twice as much money as one
who writes the same book in two. And when the pay scale is
twenty-five hundred to five thousand dollars per book, one
simply cannot afford to write a second draft.

It is also a matter of training. Many professional writers
reach a level of craftsmanship where whacking out clean copy is
as natural as hitting balls is for a professional baseball player or
dancing *en pointe* is for a ballerina. The amateur who writes
fast usually writes sloppily; the professional who writes fast will
most likely write masterfully.

Let us not forget inspiration. It is not uncommon for writers
to talk about writing as if in a trance, or feeling like a channel
through which a story is being poured from some mystical
source. Some writers rehearse a scene or story so often in their
heads that when they finally commit it to paper, it all comes in

a rush, as if they're writing from memory rather than from a sense of original creation.

All this is helped by the development of word processors, which enable their owners to write two drafts in the time it takes writers working on conventional typewriters to write one. But now that the technology is at hand, will the prejudice against prolificness finally be overcome? I'm not too sure.

For, in the last analysis, it isn't the editors or public who cling most tightly to the myth that fast writing is poor writing. It's the writers themselves. Almost all the professional writers I know equate speedy writing with money and slow writing with love, to the point where their personalities actually bifurcate and the halves declare war on one another. Authors capable of knocking off a superb genre novel in one draft will agonize over every sentence of their "serious," "important," "literary" novel as if they were freshmen in a creative writing course. They seem to believe that anyone wishing to cross the line between popular entertainment and serious literature must cut his output and raise frustrating obstacles in his own path, and that legitimacy may be purchased only through writer's block. It is futile to point out the Dickenses, Balzacs, Dostoyevskis, and Jameses who wrote as if possessed, in many cases with scarcely a single emendation, yet turned out a body of sublime classics. And they did it in longhand, by the way.

CHAPTER 10

Movies into Books

Novelizations of movies and television shows are among the most intriguing subspecies of commercial fiction. I say subspecies because they obviously cannot be spoken of in the same breath as *The Magic Mountain* or *Portrait of a Lady;* indeed, even commercial novelists look down their noses at novelizations as possessing not a shred of redeeming social value, as the literary equivalent of painting by numbers. On the spectrum of the written word, tie-ins are as close to merchandise as they are to literature. Tie-ins are kin to the souvenir, and in some ways are not vastly different from the dolls, toys, games, calendars, clothes, and other paraphernalia generated by successful motion pictures and television shows. Those who write them usually dismiss them with embarrassment or contempt, or brag about how much money they made for so little work. Yet, when pressed they will speak with pride about the skill and craftsmanship that went into the books and assure you that the work is deceptively easy. And if you press them yet further, many will puff out their chests and boast that tie-in writers constitute a select inner circle of artisans capable of getting an extremely demanding job done promptly, reliably, and effectively, a kind of typewriter-armed S.W.A.T. team whose motto is, "My book is better than the movie."

How are tie-ins created? Their birthplace of course is the original screenplay. The Writers Guild of America Basic Agreement entitles the screenwriter to ownership of literary rights to his screenplay. When he sells his screenplay he can retain the novelization rights or include them, at terms to be negotiated, in the screenplay deal. Most of the time the screenwriter sells his novelization rights to the buyer—the film's producer or a studio. The new owner of these rights now tries to line up a publication deal for the tie-in. He contacts paperback publishers and pitches the forthcoming film.

If the film has a big budget, terrific story, bankable actors, unique special effects, or other highly promotable features that promise a hit, publishers will bid for the publication rights. (In the case of television tie-ins, the producers almost always wait till a series is a hit before arranging for tie-ins. And one-shot movies of the week seldom trigger novelizations because of the brief period—one evening—in which they are exposed to the public.) A deal is then struck, the publisher paying an advance against royalties to the producer or studio.

The publisher then engages a writer to adapt the screenplay. It should be readily apparent that if the movie is indeed shaping up to be a hit, or the television show is already a hit, the publisher will be forced to pay such a high advance and royalty to the producer or studio that little will be left for the writer. That's why novelizations are generally low-paying affairs, with modest advances and nominal royalties of 1 or 2 percent. Flat fees are by no means unheard of. And, because the competition among writers for novelizations is intense, few writers are in any position to bargain. But—if the pay scale is so miserable, why do authors seek novelization assignments so ardently? Because they think it's easy money. Sometimes it is. But it's not like falling off a log, as we shall soon see.

Publishers are nowhere near as enamored of movie tie-ins as authors are, and they weigh the profit potential of such books as critically as they do that of the thousands of other manuscripts submitted to them annually. They know that most movies do not translate well into books. There are also technical and timing problems with tie-ins that are daunting to publishers. For instance, the screenplay may undergo alterations, some of them radical, right up to or even during the shooting of the film. By the time filming is complete there is insufficient time before release of the movie for a writer to write the novel and the publisher to publish it.

A notable instance of the timing problem occurred in the

filming of *2001: A Space Odyssey*. Director Stanley Kubrick insisted on complete control over the writing and publication scheduling of the novelization. The author of that novelization was a chap named Arthur C. Clarke, and since Kubrick kept changing the script as he went along, particularly the wild and mystical ending, Clarke had to keep changing the novel. His publishers bit their fingernails to the quick as the days rolled inexorably toward the release date of the movie. Worst of all, the book tie-in deal was for publication of a hardcover first, then paperback. It had been assumed that the hardcover would be brought out before the movie was released, then the paperback would be issued to coincide with the release of the film. But because of the delays there was no lead time whatsoever for the hardcover. The publisher wanted to drop the hardcover and go straight into paperback, but Kubrick insisted on hardcover. Thus we had a case, unprecedented in anyone's experience, of a hardcover novelization. The publisher did get his paperback edition out soon thereafter, but the situation was a mess and the book didn't do anywhere as well as it might have if the timing had been better.

Kubrick, incidentally, plays a role in one of the more bizarre movie tie-in stories I have ever heard. It seems that a novelist named Peter Bryan George wrote a nuclear apocalypse novel called *Red Alert*. It was acquired for the movies by a producer who couldn't put a deal together, so he laid it off on Kubrick. Kubrick adapted it, and rather broadly to say the least. *Red Alert* was a very solemn book; the adaptation was blackly humorous. He called it *Dr. Strangelove*. In fact, so different was the movie from the book that the producers decided to hire somebody to write the novelization. They hired Peter Bryan George, the author of *Red Alert*. So George *novelized the movie version of his own novel*! His novel had been published by Ace under the name Peter Bryant; his novelization was published by Bantam under the name Peter George.

Another problem for publishers is the greed that has set in at the studios. Originally, tie-ins were regarded as free publicity for movies, and publishers regarded them as little more than list-fillers. For a modest payment to the studio a publisher would get the screenplay, stills, cover photo, and promotional material, and everybody was happy. Then the studios began to smell profit.

The first big breakout tie-in was *Last Tango in Paris,* according to novelist and publishing columnist Leonore Fleischer, who has been dubbed Queen of the Paperback Novelizers for the fifty-odd tie-ins she has written. *Last Tango* was followed by a number of other hits (tie-inwise as well as box officewise) like *The Omen* and *Star Wars.* The bidding began to spiral, and the studios started charging publishers for all the material they'd formerly give away as part of the tie-in package.

The climax came with the bidding for a tie-in of *F.I.S.T.,* the Sylvester Stallone film following Stallone's smash hit, *Rocky.* Dell paid a $400,000 advance for the novelization rights, and, needless to say, took what is known in Spanish as El Batho. Soon afterward the tie-in market collapsed—"*F.I.S.T.* was your ultimate South Sea Bubble," Fleischer told me—and it never quite recovered. It has revived somewhat, principally in the area of special effects-type films such as *Alien, E.T.,* and *Raiders of the Lost Ark,* but publishers have become too cautious and sensible ever to get quite so hysterical again.

Anyone who thinks that tie-in writing is a mere matter of adding he-saids and she-saids to the screenplay dialogue has certainly never attempted such an adaptation. For one thing, most screenplays are too short to convert page for page into book manuscripts. Therefore, even if you are following the script scene by scene, you are required to amplify on character, action, and location descriptions. Any good novelist can translate a terse screenplay direction ("EXTERIOR, OLD MACDONALD'S FARM, A STORMY NIGHT") into a few pages of descriptive prose ("A bitter, shrieking north wind lashed the trees and hurled sheet after sheet of icy rain against the clapboard siding of Old MacDonald's farmhouse . . ." etc.). The problem is that when you analyze screenplays you realize that most of them don't lend themselves comfortably to scene-for-scene conversion. In fact, many of them present nightmarish challenges.

The reason is that movies are seen with one lobe of the brain, and books read with another. If you'll take the trouble to compare a novel with its film adaptation, you'll immediately realize that whole chapters have been cut or reduced to takes that last a few seconds on the screen; or that, conversely, a sentence or paragraph has been dramatized into a full-dress scene that consumes five or ten minutes of movie time. This is because some material in books is distinctly more cinematic than other material. (It also explains why few novelists make good screenwriters, and most screenwriters are dreadful novelists.)

By the same token, owing to the demands of the book reader's imagination, elaborate scenes in a movie may seem far too long to merit the same expansive treatment in a novelization; fast transitional scenes, flashbacks, establishing shots, short takes, and the like may require a novelizer to build them into whole chapters. Some years ago I was hired by Bantam to novelize John Carpenter's horror film *Halloween*. The film had already been released and was showing at only a few small theaters around the country, but the Bantam editor felt the movie was a sleeper, and he was right: It became one of the most profitable independently made films of all time.

It was most fortunate for me that the movie was already made, for in many cases the novelizer has only the screenplay to go by, or perhaps a rough cut of the film, and therefore has little visual material to aid him as he attempts to translate screenplay into book. After seeing the movie, however, I was troubled by some serious technical problems in adapting one medium to another. The movie opens with a five-year-old boy who, on Halloween, slashes his teenage sister to death with a long kitchen knife. We then jump some twenty years to show the little boy, now a grown man, escaping from the mental institution in which he has been confined, stealing a car, and returning to his hometown to go on another bloody rampage.

One of the great things about movies is that they move so fast, you don't have time to think about logic. Novels are a more reflective medium, however; at any time you can put a book down and think about what you've read. And it worried me, for instance, that my readers would put my book down and wonder how the hell someone who'd been institutionalized since he was five would know how to drive a car. So I had to concoct a whole chapter describing the fellow's stay in the asylum (which was okay, since I needed the five thousand words anyway) and showing that because he'd been a model inmate and trusty, he'd been *taught to drive a truck and use it to run errands on the asylum grounds.*

Even more serious was the fact that at the climax of the film, this malevolent individual is shot half a dozen times at point-blank range by a .357 magnum, yet steals away into the darkness leaving not a drop of blood where he fell to the ground, apparently dead; leaving, in fact, only the distinctive aroma of a sequel film. Now, all this is well and good for the moviegoer seeking a good scare, but for a book reader it raises some disturbing questions: Did the man who shot the guy from three feet away actually miss? Did he accidentally use blank cartridges? Did he simply graze him, or fail to hit any vital parts, or shoot him in such a way as to draw no blood? (Three fifty-seven magnums are so powerful they draw blood even when they *miss!*)

Or—was this maniac actually a supernatural entity invulnerable to high-calibre death-dealing sidearms?

There was no indication whatever in the movie that he was. Yet, in order to make sense out of it at all, I had to endow him with supernatural characteristics and invent a rationale, which went like this: ever since his execution during a Druid harvest ritual (whence Halloween is derived), this monster returned to earth every few years on Halloween to seek blood vengeance. My invention strained credulity to the limit, but at least it unified the book and bought me another seventy-five hundred badly needed words.

Every tie-in writer talking shop will tell you how he or she overcame similar challenges, challenges complicated by the insistence of the producer on approval of the novel or a run-in with some middle-management studio exec who demanded that whatever was in the movie must go into the book, and whatever wasn't in the movie must not go into the book. The fact that novelizations may take only a few weeks does not mean that many, many hours of thought and years of writing experience did not go into them. Novelizers earn every penny, and for all but the biggest books, pennies are what they make. Leonore Fleischer's biggest moneymaker was *Annie,* which brought in a total of some $45,000 in royalties for a labor of less than a week, but that is exceptional. Joan Vinge, who wrote *The Jedi Story Book,* a juvenile tie-in to *The Return of the Jedi,* did it for a modest flat fee for Random House. The movie was a phenomenal success, and so was the book, but Vinge was not entitled to a penny of royalty. Only by the goodness of Random House's heart, tinged perhaps with a dollop of guilt plus a healthy measure of pushing by her agent, was she awarded a $10,000 bonus.

The best advice I can give prospective tie-in writers is, if possible never write one for a flat fee, no matter how dumb the movie, no matter how quick and simple the job. Years ago, Ace hired me to write a tie-in for a perfectly dreadful and quite disgusting horror movie called *Squirm,* which portrayed in all its graphic revoltingness what happened when a small town was invaded by millions of bloodsucking earthworms. Ace offered me a flat fee of $2,500, and, seeing the prospect of earning $250 a day, I grabbed the deal. The movie came and, blessedly, went. But my book went through numerous editions for Ace, and was sold to English and other foreign publishers where it has become an enduring horror classic.

My book was better than the movie. Big deal! That and a good agent would have earned me a nice profit. Unfortunately, I don't have an agent. I don't trust them.

CHAPTER 11

Work-for-Hire

If one were to compose a Bill of Rights for authors, ownership of copyright to their works would certainly be close to the top of the list. We hold self-evident the truth that if a person produces an original book-length work, he or she is entitled to proprietorship under the law, and to full benefit of its commercial exploitation.

Yet, it has not always been so. The piracy of literature by printers, publishers, and booksellers has been common practice throughout the world from the dawn of the printed word, and was prevalent in this country until well into the present century. Until the establishment of the first International Copyright Convention in 1891 and its refinement after World War II, respect for the sanctity of copyright was largely a matter of gentlemen's agreements based strictly on self-interest: Don't steal from me and I won't steal from you. There are still vast areas of our globe where publishers think nothing of stealing and distributing works of literature from authors and publishers of law-abiding countries.

Lest you become too smug that such barbarities cannot happen here, I am compelled to report my observation that the appropriation of authors' copyrights by some publishers and book packagers seems to be on the upswing. Nothing so gross as piracy, mind you. More, I would say, like extortion. But the effect is the same: the deprivation of authors' rights to enjoy the fruits of their labors. The fruits of an author's labors include such bounties as royalties on copies of books sold, participation in reprint income, and revenue deriving from the exploitation

70

of serial, translation, dramatization, and other subsidiary rights. Not everyone shares the conviction that the enjoyment of these monies is a natural and God-given right, however. Indeed, not everybody behaves as if the enjoyment of these monies is protected by statutory law.

The engagement of writers for flat fees falls into a category of employment known as work-for-hire. Work-for-hire is a doctrine defining the relationship between a copyright owner and a writer. Note that the owner may or may not be an author; he, she, they, or it may be a corporation (like a movie studio or television production company), a syndicate of investors, or an individual who is not a writer. These entities hire writers to perform a service in pretty much the same way a homeowner hires a cabinetmaker, a painter, or a gardener, except that in this case the task is writing a text for the "boss"—the creator or owner of the idea. The owner is then free to exploit the text in any way he desires with no further obligation to the author.

Some provisions of the 1976 Copyright Act attempt to define the work-for-hire concept, but they do not do so very clearly and have left the door open to unfair exploitation of authors.

I hasten to make clear that all work-for-hire is by no means exploitive. There are numerous situations in which it may be considered reasonable and acceptable by normal ethical standards, for instance, the engagement of writers to do articles for an encyclopedia. The copyright holder of the total work is the publisher, and because it would be impractical and uneconomical to pay a royalty to each contributor, the normal arrangement is a one-time fee. As long as the fee pays for the time and effort, the author is usually content, particularly if he or she gets byline credit, for a contribution to an encyclopedia bears great prestige that helps the author endure the low wages.

Another application of the work-for-hire concept that most of us accept unquestioningly is ghostwriting. Authorities or celebrities who cannot write well or are too busy to write their own books engage writers to draft books for them. Although the principal author may agree to share some of the proceeds of the book with his ghost, the principal is the sole signatory of the contract with the publisher, thus making him the copyright owner. He then signs a separate agreement with the ghost, removing the ghost from claim to copyright and direct participation in revenue generated by publication of the book. Occasionally, what may have seemed a fair fee at the time it was negotiated with the ghostwriter may not seem so if the work demanded of him turns out to be excessive, or if the book becomes a runaway bestseller. Under ordinary circumstances, however, the ghostwriter accepts his lot as a worker for hire, and may at least secure more work for himself by telling publishers, "That book was actually written by me."

If all this seems a bit remote to you, let me point out that many garden variety authors employ other writers on a work-for-hire basis. Take the creator of a popular fictional series who, growing bored with his characters or too busy with other projects to turn out new books in his series, farms them out to other authors. He signs contracts with his publisher, then negotiates separate agreements with ghostwriters to produce first drafts or even final ones for him, which he passes off as his own. In some instances the publisher is aware of the existence of these subcontractors, in others it is not. But seldom is the subcontractor a signatory to the publication contract, and though he may receive a piece of the action as part of his deal with the principal author, it is not strictly a royalty in the sense we usually understand it, and of course the ghost forfeits any claim to copyright ownership.

Although I'm not at liberty to detail the many instances I know of authors who farm their work out, fans of those authors might be shocked to learn that their favorite books are produced, as it were, in a shop. There is in particular one bestselling male action-adventure series whose creator, to my knowledge, no longer writes his own books at all. In conjunction with his publisher, he puts the production of his books on an assembly line basis. A series "bible" describing the characters and general story line of the series is issued to writers, who submit plots for the approval of the creator and/or the publisher. Upon approval, a contract is issued to the writers. At first glance it looks like a typical publishing contract, but closer scrutiny reveals that the copyright is owned by a corporate entity; the advance is not called an advance (it's simply called a "sum"); and the royalty is not called a royalty (it's called a "bonus payment") and is expressed in cents rather than as a percentage of the list price of the book, presumably to further remove the writer-for-hire's labor from any association with creation of the work. I estimate the payments to the writer-for-hire to be approximately one-fourth to one-third of the traditional royalty that might normally accrue to him if he were the original creator of the book. I assume that the balance of the royalty is shared between the originator and the publisher.

In the above example, the originator of the series is in effect a packager. Packagers, as I have stated elsewhere, are sui generis. They are not exactly authors even though they frequently create the ideas and story lines for books; they are not exactly agents even though they take a kind of commission for their roles as go-betweens among authors and publishers; and they are not exactly publishers even though they buy the services of authors.

I've never been comfortable with packagers either in theory or in practice. Packagers are both buyers and sellers at the same time (so that "broker" might be the most apposite synonym), and there is inherent in their function the potential for mischief, abuse, and downright dishonesty. Some book packagers are as honest, open in their business dealings, and caring about authors as is possible under the circumstances. But a number are little short of rapacious, hiring authors for the smallest fees they can get away with and paying them no royalty or participation in subsidiary rights revenue whatsoever, while selling their books to publishers for very large multiples of what they pay the writers for them.

Furthermore, while these packagers manage to sell publishers on the concepts of books or series, they often contribute little or nothing by way of editorial input or guidance. An author is given the most general ideas ("How about a *Dirty Dozen* set in Vietnam!"), then is required to create characters, situations, and plots—create, in short, the entire series. The packager's argument is that were it not for his initiative in creating an idea and selling it to a publisher, writers would have no work and no pay. As the level of pay is all too frequently subsistence, the cause for heartfelt gratitude frequently escapes the writer-for-hire.

Because many publishers don't particularly care where their

product comes from as long as it is good, is delivered on time, and is not too expensive, they provide fertile ground in which packagers can flourish. That is one key reason for my concern that the packaging phenomenon, with all the implications of author exploitation that it represents, is on the rise. The other reason is that some publishers are taking their cues from packagers and doing the same thing. They cook up series ideas in their offices, produce a series bible, then hire writers to write books in the series under a house pseudonym. Because the publishers maintain that they created the series, they have been scaling back advances, royalties, and author participation in subsidiary rights for those books, and their contracts are, in fact if not in actual language, work-for-hire agreements. In many instances, the publishers offer flat fees to authors interested in writing books for publisher-originated series, take it or leave it.

You might infer that I refuse to do business with the more exploitive of packagers and publishers, but that is not the case. Some of my clients are hungry, and occasionally some are desperate for any kind of work, and though I may judge certain packagers and publisher-packagers harshly, practically speaking I don't feel it is fair for me to turn down, out of hand, work for clients who might be grateful for a few thousand dollars and a job that gets them through a financial squeeze or crisis. It's easy for an agent to tell an author, "I'd rather see you starve than accept that deal"; it's not so easy for an author to agree with him. If, after a writer has weighed all aspects of a work-for-hire deal, he or she still wants the job, then the only thing an agent can do is negotiate what few safeguards he can, such as making sure the writer is not legally liable for changes or additions to his text rendered by the packager or publisher. The quality of help an agent can render in these cases is the equivalent of telling the tenant of an avaricious landlord, "You have two choices: sign the lease or don't sign the lease."

Because packagers prosper from a supply-and-demand dynamic that is clearly—at this time, anyway—in their favor, there is little that individual authors or agents can do to roll conditions back. It must be done through collective action. Sad to say, authors and literary agents are scarcely closer to effective collective activism than they were when I started advocating it in my column some six years ago. So if you've been holding your breath, let it out.

A bill has been introduced by Senator Thad Cochran of Mississippi, however, that offers some ray of hope. Cochran's bill attempts to clarify the work-for-hire provisions of the 1976 Copyright Act by defining writers who do work-for-hire as employees of their publishers or packagers, meaning they would have to be covered by state or federal employment benefits, among other things. In a June 19, 1987, article in *Publishers Weekly*, Cochran was quoted as saying that "the need for reform in this area has grown stronger than ever," and that his bill "seeks to restore the ability of independent creators to claim authorship of their own works, and to realize profits from the exploitation of their works." Publishers, he said, are abusing the work-for-hire provision "to force both struggling and established freelance artists to sign non-negotiable work-for-hire agreements as a condition of publication."

Well said, Senator, and Godspeed to your bill.

CHAPTER 12

What Audio Means to You

In case you've been in a coma for the last few years, a revolution has taken place in the audio and video fields. After a period of uncertainty following the technological refinement of Walkman-type audiocassette players, automobile audiocassette systems, and home videocassette recorders, the audio and video industries have found their legs. Typical of the incredible growth of the audio industry is Newman Communications, which increased sales from $200,000 in 1980 to $7 million in 1984, after which the company went public. Consumer demand for audio and video electronics has permanently altered our nation's habits: People would no sooner leave their homes without their Walkman than they would without their keys, and the videotape recorder has become an indispensable component of the television set that spawned it.

Because of the close relationship between these technologies and the book publishing business, many publishers have jumped into the creation, production, and distribution of audio- and videocassettes. Most of the publishers that are allied to entertainment complexes, such as Warner, Putnam-Berkley (MCA), and Simon and Schuster-Pocket Books (Paramount Pictures), are taking advantage of the know-how, facilities, and product inventories of their affiliated companies to develop lines of book-record, book-cassette, and book-film tie-ins. Most bookstores of any appreciable size have departments devoted to selling audiocassettes, videocassettes, or both. And although the outlets for the sale or rental of videocassettes are at this time not usually connected with bookstore chains, I predict that in due time we will see a consolidation of the videocassette retail market and its eventual absorption into the bookstore chain system.

Just as political revolutions take a long time to affect the lives of rural people, the electronics revolution has only recently begun to filter down to the point where it affects the livelihood of the writers whose work is the basis for so much of the audio and video businesses. But the changes can now be palpably felt in the form of new provisions in book contracts. Language over which very little fuss was made as little as two or three years ago is now being scrutinized and haggled over by publishers. After a period of uncertainty if not downright confusion about contractual standards—agents calling each other frantically asking what was a good royalty on audio deals, and could they license the same property to two different audio companies, and should there be reserves against returns in audio as there are in the book business—some coherent trends have developed, and the time has come for authors to know what they are.

Provisions for audio and video have existed in publishing contracts for a very long time. It's just that the publishers didn't call the media "audio" or "video." Typical is a 1969 Doubleday contract in which the appropriate provisions are headed, "Sound Recording, Filmstrips, Teaching Machines, Microfilm":

> Author grants to Publisher the sole and exclusive right to sell the work or parts of it for mechanical reproduction and transmission, including, but not by way of limitation (a) sound and picture recording or any other method hereafter known or devised; (b) filmstrips; (c) programs for machine teaching; (d) microfilm and photocopying (except motion picture), or any other method now or hereafter known or devised for information storage, reproduction, and retrieval.

Today, publishers' legal advisors are rewriting contracts with more precise definitions of "audio" and "video," definitions that painstakingly differentiate those media from such kinfolk as television, radio, stage, motion picture, computer software, records, and electronic publishing. And whereas those mechanical and electronic recording rights were as often as not ceded to publishers by authors and agents who didn't see much value in them, now those rights have become serious bones of contention, and often they are deal-breakers. Several publishers that are tied to entertainment companies insist on those rights as a matter of policy whether they have any real intention of exploiting them or not. And even when they don't have any such intention, they have proven highly uncooperative in licensing those rights to competitive companies. Some publishers that are not allied with entertainment companies nevertheless try to get a position on electronic rights just in case. Bantam, for instance, has recently installed language in the boilerplate of its publishing contract stating that in the event the author controls any rights (such as movie or audio) "which Bantam has the capacity to exercise itself, the Author agrees to give Bantam the right of first refusal for the separate acquisition of such rights before licensing such rights elsewhere." In other words, if the owners of Bantam buy or start a movie, audiotape, or videotape company, you would have to submit your Bantam book to that company before being free to make a movie, audio, or video deal with another company.

Although we usually talk about audio and video in the same breath, in terms of adaptation of your work the two media are as far apart as their wavelengths are in the electromagnetic spectrum. As far as the immediate future is concerned, the chances are better that you will be dealing with audio than with video. By far, the predominant application of video right now is adaptation of motion pictures for use on home videocassette recorders. If your novel is adaptable to a dramatic medium, it will be acquired by a movie or television company, not a videotape one. If your book is nonfiction, the odds that it will be acquired by a videotape company are low unless it is a best-seller and has distinctive visual potential. Audio, on the other hand, is far cheaper to produce, requiring infinitely less technology, manpower, and capital to stimulate the listener's imagination than movies or video require to entertain the viewer. Therefore this chapter focuses on audio.

The terms for audio deals generally follow those for book deals—with some interesting exceptions. The tapes that are sold through bookstores are offered at discounts resembling those that apply to the book business—starting at 40 percent. But unlike the prevailing method of calculating book royalties on the list price, audio royalties for the most part are based on the net receipts after discount. If a tape package retailing for $50 is sold to a bookstore for 40 percent off, the licensor's royalty will be based on the $30 actually received by the tape company.

The royalty scale is generally in the area of 7 percent, and if you're weighing a royalty based on list price versus one based on net, in the above example you would be receiving $2.10 royalty per set instead of the $3.50 you'd get if your royalty was calculated on the list price. That's quite a difference! But one important factor in audiotape merchandising is that a lot of it is mail order. Nightingale-Conant, an audio company that at this time produces only nonfiction tapes, says that 90 percent of its sales are mail order. As there is usually no discount on mail order sales, the list price and the net price are the same number, and therefore you *will* be receiving a full royalty on mail-order sales of your tape.

Unlike book publishing, where royalties are accounted twice annually, audiotape royalties are accounted quarterly by many companies, and some firms send statements and checks on a monthly basis. Tapes sold via mail order are usually not returnable, but those sold in stores are, and producers therefore hold a reserve of royalties against possible returns, as in the book business.

An even more interesting and important difference is that while book publishers insist on exclusive rights in their territories, many audiotape producers will consent to your selling the same material to their competitors for distribution in essentially the same, or at least in overlapping, markets. We recently made deals with no fewer than three different audio producers to adapt the same best-selling nonfiction book for audio sold in the retail, direct-mail, and subscription markets.

When literary works are adapted to audio, the authors frequently ask to perform the reading themselves. Unless the author is a very big name and/or has a professionally trained voice, the producers prefer to employ professional actors or narrators to read or perform the adaptation. In cases where the producers do agree to let the author read his or her own work, there is usually no additional performance fee paid for the privilege.

Advances at this writing are low—under five-thousand dollars for most properties—and there isn't that much leeway even for star authors of best-selling books. That's because the volume of sales on even popular audiotapes is lower than it is for popular books. A good sale of a single cassette, an audio company representative recently told a meeting of the Independent Literary Agents Association, is a little over forty thousand units; a good sale of a six-cassette package is anything over seven thousand units.

Although the tape companies generally acquire or try to acquire world rights, translations are not much of a factor right now, and if you try to restrict the tape producer to worldwide English language rights only, reserving translation rights for yourself, you probably won't be jeopardizing your deal.

Because certain audio rights, such as exploitation of the soundtrack, are conveyed to a movie or television producer when you sell your work to one, you must be very careful when making an audio deal not to sell anything that might threaten a movie deal later on, or conflict with rights already conveyed to a movie producer. Straight reading of your book is usually okay, but when you venture into any kind of dramatization you start to run the risk of treading on territory owned, or coveted, by a movie or television producer. So use the utmost caution when negotiating your audio deal, and consult your agent or lawyer about the appropriate language to be employed in the contract.

What sort of literary material is attractive to audio producers? One of course is fiction, in the form of either dramatizations or readings. Despite my warnings about selling dramatic audio rights, most novels are *not* suitable for acquisition by movies and television, because they aren't dramatic or visual enough. Those same books may well be adaptable to the audio medium, where much drama can be made out of little content, the listener's imagination furnishing the rest of the entertainment experience.

Straight readings are also very popular, particularly if the narrator has an appealing voice. Children's audio is a very big market. Some genre fiction, like romance and science fiction-fantasy, has been adapted, but sales have not yet achieved great strength. One promising area, however, is taped interviews of star romance, science fiction, and other genre authors, which are sold to their fans.

The other important category of material sought by audio producers is instructional: self-help, how-to, and the like. Video is great for many instructional topics that call for high visual content or activity such as cooking, exercise, sports instruction, and hobbies, but for topics that don't require visual stimulation, such as language instruction, business advice, or religious wisdom, audio is the perfect medium. A critical reason is the portability of audiotapes: They may be listened to while one is doing something else, like walking to work, jogging, or commuting. For most people these are not particularly pleasurable activities, and they feel they could be using their time to improve themselves intellectually, emotionally, or spiritually. The answer, obviously, is for them to listen to a tape.

The audio business is very young, and there are a great many companies fighting for a place in the sun. A couple of years ago there was a sort of feeding frenzy as these firms snapped up all sorts of literary properties in order to have something, anything, for their lists. But a slowdown ensued as the producers, distributors, and sales outlets paused to observe just what was selling. What they discovered was that audio buyers are not unlike book buyers: They look for the familiar name or the unique gimmick or premise.

We can therefore expect an increased focus on adaptations of best-selling books and a sorting-out along the lines of the current movie, book, and recording star system. There will probably follow a consolidation of the audio companies until the little ones are absorbed by the giants. The haves will get more money for their audio rights, the have-nots will get less, and the midlist will be overlooked.

Does that scenario sound familiar?

CHAPTER 13

Multibook Deals

For many writers the term "multiple-book deal" conjures images of byzantine negotiations conducted in a smoke-filled conference room by a battery of literary agents, lawyers, accountants, and publishing executives, of telephone-number advances and thick contracts replete with state-of-the-art jargon about bestseller escalators, book club passthroughs, and topping privileges. The tyro author who would be overjoyed to get even a one-book contract must view such deals as relevant only to the gods in some literary Valhalla. What pertinence do these Ludlumian, Michenerian, Sheldonian transactions have to the humble and brutish lives of nickel-a-word galley slaves?

The truth is that many more multiple-book contracts are proffered to writers than most people imagine, and most of them are no more complicated than one-book contracts. And their terms are substantially lower than those generally associated with Olympic-sized swimming pools on the grounds of Beverly Hills estates. In fact, if you write in any of the traditional genres the chances are that sooner or later you'll be offered a multiple-book contract. Whether your specialty is science fiction, mysteries, westerns, romances, male adventure, or even popular nonfiction, it is likely that a publisher will be interested in signing you up for more than one book at a time. You may have created a character in a novel whose exploits you or your publisher would like to extend to further books. Or your publisher may like your work well enough to ask you to write books in a series created "in the house," as it were. You would do well to understand the features of such deals, if for no other reason than that, after longing to have one offered to you, you might ultimately decide that they're not that hot after all and you'd be better off selling one book at a time.

When you think about it, a multiple-book deal is simply an elaborate extension of your option clause. In a traditional contract, the publisher usually gets an option on your next book at terms to be negotiated. In a multiple-book contract, the publisher makes a commitment to more than one book and specifies the terms and conditions for the acquisition of those books. The nature of those books is usually described in detail: "Books number 4, 5, and 6 in the adult western series featuring the hero Luke Starbuck," or "Four saga-length works of fiction set on and around a Savannah, Georgia, peanut farm during the American Civil War." The general terms—"boilerplate"—that characterize a contract for one book now cover two or three or more at a time. The warranties you agree to on book number one are identical to those on numbers two and three, for instance. A few boilerplate items may be altered to adjust for the multiplicity of books in the contract. The termination clause will have the phrase "on each work" in it or something along those lines in order to account for the probability that each book in the contract will go out of print at a different time.

One of the reasons publishers like multiple-book contracts, then, is simply that they are convenient. They enable publishers to prepare one contract for several books whose terms are pretty much identical. This may seem like insufficient reason to offer such deals to authors, and in truth it is. But when you realize how much time and labor goes into the preparation of even a routine book contract, you might feel less inclined to criticize publishers for wanting to speed up the flow of paperwork, which after all benefits authors too.

The principal object of multiple-book deals is security. Ideally, they should make publishers and authors feel equally secure (agents don't mind a little security either, by the way), but things don't always turn out that way, as we shall see.

The security comes in because all parties know where they stand with each other for the duration of the contract. The publisher knows that his author is not going to leave him after the next book or the book after that. The publisher also knows he won't be hit for a high price one or two books from now if the author gets hot tomorrow, because the prices for those future books will have been fixed at the outset, when the multiple-book contract was signed. The author, by the same token, knows there will be a home waiting for his next two or three books, and can count on a specific sum of money to be paid him when he delivers them. Even if the market for his kind of books collapses, his publisher is still contractually obligated to pay him for each delivered book, whereas if the author made contracts with his publisher on a book-by-book basis, the publisher could drop him as soon it became apparent that there was no more market for his stuff.

Another important factor is scheduling dependability. Where series or other related books are involved, success rests heavily on the timing of release of the books, and that timing can be set with certainty only if the publisher can absolutely count on reliable delivery of three or four or six books. By tying the author up for that many, the publisher knows (or at least hopes) that the author won't accept contracts with other publishers that will interfere with the delivery and publication rhythm of the series.

Of course, the big multiple-book deals that make front-page headlines incorporate all of the above factors plus very big front-money. These deals are designed to nail down a best-selling author for as long as possible, and in many cases there is little or no description of the books because nobody including the author knows what they're going to be about. Indeed, the publisher may not even care what they're about as long as it's guaranteed he'll get his mitts on them.

The publicity value of a multiple-book deal may outweigh its actual monetary value. The pages of publishing trade publications and writers' newsletters are filled with references to deals that make author and publisher look good but do not necessarily stand up to intense scrutiny. A "five-figure deal" might be for $99,000—or it might only be for $10,000. Or you may read about deals that "could bring the author $850,000 per book." They *could*, yes, if they sell like hotcakes, get picked up by major book clubs, go on the best-seller list for two years, and are made into major motion pictures. The actual guaranteed money in such deals might be quite modest, but the built-in escalators, bonuses, and similar features enable the publishers to wring the most publicity out of them.

And of course, deals that may seem relatively small to the public at large can be most impressive in the author's "hometown"—that is, the genre in which he writes. A three-book deal for $75,000 advance might be sneezed at by *The New York Times*, but if the books are science fiction, romance, westerns, or some other genre, the writers and editors who read about such exploits in the trade papers will sit up and take notice.

Big deals or little, the underlying accounting principles are the same. Let's examine them.

There are several ways in which the accounting may be set up in a multiple-book contract. The first is to fix the advance for each title in the contract, and to keep the royalty accounting on each book separate from that on the other books in the package. Thus you might have a three-book, $30,000 advance contract, with the advance per book pegged at $10,000. When book number one is published and earns more than $10,000 in royalties, the author will collect the overage in royalties even though the second book, say, has not yet earned back *its* $10,000 and the third book has not even been published.

The other way to structure a multiple-book deal is to "jointly account" the advances on each book. Joint accounting (also known as "basket accounting" and "cross-collateralization") creates a common royalty pool for the earnings of *all* books in the contract. This means that royalties earned over and above the advance on one book in the contract will not necessarily be paid to the author but will instead be applied to the unearned advances on other books in the contract. Until the total of advances in that contract has been earned out by royalties from any or all books in that contract, the author will not receive additional royalties. For instance, suppose we have that $30,000 advance deal for three books, but with joint accounting. Book #1 is published and earns $15,000. Does the author receive royalties? No, because the three-book combination must earn a total of $30,000. Suppose, further, that the second book earns $15,000 too. Does the author now receive royalties? Again, no, because the two books have earned, together, no more than the

$30,000 originally advanced to the author. Now book #3 is published and earns $4500 in royalties. Does the author *now* get anything? Yes, he gets $4,500, for the total royalties earned by the three books is $34,500, or $4,500 more than was originally advanced. Of course, it can work the other way around too. Suppose the first book in the package was a wild success and earned $35,000. The author would then collect $5000 royalties on his three-book contract even though the second and third books weren't yet published. And when those books *were* published, all royalties they earned from the very first dollar would go to the author, because his $30,000 advance would have been earned out on the first book.

In a jointly accounted multiple-book contract, then, the advance per book becomes meaningless, for as we've seen, one book in the series could earn more than its proportionate share of royalties but pay the author no money over and above his advance; and in other cases a book could earn considerably less than its proportionate share of royalties but the author would get all the royalties from that book. Publishers will still, however, assign a value to each book in such a contract for a different reason. Suppose we have a three-book $30,000 contract with joint accounting, and after delivering the first book the author fails to deliver the second one, or screws it up beyond repair. The publisher wishes to cancel the contract, at least for that book: How does he figure out how much the author must repay him? Well, if for this purpose (and this purpose alone) he assigns each book in the contract a value of $10,000, that task becomes easy. If the author delivers all three books in the contract, though, and the publisher accepts all three, then the $10,000 per book evaluation becomes meaningless.

There are pitfalls for both author and publisher in multiple-book deals, for such deals are like long-term commodity investments. If you bet that a commodity will be worth X dollars one year from now, and between now and then the value soars far beyond what you estimated it would be, you will be left holding a considerably undervalued contract. Apply this to the case of an author who grabs a three-book contract for $30,000 advance. The advance is paid in four equal installments of $7,500 apiece, the first on signing and the next three on delivery of each book.

The first book is published and becomes a wild success—book club, reprint, movie, the whole bit. Now he delivers the second book and what does he get—a mere $7,500. He may be mad at himself (to say nothing of his agent) for tying himself up for so long for so little. Of course, the difference between an author and a pork belly (and perhaps the only difference) is that the author at least has the opportunity to make up in royalties for the inadequate advance he negotiated two or three books ago when he was just another lowly writer in the crowd. Thus he may only collect $7,500 when he delivers book number two, but a few months later he may collect $50,000 in royalties earned on book one.

Bear in mind that by the same token the publisher stands to lose if the commodity—the author, his books, and the market—go short, that is, drop below what the publisher projected when he tied the author up for all those books. If a publisher signs you up for that four-novel peanut-plantation saga, and just around the time you're delivering the first one the market for plantation sagas collapses and your publisher can't give them away—well, there's going to be much rending of garments and maybe of jobs at that publisher's office.

So it's a bit of a crapshoot both ways, and if you feel your books are going to be worth far more than the per-book advance you've been offered in a multiple-book deal, then turn that deal down. If the publisher doesn't agree with your appraisal of your future value, then *he'll* turn the deal down. Sometimes you can forge a compromise. If your publisher feels that the individual value of the books in a three-book deal is $10,000, and you feel it's $15,000, you can split the difference by structuring advances of $10,000 on the first book, $12,500 on the second, and $15,000 on the third. If the deal is jointly accounted, you'd simply add these advances up for a total advance of $37,500.

Once a publisher has a good writer in his stable, he may be willing to pay high, even to overpay, to keep him there for a long, long time. I remember negotiating with a publisher for an author he coveted, and I fixed a price of $225,000 for a three-book contract.

He winced. "That's awfully high."

"What can I tell you?" I said with a shrug. "That's what I think he's worth, or will be by the time he writes his third book."

"Who knows how much he'll be worth two years from now?" the publisher sighed philosophically. "We could all be dead two years from now."

"That's true," I replied. "So why don't we just make a deal for one book and see how that one goes?"

The man sat bolt upright in his chair, a stricken look on his face. "Don't do me any favors." Alarmed at the prospect of having this rising young author for only one more book, the publisher quickly met my terms.

CHAPTER 14

Payout Schedules

While the size of the advance is the criterion by which most authors measure the commercial value of their books, the size and timing of the installments in which the advance is paid are just as significant, and sometimes more so. Because the "payout schedule" directly affects the cash flow of publishers and authors, it is often a bone of bitter contention in negotiations, and many a player has walked away from an otherwise good deal because the payout schedule nullified advantages gained in the negotiation.

With few exceptions, advances are paid in installments. Part of the total money is payable upon signing the contract, the balance payable on acceptance of partial, complete, or revised manuscript; on certain calendar dates; on publication; and even after publication. Although the payout formula may be fairly simple when the advance is small, publishers and agents devote a great deal of attention to it when the stakes get high. The reason, of course, is the cost of money.

Until recently, when the inflation rate ground to a comfortably low single-digit crawl, it could be projected that the value of one thousand dollars deferred for one year was nine hundred dollars. At the same time, double-digit interest rates until late 1985 appreciated the value of that thousand dollars to something like twelve hundred in a year. Thus, between inflation and interest, a year's postponement of payout to an author meant a swing of some 30 percent in the value of that money.

Both interest rates and inflation have, at this writing at any rate, returned to manageable levels, but for both publishers and authors, even 10 percent per annum is worth fighting over and may indeed make a significant difference to their balance sheets.

Let's take a closer look at payout schedules installment by installment and sketch some ways authors may improve their position when the haggling begins.

• *Payment due on signing of the contract.* All contracts large and small require a consideration to be paid on signing, even if it be no more than one dollar, in order to bind the agreement. If the total advance is small enough, it may be payable in full upon signing. Most publishers today, however, have policies prohibiting payment in full on signing, and editors are ordered to defer some part of the advance in negotiations. Even if your book is a flawless gem requiring not a jot of revision, an editor may contrive to pay a second installment of your advance "upon acceptance of revisions" in order to satisfy company policy. Then, a week or two after vouchering the signature installment, the editor will put through the acceptance installment as well.

If the contract is for an unwritten book, the advance will be divided at least into an on-signing payment and an acceptance one to create an incentive for the author to deliver the work. The publisher may try to divide the advance even further, into installments payable on delivery of a partial manuscript or first draft.

You will have to do some solid reckoning before accepting too small an installment on signing, otherwise you'll run out of money before you turn in material qualifying you for the next installment. First you must subtract your agent's commission if any, then calculate the amount of time that will pass until you are entitled to the next payment. You then have to figure whether your living costs (including anticipated lump sum payments like school tuition, income taxes, or insurance premiums) during that period will be covered by what you collect when you sign your contract. A $50,000 advance may seem attractive to you, but if your publisher wants to pay you $10,000 on signing and it takes you six months to write the book, and your monthly nut is $3,000, you're going to be up the creek halfway through the writing of the book. So you must bargain hard for a down payment that will sustain you until you've turned your manuscript in.

• *Payment due on delivery of partial manuscript or first draft.*
These installments are generically known in the book trade as
"satisfactory progress" payments. To help bridge the gap between the on-signing and the acceptance checks, and to encourage or compel progress, publishers frequently negotiate installments payable when the author turns in part of the book. A
typical deal might be structured: one third on signing the contract, one third on delivery of half the manuscript, and one
third on delivery and acceptance of the complete manuscript.

Of the many ploys cooked up by publishers to stretch out
their money, "satisfactory progress" is the least effective, and if
it weren't so dangerous it would be just plain silly. At the very
least, "satisfactory progress" is satisfactory neither to authors
nor publishers, and the only thing it does for progress is halt it.

In a "satisfactory progress" situation, an author faces a number of choices, all of them terrible. He can turn in a rough
draft, which is usually an embarrassing mess that will send most
editors into respiratory arrest, or at least provoke them to
request revisions that the author would ordinarily make on his
own when tackling the final draft. Or he can stop work in the
middle of the book, polish and retype what he's done so far,
and turn a partial manuscript in. Either way, he will have to
suspend work on his book until he has received some feedback
from his editor. Even if his editor offers no feedback whatever,
it may take weeks or longer to get that editorial reaction, and
such delays are inevitably harmful to creativity and cash flow. If
the editor does have criticisms, the author may be required to
rework what he's turned in in order to get his hands on that
money. To avoid all that hassle, therefore, an author may
choose to forgo his "satisfactory progress" payment and forge
ahead with the rest of the book, which defeats the purpose of
such interim payments. Most authors do not polish chapters
after drafting them, but prefer to finish a rough draft and polish
it in the final draft. Thus the time between the completion of a
first draft and a final draft, or delivery of half the manuscript
and all of it, may be so brief that the machinery for putting
through the "satisfactory progress" installment will scarcely
have begun turning when it will be time to put through the final
acceptance payment. Furthermore, many editors feel it's silly to

read a partial manuscript or first draft when the final product will be turned in a few weeks or a month later.

In short, "satisfactory progress" payments reflect little understanding of how authors work and pose a genuine threat to both the quality of a book and the timeliness of its delivery. Ultimately, this ends up hurting the publisher as badly as it hurts the author.

If there is no way that you can avoid this onerous arrangement, at least negotiate for a time limit on editorial approval of your partial manuscript. If you've had no word in, say, four weeks, then the material you've turned in should be deemed satisfactory and the check due at that time must be vouchered.

• *Payment due on acceptance of the manuscript.* Whenever possible, the balance of the advance on a commissioned book should be payable no later than upon acceptance. A number of contracts stipulate that a manuscript is deemed acceptable unless the publisher notifies the author to the contrary within a period of time, thirty days, sixty days, or thereabouts. This is a very desirable feature and one worth fighting for if it does not appear in the boilerplate of your contract.

In most contracts the definition of acceptability embraces revisions. If serious revisions are required by a publisher, the acceptance segment of the advance may be delayed until satisfactory revisions are turned in. If the revisions are minor, however, the publisher can often be prevailed upon to put through the acceptance money and take it on faith that the author will turn in acceptable revisions. There is an in-between state where revisions are necessary but the author cannot afford to do them without some sort of financial relief. In such cases the publisher may be persuaded to release some of the acceptance money to carry the author during the revision period.

I'll express myself in a later chapter about the prevailing requirement in publishing contracts that an author must repay the on-signing installment of his advance if his manuscript is rejected. But in case you can't restrain your impatience—I think it stinks. The on-signing advance should be regarded as a forfeitable investment, not a refundable loan. Needless to say, hard-headed (or hard-hearted) publishers will see things quite differently.

• *Payments due on publication.* The purpose of publication installments is to enable publishers to start recouping what they've paid the author as soon as possible after disbursing his advance. Publication payments used to be the norm in American publishing. Then the rise of strong agents in the 1960s drove publication payments out of favor. But when money started to get expensive again in the 1970s, publishers pushed the agents back, and it is now common for publication installments to be paid. In some foreign countries such as England, the publication installment is an article of faith.

The most common mistake authors make when agreeing to publication payments in a negotiation is failing to fix a time limit on them. Unacceptable language is, "$5,000 payable upon publication of the Work." Acceptable: "$5,000 payable upon publication of the Work or twelve months after acceptance, whichever date is sooner." The reason should become obvious if you think it through. Few contracts require publication of a book in less than twelve months after its acceptance, and many allow for publication in eighteen or even twenty-four months. Tacked on to these times are grace periods giving publishers an additional six months or more beyond the deadline to publish the work upon notification by the author that the deadline has passed. A publication payment may therefore not be due for as much as three years after a book has been accepted.

What is worse, publication of a book may be cancelled entirely for any of a number of reasons: staff changes, new policies, or events or trends that date the book. That means that the publication portion of the advance will not be payable at all, at least not according to the publisher's interpretation of the contract. I don't know if the point has been tested in court, but it can certainly be argued that if you sell a book to a publisher for $25,000 and the publisher cancels publication—well, you *still* sold the book for $25,000 even if some of that sum was to have been paid, for the publisher's convenience, on publication. Therefore, whenever you negotiate a publication advance, you should always stipulate that the installment will be due on publication *or X months after acceptance, whichever date comes first.* The X is negotiable, but should be no longer than the outside date by which the publisher is required to publish your book.

• *Postpublication payments.* Publishers have devised a fascinating array of gimmicks to postpone the day of reckoning to authors. Among these is the postpublication advance. Such installments may be payable on a specific date—X months after publication, say—or, in the case of a hardcover-softcover deal, one installment may be payable when the hardcover edition is published, another when the paperback edition is brought out. There are other creative variations on this theme, but because a book begins earning royalties from the date it's shipped, all postpublication advances amount to the same thing: paying authors with their own money.

Authors may want to try to negotiate payout schedules advantageous to their income tax statuses. An author who has already made a lot of money in a year may not want to receive a large on-signing payment that same year. A deal can be structured, therefore, so that only a token amount is paid on signing and the balance of the on-signing advance paid on January 2 of the following year. Not surprisingly, publishers like such setups, since they enable them to keep authors' money for several months. Literary agents, however, are not always thrilled to have their commissions deferred just because a client is enjoying a good year, so I don't feel your agent is out of line to request his commission on the full on-signing advance now, and to take no commission when your money comes in in January. Suppose the on-signing advance is $10,000 but you don't want any of that money until January. If your agent wants his commission now, he could negotiate $1,000 on signing of the contract to be retained entirely by him as commission (assuming a 10 percent commission), then $9,000 payable in January on which he would take no commission at all.

If you do want to structure installments in a way that you feel is advantageous to you taxwise, and your publisher is agreeable to the arrangement, the time to do it is when your contract is negotiated. If a contract is already in force and you ask your publisher to defer until next January a payment that is due this October because you don't want more money this year, the Internal Revenue Service may disallow it if you are audited and your publishing contract is examined. The same holds true of requests to agents to hold money until the following January.

The law makes it quite clear that money received by a fiduciary—a literary agent, for example—is construed to have been received by the author. This is not to say that publishers and agents do not hold money for authors in such circumstances, but getting away with it doesn't alter the statutes concerning "constructive receipt," and you may be liable for an adjustment in tax for that year plus interest and penalties.

Not long ago a publisher approached me with an intriguing idea for payout of the advance on a deal with a superstar client. He suggested structuring the terms in the same way that they are structured for superstar ballplayers to help prevent them from paying too much in taxes in any given year. A $2 million advance, for example, might be payable over twenty years to hold the tax bite down. However well or poorly the book did, the publisher reasoned, and whether the author was working or retired over the next twenty years, he could look forward to a check for $100,000 every year.

I said, "Thanks but no thanks." For one thing, between inflation, interest, and revenue earned on the book, the $2 million advance would actually cost the publisher close to nothing. Second, most authors who have achieved superstar status will probably have incorporated themselves, and deferred compensation for corporations is not as desirable as it is for mere mortals.

Even if you are nothing more than a working-stiff-type writer, it's still a good idea to get as much money up front as you can. A smart agent and a smart accountant will help you to structure your cash flow so that your hide is relatively intact every April 15. Don't let publishers earn interest on your money. Remember, the sooner you get your hands on it, the sooner you can start blowing it on stupid investments.

CHAPTER 15

Escalators

A term commonly heard in discussions of book deals is "escalator." For instance, "Her book was bought for an advance that, *with escalators*, could exceed $1 million." Escalators are additional advance payments made by publishers to authors if and when certain contingencies occur. What are those contingencies? How much are they worth? And what, if anything, is their real value?

Escalators were created to bridge the gap between author and publisher when negotiations reach an impasse. You strongly believe your book will be a best-seller or will be bought by a major book club or made into a motion picture, and you feel that your advance should reflect the same optimism on your publisher's part. Your publisher, on the other hand, hopes and prays you're right, but has seen many a slip 'twixt the cup and the lip. He cannot afford to overpay authors on the strength of hope alone. Of course, if your track record justifies it—if your last five books have soared to the top of the best-seller list, been main selections of major book clubs, and been made into hit movies—he will be greatly disposed to pay you a lot of money up front. But let us say, for the sake of argument, that this is not the case.

The answer is for the publisher to offer you escalators. These bind him to pay you scheduled sums of money if, and only if, your optimism turns out to be justified; if it doesn't, he owes you nothing beyond whatever royalties your book may earn over its original advance.

Although the terms "bonus" and "escalator" are used interchangeably in Publishingese, and I'll use them that way here as well, these extra payments are not really bonuses in the usual sense. They are always recoverable from royalties and subsidiary income generated by a book; they are, in other words, additional advances. If your original advance was $50,000, say, and your contract calls for a $10,000 escalator to be triggered by the release of a movie adaptation of your book, then your advance becomes $60,000. The $10,000 escalator is, in effect, a prepayment of royalties that your publisher hopes your book will earn as a result of the movie.

It would seem, then, that you are being paid with your own money, and in certain cases that is true. Suppose you sold your book to a publisher for a $25,000 advance, and your contract calls for a $10,000 escalator to be paid if your book is sold to a paperback reprint house for $100,000 or more. Further suppose that the book is auctioned off and sold to a reprinter for $150,000. If the traditional fifty-fifty split on reprint money obtains, your share of the reprint money will come to $75,000.

Okay, the reprint deal triggers your $10,000 escalator. Now you've received a total of $35,000: your advance plus your escalator. But it is no hardship for your publisher to pay that escalator to you, because you are guaranteed $75,000 as your share of the reprint deal!

Other escalators are riskier for publishers and can end up losing money for them. Take another hypothetical case where you sell your book for a $100,000 advance, and the contract calls for a $25,000 bonus if a movie is made from your book. Let's say that both book and movie flop, and your book doesn't even earn back its original advance, let alone the advance plus the escalator. This is a case where the publisher was *not* paying you out of guaranteed monies, but is genuinely out of pocket.

A few years ago, when negotiations with a publisher over a science fiction novel became deadlocked, I proposed a solution that would require the publisher to pay a smaller advance up-front, then additional advances when the number of copies *in print* exceeded certain scheduled levels. That way, the publisher would recover the escalator payments as soon as the books were distributed. Unfortunately, the publisher did not make adequate allowances for returns on distribution of new printings. While new printings normally generate royalties that reduce an unearned advance, the paradox in this case was that with each new printing the unearned position grew larger and larger. The more copies the publisher sold, the greater the deficit became!

Escalators fall into a number of categories. The most common is the best-seller bonus. The best-seller list usually used to determine escalators is the one in the book review section of the Sunday edition of *The New York Times*, though sometimes the one in *Publishers Weekly* is also used.

There are several ways to structure best-seller bonuses. One is the length of time that a book is on the list, another is a book's position on the list. It is desirable for a book to be on the best-seller list for a long time, of course; it is also desirable for a book to be high on the best-seller list. Bonuses can be structured to reward length or position or both.

A long run on the list, even at the bottom, can be significant, both because it means the book is selling strongly over a long period of time, and because it enables the publisher to boast, "———Weeks on the Bestseller List!"

Just as important is position on the list. The higher your book rises, the better it is, naturally. But the book that reaches the number one position causes a quantum leap in promotional value, even if it drops down or off the list the very next week. Therefore, many escalator schedules in book contracts are heavily weighted in favor of the number one slot.

The actual sums paid at the various stations of the list can vary widely. I have negotiated best-seller escalators for as little as a few thousand dollars. I have also negotiated the following:

> If the Publisher's edition(s) of the Work is listed on *The New York Times Bestseller List* the Publisher agrees to pay to the Author as an additional advance against and on account of all monies accruing to the Author under the terms of this agreement, the sum of up to but no more than one hundred and fifty thousand dollars ($150,000.00) payable as follows:

> Listed as #11, 12, 13, 14, or 15: the sum of five thousand dollars ($5,000.00) for each week so listed.

Listed as #6, 7, 8, 9, or 10: the sum of ten thousand dollars ($10,000.00) for each week so listed.

Listed as #4 or 5: the sum of fifteen thousand dollars ($15,000.00) for each week so listed.

Listed as #2 or 3: the sum of twenty thousand dollars ($20,000.00) for each week so listed.

Listed as #1: the sum of thirty thousand dollars ($30,000.00) for each week so listed.

The Publisher agrees to pay the Author the appropriate amount due within thirty (30) days of the Work being so listed on *The New York Times Bestseller List.*

You'll note two features in this provision that I haven't discussed. The first is a ceiling of $150,000. Almost all escalator deals place a limit on the total extra money payable to the author. The other is that the escalators, or escalator installments in this case, are payable within a short period of time after the event. In this case, that's thirty days, and thirty days is as long as it should take for most bonuses, otherwise the publisher will be taking back in interest what he owes you in bonus money. If a publisher waits until royalty time to pay you your escalators, that's not much of a bargain.

Another form of escalator is book club or paperback reprint, wherein your publisher agrees to pay you additional advance monies if a book club or paperback reprint deal on your book exceeds a certain amount of money. As we've seen, such escalators are almost invariably of the pay-you-with-your-own-money variety, because your publisher is guaranteed recoupment of the bonus out of the money he will eventually collect from the book club or reprinter. The only thing he loses is interest on the prepayment to you of money he would otherwise have paid in the normal six-month royalty cycle.

Then there are movie bonuses, which are usually payable upon national release by a major distributor of a theatrical motion picture based on your book. There's a mouthful of contingencies crammed into that sentence, so let's analyze it. First, the movie has to be released. Of course! you say, but many authors believe that a movie *deal* on their book ought to be enough to garner them a handsome bonus from their publishers. I'm sorry to tell you otherwise. Although there is some promotional value for a publisher to be able to boast, "Acquired for motion pictures by Dino DeLaurentiis," it scarcely does a thing for sales. Thus, escalators are usually not payable when movie rights to your book are optioned, or when the option is exercised. In fact, they are not even payable when your movie goes into production. Publishers have seen too many movie deals fall through to get excited when Meryl Streep or Eddie Murphy or Steven Spielberg takes an option on a book property. They have learned to their sorrow that many movies that go into production are not completed or released. So, in order to trigger that escalator, the film must be distributed.

And it must be distributed by one of the big distributors, Twentieth Century-Fox or Warner or MGM-UA and the like, rather than any one of the thousands of little ones that service the movie community. And finally, the movie must be released nationally, as opposed to locally or regionally. The premiere of a film, even a high-budget one made by a great director with superstar actors and actresses, is not going to boost sales of the book from which it is adapted if it's shown only at a few elite showcase theaters in New York and Los Angeles. In order for the film to have impact on mass market book sales, it must be shown at hundreds or thousands of theaters around the nation.

The prices for movie escalators vary widely, from modest—in the low five figures—to very large in the case of authors with long track records in the area of books made into hit films.

Related to theatrical movie bonuses are television-movie escalators. But while the market for television adaptation of books is a very active one, the stimulus to book sales is usually minimal. Even though the exposure is tremendous, far greater than that of a theatrical movie, it is also ephemeral: an evening or two (repeated once, six months or a year later) and it's gone. For publishers this presents serious problems of distribution and promotion. The books must be in the stores precisely on the day of or the day after the airing of the film, and the film must be so heavily publicized that consumers will be motivated to buy the book at the time of the airing. This is expensive, inefficient, unpredictable, and usually, therefore, unsuccessful.

For a television movie to mean anything in terms of tie-in value, it must first of all be an event, one absorbing a minimum of four hours but preferably spanning a whole week of evenings. It should also be based on a bestselling book such as *The Winds of War* or *North and South*, so that viewer recognition of both the book and movie stimulate each other: You've read the book, now see the television movie, you've seen the movie, now read the book. Because very few books are converted into television events on the magnitude of, say, *Shōgun*, the prices for escalators in this medium are considerably lower than they are for release of a major theatrical film adaptation of your book. The conditions are that the TV film be of at least four hours, run on consecutive evenings, and be aired originally on a major television network.

There are other contingencies that may trigger escalator payments. Some contracts call for bonuses to be paid if a book wins a major prize or award that has promotional value: Pulitzer, National Book Award, and the like. In some science fiction book contracts, I have negotiated bonuses for winning Nebula or Hugo awards, and in a few cases I even worked in bonuses for *nominations* for those awards. To science fiction fans the words "Nebula" or "Hugo" on the cover of a book are powerful inducements to buy that book, even if the word "Nominee" is printed beside them.

Obviously, not all books are suitable for escalators. Midlist books, most genre books, and books in category series seldom have escalation provisions in their contracts. For the occasional *wunderbuch*, the midlist novel that becomes a word-of-mouth best-seller and gets made into a hit movie, the author who did not have escalators in his contract can nevertheless look forward to royalties in the usual course of things. Of course, the next contract he negotiates will, you can be sure, contain more escalators than Macy's department store.

There's no harm in your trying for escalators when you negotiate your next contract, because it's no skin off your publisher's nose to give them to you: He only has to pay them to you, as they say in Las Vegas, "on the come." So what the hell: Go for it. That way, you too will be able to brag that you have sold your book—with escalators—for a million dollars.

CHAPTER 16

Acceptability

A great quantity of ink has been spilled in recent years about the "acceptability" clause of publishing contracts, and I'm afraid I must beg your indulgence while I spill a little more, for there is still considerable confusion about it. I have read many legal briefs and trial transcripts and have even testified as expert witness in cases involving this issue. Yet, little of what has been spoken and written has cleared up this confusion. But as acceptability is the keystone of the relationship between author and publisher, it seems worth making one more attempt at elucidating it.

The acceptability provision can be summarized as follows: A publisher engages an author to write a book, stipulating in the contract that if the manuscript is not acceptable in the publisher's sole discretion, the publisher may reject it and require the author to repay in full the advance he was paid on signing the contract. Until that advance is repaid, the publisher will not release the author from the contract, thus restricting the author from entering into a contract with another publisher for that (and perhaps any other) literary work.

Inherent in this provision are three potentially explosive elements. The first is that acceptability depends entirely on the arbitrary editorial judgment of the publisher. The second is that the author is required to repay every penny to his publisher when his manuscript is determined to be unacceptable. The third is that the author is restrained from selling his book to another publisher until his original publisher has been repaid, or at least until satisfactory provisions for repayment have been made. (And if there is an option clause in the original contract, the author may be prohibited from selling *any* other work to another publisher until satisfactory refund arrangements have been made with the publisher of the first part.)

This mixture has indeed exploded on numerous occasions, and with growing frequency as the stakes in our business have grown higher. But there is a qualitative difference between disputes over acceptability and those over most other items in publishing contracts. Whereas 99 percent of the quarrels that arise between authors and publishers end up being negotiated, settled, or compromised, those over acceptability often end up being litigated to final judgments. Now, publishers are loath to spend money on lawsuits, especially against authors, because it is expensive and makes for poor public relations. But when it comes to the question of acceptability, a publisher may be counted on to fight like the devil even though it looks lousy to dun and sue authors and the legal costs exceed the prospects of recovery of the money paid to the author. And authors who might otherwise shrink from the expense of prosecuting or defending a lawsuit have been known to dig in against all reason to wage war over the acceptability provision. Both sides seem anxious to make law on this issue. And when that happens, it usually means that a principle is involved that transcends money.

Authors frequently balk over the seeming right of life and death accorded in the provision that gives publishers the sole discretion to accept or reject a manuscript. But if the publisher doesn't have that right, who else should have it? The author? *Of course* a publisher is entitled to that right. As in any other business enterprise, the party that commissions a work is entitled to approval of the merchandise. It's only the potential to abuse the right that makes authors anxious, and there are enough instances of abuse to justify that anxiety.

In defense of publishers, it must be said that abuses occur less frequently than might be expected, and for two reasons. The first is that most publishers are extremely cautious about engaging authors to write books. Before contracting for an unwritten book a publisher will require ample evidence of the author's track record, writing skill, and reliability so as to minimize the possibility that the author will not deliver, will deliver late, or will deliver a problem manuscript.

The second reason is that most publishing companies today are run by committee. Just as the decision to hire a writer is not left to one editor, neither is the decision to accept or reject the finished product. Rather, the manuscript is circulated among members of the editorial board. This is particularly true when the sponsoring editor has doubts about the quality of the material. That editor's judgment is on the line, for he was responsible for advocating the company's investment in the project to begin with. If he rejects it, wasting his firm's time and raising the possibility that the money paid the author thus far won't be recovered, he loses face, prestige, and authority with his colleagues and employers. Sometimes he loses his job. Therefore, the editor who feels negatively about a delivered manuscript will seek backup from others on the editorial board, just as he solicited that backup when he acquired the book. And unless the manuscript is truly a stinker, the board may vote to go ahead with publication or revision despite its reservations. So there are fail-safe mechanisms operative at publishing companies that can reduce the potential for arbitrary rejection.

Nevertheless, abuses of "sole discretion" do occur. I can recall more than a few occasions when a publisher contracted for an unwritten book, then rejected the manuscript because the subject was no longer as timely or relevant as it was when the publisher signed up the author, or because the editor who commissioned the project was no longer there to lend support and enthusiasm to it. A notable example of this occurred when William Morrow rejected William Safire's manuscript of a book about Richard Nixon. Safire contended that the real reason Morrow found his book unsatisfactory was that between the time Morrow commissioned the book and the time Safire completed it, Richard Nixon had become persona non grata with the American public.

Agents and authors can cite numerous instances of publishers using the acceptability clause to renege on high-priced agreements. These publishers will agree to whatever terms it takes to get a hot author or property. Then, when the manuscript is turned in, the publisher may decide for any number of reasons that it overpaid. The publisher then threatens to reject the manuscript unless the author agrees to renegotiate the contract. The real reason for rejection may be that the publisher doesn't have, or doesn't want to spend, that much money. Thus far the courts have favored the publishers' argument that they should not be compelled to publish a book that they are certain is going to lose money.

It is extremely difficult for an aggrieved author to prove in a court of law that his publisher acted in bad faith in rejecting his manuscript. The parties cannot ask judge or jury to read the manuscript, because this involves matters of taste that are beyond a court's jurisdiction. So it's incumbent on authors and their lawyers to demonstrate that the publisher was motivated by bad faith, and I'm happy to note a trend toward admitting good and bad faith as factors in lawsuits over the acceptability clause. Admitting those factors in turn opens the door to questions of a publisher's editorial responsibilities, its obligations to furnish authors with editorial guidance, opportunities to rewrite, second opinions by other editors, arbitration and appeal, and other procedures designed to insure that authors are not placed totally at the mercy of publishers whose motives may be impure.

This also means that the stipulation requiring authors to repay their on-signing advance if the publisher rejects their manuscripts is coming under closer scrutiny by the courts. For if it can be shown that a publisher acted in bad faith when it turned a book down, a court may decide that the publisher is not entitled to a refund, no matter what the contract may call for. This very thing happened in a dispute between author Julia Whedon and Dell, in which the court supported Whedon's contention that Dell had acted in bad faith by rejecting her manuscript without affording her the benefit of editorial guidance, rewrite instructions, etc. The court not only allowed her to keep the advance Dell had paid her on signing the contract, but even ruled that she had not breached her contract when she sold the rejected manuscript to another publisher before being released from her Dell contract. In fact, the court ruled that when Dell failed to furnish Whedon with adequate editorial help, *Dell* breached its contract and at that point the author was released with no further obligation to repay her advance.

These developments are extremely promising from the view-point of authors even though, at this time, they still have to fight and even go to court to gain protection that should auto-matically devolve on them in the boilerplate of every publishing contract. At the same time, all this legal wrangling over sole discretion only serves to obscure the real issue in the war over acceptability: Is an advance a loan? *Or is it, rather, an investment?*

As things stand now, publishing contracts are nothing more than free options on an author's time, talent, and services. If, after the months or years it takes for an author to produce a book, the publisher turns the manuscript down, that publisher is entitled to get its money back in full. The only sum the publisher is out of pocket is the cost of the money—the inter-est, that is—that it "loaned" to the author while he was writing his book. Now, money-back guarantees are fine if you manu-facture soup, soap, or spaghetti sauce. But it's quite something else if you write books. The principle of repayment on which the acceptability clause rests is a thoroughly odious one and de-serves to be fought by any means at an author's disposal.

An advance is *not* a loan. It is a nonrecoverable investment, no different from an investment in a stock or bond issue, a mining or drilling operation, a Broadway show. A publisher reviews an author's "prospectus," his writing credits, sales rec-ords, reputation for reliability, and samples of the proposed work. If the publisher determines that a book by this author is a good investment, he puts money on it. As we have seen, the publisher truly examines book proposals as carefully as if they were "at risk" investments. Why should a publisher be entitled to get his money back while investors in every other type of offering stand to forfeit theirs? If for any reason the manuscript is disappointing to the publisher, the company has the right not to pay the balance of the advance due on delivery and accep-tance. But the down payment must be forfeited and the author automatically released from his contract.

I realize that this is a hard line, but only by taking it will authors force publishers to demonstrate good faith when com-missioning books. The publisher who knows he can recoup his full investment is going to have too many escape hatches when the book is delivered. He will have far fewer if he stands to lose money.

To a small degree, publishers have conceded the fairness of this position by modifying the requirement that the author promptly refund his down payment. Many houses now stipulate in their contracts that the refund may be paid out of the "first proceeds" received by the author from the sale of the rejected manuscript to another publisher. This is scarcely better than having to repay the advance at the time it's rejected. All it means is a postponement of the day of reckoning, an extension of the date when the publisher's "loan" must be repaid by the author.

Many authors and agents who understand the nature of large corporations know that if they determinedly resist or ignore a publisher's demand for repayment, the matter will eventually drift to the bottom of the publisher's priorities, to be covered like the bones of some dead creature by the sediment of more pressing and less unpleasant things. They then sell the book again and pray that the original publisher won't notice it's been published by another house, won't realize the advance was never paid back, or simply won't care enough to unleash the hounds in pursuit of the delinquent author. This is a risky solution, for at any given time the unresolved problem may be rediscovered and revived by some zealous minion of the publisher's legal department. It *is* one strategy, though, and sometimes it works. I know of one case where Doubleday commissioned an author to write a book, and when it was delivered the editor rejected it. "Why?" the agent demanded to know.

The editor shrugged. "I just don't like it, it's not what I had in mind when I hired the author."

"It follows the outline precisely," the agent argued.

"Yes, but it doesn't *feel* right. Anyway, there's no arguing about taste, so I'm afraid we have to turn the book down and request the down payment back."

"Over my dead body," said the agent. "If you can't articulate what you don't like about the book, and give the author a chance to revise it, we're not giving the money back."

"Well then, we won't let your author out of her contract with us," replied the editor.

"We'll see about that," said the agent.

The agent conferred with his client and they decided to defy the publisher. They circulated the rejected manuscript and before long found a publisher who liked it a great deal. A contract was signed, and when the advance was paid, the agent spoke to the author again. "Do you want to repay Doubleday?"

"No," said the author. "Let them find out I sold it to somebody else. Let them come after me."

Shortly after the book was published, the agent got an excited phone call from the new editor. "Good news! The book has been taken by a book club!"

"Great!" said the agent. "Which one?" The editor mentioned the name of the club. The agent gulped. "Uh, if I'm not mistaken that book club is owned by Doubleday, right?"

"Yes," said the editor. "I hope you're pleased."

"Oh, I am."

"Why are you laughing?"

"Just a private joke," said the agent.

For years until it went out of print, the author's book earned Doubleday book club royalties on a book that Doubleday rejected but which Doubleday still, legally, owned.

Section Three

❋ ❋

Busting Out

CHAPTER 17

✿ ✿

Are Editors Necessary?

There's been a lot of talk lately about the decline of editing. These are fighting words.

The problem with evaluating this allegation is that everything editors do today is invidiously compared to the accomplishments of that quintessential master, Maxwell Perkins. Perkins practiced his art at the offices of Charles Scribner's Sons from 1914 until late in the 1940s and midwifed the masterpieces of such immortals as Hemingway, Fitzgerald, and Wolfe. "Where are today's Maxwell Perkinses?" is the plaintive cry of authors who discover horrifying grammatical, syntactical, factual, and typographical errors in their freshly minted books, or, worse, have them gleefully pointed out by friends and critics. Every such erratum is a rebuke to the hallowed memory of that figure who has been depicted as gracious, patient, erudite, nurturing, precise, demanding, polite, and modest, a man whose love of authors was exceeded only by his love of good and well-made books. Let's assume that he truly did possess all of the virtues ascribed to him, and more if you wish.

I have no desire to desecrate either his memory or his achievements. I just don't happen to think that "Where are today's Maxwell Perkinses?" is a very good question. It oversimplifies editing both then and now, and fails to take into account the fact that today's editors simply don't perform the same tasks that their forebears did. I know a number of great editors working today, but they're great in many significantly different ways from the great editors of yesteryear.

Just about every aspect of publishing has changed since Perkins's era. The types of books published are different. Agents exert far more influence. The paperback industry has revolutionized the marketing of books. Computers and word processors have been created and refined. Bookstore chains have swept most independent bookshops out of business. Printing technology has improved immensely. Books today are not acquired, edited, produced, printed, or distributed the same way they were earlier in this century. They are not even written the same way.

We must also define "editors" before we apply the word irresponsibly. Editing is a highly complex set of functions, and no single individual is capable of exercising them with equal aplomb. The editor who wines and dines agents and charms authors may be a clumsy negotiator; the brilliant dealmaker may have no patience for the tedious and demanding word-by-word task of copy editing; the copy editor who brilliantly brings a book to life word by word, line by line, may be completely at sixes and sevens when it comes to handling authors.

It is certainly easy to wax nostalgic about editing in the Good Old Days (which really ended only about twenty or twenty-five years ago). If accounts and memoirs of that era can be trusted, editors then were steeped in fine arts, philosophy, languages, and the classics. They were a breed of compulsively orderly and fanatically precise individuals who ruthlessly stalked and destroyed typos, solecisms, and factual inaccuracies, and who conducted prodigious debates with authors about linguistic nuances. Their pride in their labors matched—and sometimes exceeded—that of the authors themselves. And when it came to money—well, they placed literature high above crass commerce, and discussed author compensation with the same delicacy they reserved for childbearing.

Christopher Lehmann-Haupt, a book critic for *The New York Times*, in an article about the vanishing breed of editors, quoted Harper and Row editor Dolores Simon as observing that ". . . there simply isn't the old interest in grammatical precision among young people any more." And Joseph Smith, an editor at Simon and Schuster, said that although good editors are still coming into our business, they are not "fastidious" in that "quaint way" we associate with oak-paneled editorial offices of yore. Lehmann-Haupt, himself a former editor, described strolls through Times Square in which he obsessively edited billboards, neon signs, the printing on the sides of trucks, and even sidewalk graffiti. David Leavitt, in his novel *The Lost Language of Cranes*, captured the ideal editor's profile, describing her as driven by the instinct "to put the world in order" and "possessed of the rare capacity to sit all day in a small cubicle, like a monk in a cell, and read with an almost penitential rigor."

Trumbull Rogers, a freelance technical copy editor writing in the "My Say" opinion column of *Publishers Weekly*, observed:

> When I landed my first job in publishing in 1970, my boss sat me down at a desk and told me to spend the first day learning the house style. The style was important because all the articles I would copyedit had to conform to it—no exceptions. The emphasis of my training was on economy and clarity of marking . . . , accuracy and attention to details. Although the journals were set in hot metal, we still made punctuation corrections in page proof, a very expensive process, but we felt it was worth it to create a product we could be proud of.

Today's editor, industry critics claim, no longer has that pride and painstaking compulsiveness. Indeed, it has been contended, editors today do everything but edit. The nurturing of authors has given way to the acquisition of properties. Editorial taste and judgment have been replaced by the application of success formulas devised by editorial committees. Risk-taking, hunches, and commercial instincts have yielded to the conservative application of bottom-line buying policies dictated by bookstore chain managers and implemented by rigid computer programs. The new breed of editorial animal, it is asserted, looks down his or her nose at line editing and production details. The time and money pressures of today's monolithic and highly competitive publishing business have devalued good book-making. The result is books that fall apart, prematurely yellow with age, and are scandalously rife with typos. "Years ago," Rogers wrote (his "My Say" piece was entitled "On the Road to Mediocrity"), "you rarely saw a typo in a book; now you rarely pick up *any* book that isn't riddled with every imaginable kind of error."

Invited to comment on the transformation of the editing profession over the last few decades, author Harlan Ellison had this to say:

> In large measure because of the niggardly wages paid to entry-level personnel, the caliber of daring, intelligence, and expertise has decreased alarmingly over the past twenty-five years, in my opinion. With the takeover of this "gentleman's sport" by multinational corporations obsessed by the bottom line, those rare urbane individuals who looked on editing as a holy calling have vanished. Priced out of the market. The Maxwell Perkinses, Walter Fultzes, Ben Hibbses and others are no longer with us, nor will the arena permit their sort to reappear. Now, with editors being drawn from a pool of business school graduates, we find entry-level editorial personnel who are semiliterate and understand debentures better than declensions.
>
> Editorial success today means climbing the corporate ladder, passing through the sweaty environs of editorial responsibility. But it is, sadly, a case of the lame leading the halt; because most of the people with whom these arrivistes must work are already working writers. So where is the guiding intelligence a writer looks to in his or her editor? In my view, with modern technology overtaking the scutwork of editorial responsibility, virtually the only value an editor has for a professional writer (first novelists are another matter) is in the generation of "in-house interest," the ramrodding and championing of a book through the labyrinth of publishing house indifference, ineptitude, and chance. And when the editor hasn't the in-house rep or clout to get that enthusiasm translated into promotional and advertising dollars his/her value is damned near zero.

Ellison's criticisms go true to the mark, as they usually do. But they must also be evaluated in a larger context.

Unquestionably, a shift has taken place in the role of trade book editors from what is generally characterized as line functions to that of acquisitions. The earlier role, the one that we most sentimentalize, combined nurturing parent and stern taskmaster, a person who could get a great book out of an author, then groom and curry the text until it virtually sparkled. Although editors then, as now, worked for publishers whose profit agenda seldom coincided with that of their authors, the editor was thought of as the author's friend, protector, and advocate.

The emphasis today on the acquisition role of editors places them in a more adversarial role with authors. Negotiation often pits them against each other, and the residue of resentment and distrust that remains after the bargain is sealed makes it difficult for authors to feel completely comfortable with their editors.

The paternalistic treatment of authors by editors in earlier times, however, produced its own set of inequities, for publishers took advantage of many authors who were too ignorant, shy, or well-bred to demand good terms of their editors. Knowing that most authors write for love, publishers tended to assume that they didn't need to write for money.

Resentment toward publishers over their exploitation of authors created the conditions for the rise to power of literary agents, and though new authors today are still at a disadvantage, the balance eventually shifts when they engage agents and become more successful. Good agents often insist on a large measure of control over the author-editor relationship, holding authors at arm's length from their editors to protect them from being taken advantage of. And what has happened in the four or five decades since this transformation occurred is that the agents have begun to take over the role formerly played by editors. Today's agents nurture authors, work closely with them in the development of their work, perform a great many editorial tasks, and lend strong emotional and psychological support. And, perhaps most important of all, in a turbulent world of publishing mergers and takeovers and editorial musical chairs, agents have become the islands of stability and reliability that were once the province of editors. So, if the importance of editors in this respect has diminished, the loss has not necessarily affected authors for the worse.

Or, take the tasks of copy editing manuscripts and proofreading galleys. Although these still fall upon the employees of publishing companies, the high costs of running businesses have caused a shift from in-house line editing to freelance work done at home. Many copy editors are former employees of publishers who have managed to adapt their responsibilities to their domestic schedules. But the pressures of producing large numbers of books annually have forced publishers to overload editors with work or to seek less-experienced people to do these highly demanding jobs. Some publishers just can't afford the time or expense to train copy editors, supervise them closely, review their work, and instill in them a grasp of house style, a knowledge of company tradition, and a sense of pride. English is not even the first language for many copy editors. And those who are fluent in English may not have the patience, precision, and skill to be good editors.

Whether we like it or not, the responsibility for well-edited books is shifting to authors. Actually, they have always borne much of that burden. In hardcover publishing particularly, most authors are given the opportunity (if not the contractual right) to review copyedited manuscripts and to proofread galleys, and if an author doesn't care enough to double-check every fact, every dubious grammatical construction and spelling, indeed every word of his manuscript and galleys, he has no one to blame but himself for a flawed product.

It is harder for authors to control errors in paperback originals and reprints, however, because tight publication schedules make it prohibitive for publishers to furnish galleys for review by authors in many cases. Also, authors rarely get to see galleys of paperback reprints of their hardcover books. But authors and their agents can and often do demand the right to examine galleys in exchange for a promise to turn them around promptly. Thus, even paperback authors have a chance to bring out unblemished books.

The development of computerized editing and word processing hardware and software promises to eliminate many problems for authors and editors. Although numerous technical, financial, labor, and other obstacles have impeded the automation of some important editorial functions, I'm reasonably certain that these will be overcome in the foreseeable future, making clean copy in both manuscript and galley an everyday occurrence. The same is true for style, design, composition, and other aspects of the publishing process that are now in the hands of a diminishing number of expert craftspeople. In short, emerging technology will replace a good deal of the mental and manual labor involved in producing books.

What do all these changes leave for editors to do? The answer is, just about everything. Unlike those of the older generation, today's editors must master an entire gamut of disciplines including production, marketing, negotiation, promotion, advertising, publicity, accounting, salesmanship, psychology, politics, diplomacy, and—well, editing. But into that last designation goes a bewildering variety of activities, many only remotely connected with the stereotyped one of sitting in a monastic office hunting for typos. "I don't know what *you* mean by editing," one editor said to me, "but among the responsibilities found in *my* job description are proposing ideas and subjects to authors, soliciting authors and experts for projects I'm developing, dealmaking, line editing, packaging, lobbying in the house for books I love, boosting those books to anybody in the trade who will listen, preparing profit and loss projections, and . . . well, how many hours do you have to listen to what else I do?"

The dizzying pace and complexity of modern publishing makes it neither possible nor desirable for editors to sit all day reading or conversing with authors. They must be worldly and sophisticated, capable of shepherding the projects they sponsor through a gauntlet of technical, financial, political, and other hazards. Though editors are often criticized for being corporate animals, in this respect at least we should thank our stars that they are. For they and they alone understand how to work their systems, to maneuver, coax, and sometimes ram their beloved books— *our* beloved books!—through the corporate obstacle course. Today's editors are professional company men and women, and if they don't have a problem with that characterization, I don't see why we should.

Jennifer Brehl, a young editor at Bantam Doubleday Dell known for her ardent advocacy of the projects she sponsors, expressed what she believes an editor's role today must be. "I don't care how many editorial functions agents have assumed, authors still need someone in the house to see their books through at every stage. We must work, and work well, with every department. Among the many things we are, are expediters and facilitators." When I asked her if she thought her attitude was typical of her generation of editors, she nodded vigorously. "Lord knows we're not in it for the money. You can't be a disinterested party when it comes to writers. You have to love books; a writer needs someone in the house who loves his or her work."

I believe she has identified the critical factor in the makeup of all good editors, and though her style of dealing with books and authors may be light-years apart from that of Maxwell Perkins, he undoubtedly would recognize the underlying passion.

There are many editorial qualities that are irreplaceable. Among them are taste, discrimination, personal emotional response, a sense of order and organization, determination, devotion, and tender loving care. In these respects, no one has discovered anyone or anything that can remotely take the place of an editor. Agents can't do it because they're outsiders. Computers can't do it because they're heartless.

But none of those virtues means anything if editors are lacking in courage. The biggest threat to the health of our industry is not mergers and acquisitions. It is failure of nerve on the part of its editors. The evolution of publishing from a profession run by individuals to a business managed by committees has created a population of editors preoccupied with holding their jobs. The pressures they live under are constantly forcing them to lower the common denominator when selecting the projects they wish to sponsor. This means that it is easier to say no than yes.

The way that this attitude manifests itself for me is editors' resistance to acquiring books that are even slightly flawed. It was not long ago that the prevailing attitude among editors was, "This book has some problems, but the author is so talented that I'd like to buy it and work with him." Today such words are rarely heard. A book with problems is a book rejected, and more and more one hears editors say, "Let the author revise it, then we'll decide if we want to buy it." Many of them have confided in me that they would love to buy the book, but the prospect of bucking the system is simply too daunting.

"In order to acquire a book I love," another editor told me, "I have to fight. I have to fight with my colleagues, my bosses, with a battery of nay-sayers telling me, 'This will never work,' 'That will never work,' 'This doesn't fit our formula,' 'That's too hard to do.' A person can get weary and beaten down. Sometimes we all wonder if it isn't easier to say the hell with it and turn the damned thing down."

It takes as much courage to love a book, in many ways, as it does to love a person, and sometimes there is as much at stake. But there can be no love without responsibility, and no responsibility without fortitude. "I'm responsible for my books," Macmillan editor David Wolff proudly declared to me. "And I *want* to be responsible for them."

When I asked an agent colleague of mine, Betty Marks, whether she thought editors were necessary, she quipped, "Of course they are. Who else can take agents to lunch?" If editors are to remain more than entertaining luncheon hosts, if they are to be not merely necessary but indispensable, they will have to continue resisting the pressures toward homogeneity and mediocrity that are arrayed against them by the monolith of Big Publishing.

I sincerely wish them luck.

CHAPTER 18

Sales Conference

Many businesses are seasonal in nature, rolling through predict-able cycles not unlike agricultural ones, when there is a time to sow, to grow, to reap, and to leave fallow. In the garment industry, my father's trade in which I briefly apprenticed, there is the spring season, the fall season, and the resort season, and the rhythms of designing, cutting, manufacturing, selling, and shipping are printed so indelibly on my memory circuits that even today I sniff the air and say to myself, "It's time to cut goods for the fall line."

The "seasons" in the publishing business are nowhere as sharply delineated. Publishers' catalogues are still designated "spring" and "fall," but such distinctions seem to have lost much of their meaning. A deal may be cut, a book published, a best-seller soar to the top of the list, on any given calendar day. There are of course certain events that figure significantly in the lives of publishing people, such as the Frankfurt Book Fair every October and the American Booksellers Association Convention every Memorial Day weekend. From the viewpoint of myself and other literary agents, the only seasons worthy of the name are the April and October royalty periods, when most publishers report authors' earnings for the accounting periods ending December 31 and June 30 respectively.

But twice every year, around mid-May and mid-December, a curious lull befalls the frenzied lives of literary agents, like those abrupt silences that occasionally muffle a party when everybody, inexplicably, stops talking at exactly the same time. I've experienced enough of these semiannual brownouts so that

I ought to expect them by now. Yet they always take me by surprise, and I can predictably be heard at these times barking to my staff, "Is there something wrong with our phones? Is this a mail holiday or what?" At length it occurs to me: It's sales conference season. I then take advantage of this hiatus to catch up on paperwork.

Recently, however, I contemplated the meaning of sales conference, and asked some participants to tell me what happens at them and what significance they hold for authors. I came away realizing that it is unquestionably the most important event in the life of your book. Since most authors think of sales conference merely as the period during which it's even harder to get their editors on the phone than it is during the rest of the year, I strongly urge you not to pass up this particular lecture.

Sales conference is the time when a publisher's list of forthcoming books is introduced to the company's commissioned sales representatives, who then go forth to the stores in their territories and line up orders. Since this is the point where the editorial process interfaces with marketing and distribution processes, it may literally be said that the fate of your book, and possibly your career, is cast at sales conference.

For the people who work at publishing houses, these convocations are red-letter days, major events in their corporate lives. For the past six months they have been sweating, suffering, beating thier breasts, and rending their garments over the books they have acquired. Now they are going to pitch them to the folks who actually get them into the stores. This is a time of intense anxiety, for the presentation of the list is by no means a matter of handing the sales reps a set of proofs and saying, "Read it, it's terrific." Indeed, it's uncommon for the reps to read any but the most important books on their publishers' lists. Nor is it necessary.

If they don't need the book itself, however, they do need information about it, and in the weeks leading up to the conference editors scurry frantically about the halls of their companies, rounding up cover proofs, advertising copy, promotional quotes, author-tour itineraries, and anything else that will make their books look and sound irresistibly tempting to sales people, store buyers and distributors, and ultimately to consumers.

The conferences are held in different locations around the country. Many companies hold their winter conferences in Florida, Puerto Rico, and other tropical climes, giving participants a chance to relax in the sun after work sessions and making the event in part a paid vacation. Other publishers hold conferences closer to home, in resort hotels within easy driving radius of New York City. Some publishers conduct them in the city itself. The more distant the conference, the fewer employees may be permitted to attend due to the costs of air fare and accommodations, and therefore the privilege of attendance is one of the ways an editor's status at a publishing company is determined. Conferences held in New York City enable all staff members to participate. From the viewpoint of sales reps these may be great fun, entitling them to a week in the Big Apple with a publisher picking up the tab. But for the publishers themselves, New York City-held conferences are harder work, as there is little letup from the grueling labors of conferring and ingratiating themselves with the sales representatives.

Each publisher has its own style, format, and strategy for sales conferences, but typically the days are divided into morning and afternoon sessions. At these, the editors sponsoring the books, or perhaps the heads of editorial divisions, present each title with a brief description of the contents and salient sales features. What successes have the author's previous books enjoyed? Is the book tied into some trend or fad, some event such as an election, opening of the baseball season, a disaster, a war, a trial, a scandal? Is there a movie or television adaptation in the works? Are author appearances planned? Is the author engaging, promotable, famous?

The editor's spiel is fortified by a variety of supplementary material: cover proofs, bound proofs of the book itself or excerpts or condensed portions, inside illustrations, an agenda of the author's tour, posters or mockups of advertising copy, plugs by famous authors or other celebrities, trailers from movie or television tie-ins, slide shows, audiocassettes, and all manner of gimmicks such as buttons, pens, and bookmarks. Sometimes the publisher will stage a real dog-and-pony show, with professional entertainment, elaborate skits written and performed by the publishing staff, and even cameo appearances by star authors.

If the publisher's list is a big and multifarious one, the work sessions may be broke down into specialized seminars in which the sales reps, distributors, or chain store buyers may educate themselves as to the nature of such categories as science fiction, westerns, or romances, or focus on strategies for one or two blockbluster lead titles.

All of this activity is designed to impress and enlighten the sales reps, help them to understand the publisher's aims and problems, give them an opportunity to offer feedback garnered from experiences in their territories, and inspire them to get behind the publisher's list with every fiber of their being.

What makes these sessions so critical to the success or failure of your book is that they bear directly on the number of copies that will be printed and distributed, and on the energy that will be expended on the marketing. Thus, sales conference is the week of reckoning for the list, during which time it is inscribed which books shall fly and which shall bomb, which shall be raised up to the best-seller list and which cast down to the remainder bins, which shall be stacked near the cash registers in pyramids of pharaonic magnitude, and which secreted spine-out in quantities of two or three in the wrong department of a bookstore.

Broadly speaking, there are two ways in which printings are determined by the activities at a sales conference. At the one extreme are those books for which printings and sales goals are somewhat nebulous in the publisher's mind. These books are presented as vigorously as possible in the hopes the sales reps will get turned on and bring in a surprisingly large number of orders. At the other end of the spectrum are those titles for which the publisher has set specific printing and sales goals and the sales reps are expected to fill their quotas.

Most of the books on any given list fall somewhere between these two approaches, and not all the books get fair shrift. This is particularly true of first novels, midlist books, experimental works, and books that are part of a series. There is only so much you can say about a first novel, or about the latest Regency romance, or a book about costumes of colonial Virginia, and there's no sense in trying to tell these highly sophisticated sales people that such books are going to leap off the

shelves by the score. On the other hand, as there is a steady market for such books, it can be expected that a minimum number of copies will sell without undue effort on the publisher's part. Still, it's easy to see how the best-seller mentality can affect your book in a sales conference situation as it does in the editorial boardroom, the review media, and in the bookstores.

Armed with all this information, with press kits, cover proofs, promotional gimmicks, and inspiration, the sales reps go forth to the stores and sell, sell, sell. Although the publisher may have outlined a sales strategy for the list, the handling of sales is largely left to the discretion of the reps. Conditions in each territory vary widely: Consumers may buy westerns by the truckload in the southwestern region, but the same books will lie in great untouched stacks like dead fish in the bookstores of the Northeast. They may adore Ludlum in Cleveland and ignore him in Topeka. A book on the hottest new rock group may march out of California stores in regiment strength, but in Bible Belt bookstores will molder in unopened cartons.

The sales reps servicing these territories understand the tastes of the readers there, and know how to "play" the books in their sales kits like so many cards in a rummy game. Like authors, agents, and publishers, the salesman or woman makes the most profit on best-sellers, and so these titles may be expected to muscle out the rest of the list. The salesperson may make all sorts of bargains to induce store buyers to take that quota of the big book: special discounts, relaxation of strict return policies, a little coaxing here, a little coercing there, and some trading off of little books for big ones elsewhere. Among the little ones may be your book. Or maybe it's the other way around, and you're the lucky author whose big book will push the little ones off the boards. This is, you must realize, a jungle, however civilized the product being sold. Someone once said that the wise man never looks too closely at what goes into his laws or his sausages; perhaps best-selling books should be added to that list.

Although business is not conducted around the clock at sales conference, it is never far away at breakfast, lunch, or dinner, at cocktail time, out on the beach or the golf links, or in the evening at the theater or floor show. Sales conference is a time

for everybody to get to know everybody else a little better, creating a sense of teamwork and harmony. Many editors tell me they come away from these occasions with an enhanced sense of "family" about the people they work and deal with. You may know next to nothing about someone in an office down the hall from you, but in the relaxed informality of a resort setting, that person may tell you something about himself or reveal aspects of his character that have been held in tight check by the requirements of office decorum and the hurly-burly of the business day.

Sales conference is the place where an editor can bestow a personal touch on a sales campaign, and that can make the difference to a book's success. "I know books like this don't ordinarily work in your region," an editor might say to a sales rep he or she has buttonholed at the bar, "but this particular novel has some aspects that will appeal to the stores you service." It works the other way around, too. Sales reps, knowing their particular market a lot better than the publishers do, will pull an editor or sales manager aside and say, "My customers can't keep science fiction in their stores; are you going to increase the number you publish?" Or, "Everybody in my territory wants to know when the next book in the Hieronymus Bosch detective series is coming out." Or, "Dell and Berkley are doing really well with a certain kind of romance, so how about our starting a similar line?" In short, sales conference is the time and place for important dialogues among staff members of publishing houses, among sales people, and between publishers and sales reps, distributors, or bookstore and chain store personnel.

Is there any place for authors at sales conference? Except for the very biggest names, authors are seldom invited to the ones held outside New York City, and because of the expense of bringing authors to New York, any that are invited to the conferences held in the city are usually people who live in or near the city to begin with. Invitations are not automatic, however, as few authors are dynamic, attractive, and promotable enough to make a strong positive impression on the sales reps. There is still much you can do, though, to cooperate with your editor in furnishing him or her with information and sales

features about your book, anything and everything that will enable your editor to highlight your book when the presentation is made.

Maybe, then, you too should become aware of the onset of sales conference season, and instead of writing it off as a period of downtime in your calendar, get yourself involved in the preparations. It need not cost you a lot of money. One of my clients, author of a tragic romance novel, bought a small carton of tissue packets for her editor and urged her to hand them to the sales reps with the other material in the promo kit for her book. "Tell them to have a good cry," the author said. It proved quite effective.

Perhaps you can think of something equally creative. After all, why on earth would you want to go to a tropical resort, all expenses paid by your publisher, anyway?

CHAPTER 19

"P & L"

One of the least pleasant duties that agents are obliged to perform is explaining to their clients why their books have flopped. And there is no dearth of reasons: The editor was fired, the company was taken over by a conglomerate, the salesmen didn't understand the book, someone stuck a lousy title on it, they didn't advertise it, they didn't advertise it enough, they underprinted it, they brought it out too soon, they brought it out too late, there was an Act of God, there was an Act of Satan—an agent's files are a veritable Grand Guignol of publishing horror stories.

The one thing it does not always occur to agents to tell their clients, however, is that their books have not really flopped, at least not from the publisher's viewpoint. Maybe your book wasn't a best-seller, but that's not to say your publisher didn't make money on it. Most authors and a great many agents tend to equate the earning-out of an author's advance with the recoupment of a publisher's investment. It's an understandable misconception, for to authors, royalties are profits. If their books start earning profits, they assume the publisher has started making profits too; and conversely, they figure, if the advance doesn't earn out, the publisher must have lost money on the book.

Seldom is this equation true. Although royalties are a gauge of success or failure for an author, publishers use an entirely different system to determine how well or badly a book has done for them. In that system, authors' royalties are only one element of the profit picture, and it is entirely possible for a

publisher to make a big profit on a book whose advance has not earned out, or to lose money on a book whose advance *has* earned out.

Because I have never worked for a publishing company, it's taken me a long time to grasp this distinction. But because it's a terribly important one, explaining as it does why publishers often *seem* to be doing everything they can to lose money on their books, I've tried to educate myself in basic publishing economics and would like to share my findings with you.

In most cases today, publishers prepare profit-and-loss projections for books that they are considering acquiring. The calculations differ widely from company to company, from type of book to type of book, and even from book to book. The database for an illustrated book is quite different from that of a hardcover novel, which in turn differs from a paperback novel; and even within the genus paperback novel are such species as lead novel, category novel, movie tie-in, etc.

Many staff members may be involved in producing these estimates: editors, production people, sales managers, sub-rights directors, advertising and promotion personnel, the company comptroller, art director, and so on. Each tries to factor into the profit-and-loss worksheet the best-case and worst-case numbers that will help their firm formulate as accurate a picture of a book's potential as is possible in our unpredictable business. The worksheets are really a tool, and their data may be manipulated and negotiated so that costs trimmed from one area may be applied to another in the hopes that enthusiasm for the book will not be dampened by discouraging figures from one or two precincts. If, however, all or most of the committee members come in with poor profit projections, it's unlikely that hearts will prevail over heads when the votes are cast at the editorial meeting.

I may be romanticizing the past, but these complex formulations don't seem to be much of an improvement over the intuitive judgments reached by the founders of such illustrious houses as Knopf, Harper, Scribner, Random House, and Simon and Schuster. Be that as it may, publishing decisions today are reached by computers, consensus, and committee, and we may

consider ourselves lucky if someone remembers the love factor when the bottom line is being examined.

Love aside, what are the elements of a profit-and-loss projection? What kind of "P & L" figures are resting at your editor's elbow when he phones you or your agent to commence negotiations on your book?

The key figure on the positive side of the ledger is revenue to be realized from sales of the book. You get this by multiplying the number of copies sold by the wholesale price of the book, that is, the actual price received by your publisher after he discounts it to the book trade. If the list price of the book is $20, and the average discount offered by your publisher to the stores is 40 percent, the actual price received by your publisher will be $12 per copy.

"Copies sold," remember, means net sales after returns, for in the publishing business books are sold on a returnable basis. So, if a publisher prints and distributes 25,000 copies of a book but 30 percent of them are returned, the actual number of copies sold (what publishers call the "sell-through") will be 17,500. Multiply that 17,500 by the $12 per copy that your publisher is getting and you get the publisher's gross sale. In this example, that comes to $210,000.

To this figure is added the publisher's anticipated share of subsidiary revenue: book club, paperback reprint, first or second serial, foreign rights, etc. Depending on how liberal or conservative the firm's fiscal policy is, these numbers range from wishful thinking on the one hand to zero if the publisher doesn't want to count on income that is not absolutely guaranteed at the time the book is acquired. More and more publishers tend to take a highly conservative position in prognosticating sub-rights income. For one thing, agents have grown tougher over the last few decades about permitting publishers to participate in that income; and for another, the collapse of the paperback reprint market early in the 1980s forced hardcover publishers to count on nothing but hardcover sales when preparing their projections. These are significant factors in the driving-out of midlist books from the hardcover marketplace.

Another source of revenue for publishers derives from the

sale of remainders. If the undistributed or returned copies of a book, such as the 7,500 copies in the above example, are sold to remainder jobbers they will bring in a few thousand dollars for the publishers, and that goes into the plus side of the P & L.

Now for the minus side. From the income generated by sales of the book, remainders, and sub-rights income, your publisher subtracts his costs. These fall into several categories that are reckoned by formulas drawn from company and industry experience and the counsel of the firm's financial officers and accountants. One category is plant costs: typesetting, color separations for the cover or for color illustrations, preparation of halftones for black-and-white illustrations, and all other procedures up to the actual printing of the book.

The second category is manufacturing costs, lumped together as "PPB": printing, paper, and binding.

A third is overhead. Included here are rent or mortgage payments on the publisher's offices, electricity, salaries, telephone, office supplies, the cost of money, warehousing, sales commissions, insurance, and the many other expenses required to run a business. Because each publisher includes or excludes different items when calculating overhead, the fluctuations in overhead allocations differ widely from one publisher to the next. A safe guess is that most houses allocate between 30 and 40 percent of gross sales.

The next category is author's royalty. This figure is fixed by contract. Royalties represent a big chunk of a publisher's costs. An eight percent royalty on a $3.95 paperback comes to about 32 cents. But remember that the publisher sells that book to the trade at a discount. If the discount is 50 percent, or two dollars a copy, the royalty will absorb about 16 percent of that revenue.

Then there are some miscellaneous costs such as outside design, cover art, copyediting, indexing, illustrations, and the cost of free and review copies.

And finally, there is the cost of advertising and promotion.

As I mentioned, accounting practices vary widely when it comes to allocating costs to specific books on a list. Should the publisher allocate the same share of his total costs to every

book regardless of its importance, profitability, and actual share of the company's investment? Or should big books carry a proportionately larger share of the cost load than routine ones?

Because publishers don't agree on the fairest way to deal with the question, their allocation formulas vary widely, and a good example of this is advertising and promotion. Some publishers simply average out the cost of advertising and promotion for all books on their list and add some percentage points to the overhead charge on each book. For other publishers, it makes no sense to allocate to a routine book a percentage of the enormous cost of pushing a best-seller. These publishers therefore "break out" the advertising and promotional cost of each book and show it on their profit-and-loss worksheets as a separate item from overhead.

Okay, we're ready to do some calculations. Take the gross sales of your book, add remainder income and anticipated subsidiary rights revenue, and you have an income projection for your book. From this you deduct your plant and manufacturing costs, overhead, royalties, advertising and promotion, and miscellaneous costs. What you end up with is projected profit or lost.

Recently the Independent Literary Agents Association conducted a panel discussion on the subject of "Publishers' Profit and Loss Formulas," and one of the editors kindly furnished a sample "Book Profitability Worksheet" with some hypothetical figures inked in to give us a picture of the projections for a $14.95 novel of average expectations. I reproduce it here to illustrate some of the dynamics we have been discussing.

In this example, the publisher's overhead is not included. And so, after deducting costs from sales the publisher is left with what he calls an estimated "profit contribution" of $30,929. This sum goes to pay off the publisher's overhead, and what's left is real profit. If the profit contribution, or the actual profit, is marginal, this publisher will either turn the book down or take a harder look at some of the profit or loss items to determine how the book could be made more profitable. In this case, while the author might look forward to an advance and royalties totalling $16,300 plus another $7,000 as his share of

BOOK PROFITABILITY WORKSHEET

TITLE: AVERAGE NOVEL   EDITOR_____
AUTHOR: _____   PUB DATE_____

PRODUCTION INFORMATION

Number of Words:_____ Number of Pages: 256 Book Dimensions: 5½" × 8¼"
Illustrations:_____ Format: Hardcover _____
Special Requirements:_____

	Amount	% Net Sales
Retail Price	$14.95	
Price Received (% Retail 52%)	7.77	
Minimum Gross Sale: No. of copies 12,500		
Less returns (% Gross 20%) 2,500		
Net Sales 10,000	$/77,700/	
Cost of Sales		
Plant (excluding design)	$8,500	
Outside Design & Cover Art	$1,000	
Permissions, Illustrations, etc.		
Printing, Paper, Binding Gross Sales ($1.30 per copy)	$16,250	
Royalties:		
Earned Royalties	$16,300	
Unearned Advance	N.A.	
Total Cost of Sales	$/42,050/	
Gross Profit	$ 35,650	46%

Other Direct Expenses

Outside Copy Editing ($350 c/e, $200 proofread)	$550
Other Editorial (describe:_____)	
Advertising & Promotion	$12,500
Free Copies (No. of Copies: 200 @ $1.95)	$390
Total Other Expenses	$/13,440/

Other Income (Publisher's Share)

Reprint Rights (50% Publisher's Share)	$5,000
Other Rights (Describe: Quality PB Club 50%)	$2,000
Gain on Special Sales:	
Remainder Value	$1,719
Total Other Income	$/8,719/
Profit Contribution	$/30,929/ 40%

Earned Royalties

Contract Terms		Computations		
Sales Levels	Rates	Copies Sold in Level	Earned per Book	Earned Royalty
-0- to 5M	10%	5M	$1.45	$7,250
5M to 10M	12½%	5M	$1.81	$9,050
Over 10M	15%			
Total		/ 10M /		$/16,300 /

Unearned Advance Royalty

Total Advance Royalty	$15,000
Less: Earned From Sales	$16,300
Less: Author's Share of Rights	$7,000
Unearned Advance (Zero if Negative)	$/ -0- /

subsidiary rights income, from the publisher's viewpoint the profit projections are dangerously close to marginal; that $30,929 will be eaten up by overhead, leaving a real profit of around 10 percent. The publisher might tinker with some of the items to make his profit picture look rosier, but if there isn't much to tinker with, he may have to turn the book down. Here is a vivid example of why first novels, experimental, and other midlist books are being driven out of the marketplace. The publisher who furnished this worksheet stated that only one out of twenty books earned a profit for his firm, and that's why he and his staff have become increasingly best-seller-conscious.

The illustration given here is for a hardcover book. Hardcovers are harder to do projections for because of the special, often individual, attention they require in terms of design, choice of paper, typeface, and the like. This is doubly true if the book is illustrated, and quadruply true if the book is illustrated with color. In mass market paperback, many of these problems are minimized. Paper quality and typeface don't vary from book to book; many categories carry books of precisely the same length; and the books are seldom illustrated.

Unfortunately, the paperback publisher who appeared at the ILAA panel discussion was not permitted to reveal figures on his company's worksheet. He did, however, furnish a blank worksheet that took into account such variables as whether the book is a lead or ordinary title; a reissue, reprint, or original; whether the book contains photo or other inserts; has a foil cover or uses a special cover stock; it also projects when the book is scheduled and how many pages long it is. From discussions with a number of paperback editors, I've been able to piece together a profit projection on a routine book. One of the key figures, according to those I spoke to, is the projected number of copies printed over the life of a book. A paperback that goes through one modest printing will have a lower profit potential than one that goes through a large first printing and two or three more printings of good size.

Let us suppose a good first novel of lead length—100,000 words or so—for which the publisher can charge $3,95 (prognosticating book prices at publication dates a year or two down the road is an important aspect of P & L preparation). This novel won't be the lead book in the month in which it's published, but it might be the second or third lead.

If we figure that the publisher will give an average discount of 45 percent to store chains and wholesalers, we come up with a net price per copy of $2.17 ($2.1725 to be precise) received by the publisher. Now, the publisher has projected a first printing of 100,000 copies and two further ones of 25,000 copies each over the life of the book, for a total in-print figure of 150,000 copies. In his experience, 40 percent of all copies of books like this one will be returned, meaning a 60 percent "sell-through," or 90,000 copies actually sold. Multiply 90,000 by the $2.1725 per copy the publisher is receiving and you get a gross sale of $195,525.00. Let's assume for simplicity's sake that there is no subsidiary income.

The first item to be deducted by your publisher is plant and manufacturing cost. The publisher reckons an average of 40¢ per copy, or $60,000.00 for the 150,000 copies printed.

The next item is royalty. Let's say it's 6 percent on the first 150,000 copies, or $0.237 per copy. A sell-through of 90,000 copies will cost your publisher $21,330.00 in royalties.

Then there is overhead. In this case the publisher includes advertising and promotion costs in his overhead calculations, and attributes 35 percent of gross sales to overhead. That comes to $68,434.00.

Deducting costs from the gross sale, the numbers look like this:

Gross Sale (90,000 copies × $2.1725 per copy)	$195,525.00
Manufacturing cost	60,000.00
Royalty	21,330.00
Overhead	68,434.00
Profit on sales	$ 45,761.00

On this particular title, the publisher can project a profit of $45,761.00.

Because many readers of this book are interested in writing category paperbacks, I've sketched some figures for a $2.50 book in a genre such as romance, western, or male adventure.

Here we figure the publisher offers a 40 percent discount, meaning he actually receives $1.50 per copy. Printings of these routine books are low, and there is seldom more than one printing. Let's say 60,000 copies printed. Returns on these types of book often run high, so let's posit a 50 percent sell-through, or 30,000 copies actually sold. We multiply 30,000 by $1.50 per copy and get a gross sale of $45,000. From which we deduct costs, to get the following picture:

Gross sale (30,000 copies × $1.50 per copy)	$45,000.00
Manufacturing cost (35¢ per copy)	21,000.00
Overhead (30% of gross sale)	13,500.00
Royalty (6%, or 15¢ per copy)	4,500.00
Profit on sales	$ 6,000.00

These figures are extremely rough, of course, and don't take into account many factors on both the income and outgo sides of the ledgers, such as corporate taxes, inflation, damaged copies, losses due to strikes, fire, and flood, interest earned on royalties banked between semiannual royalty periods and on reserves against returns, and much, much more. Still, it would appear that paperback publishers earn something like 15 to 20 percent pre-tax profit on routine books. And, because unit costs go down and sales volume goes up on best-sellers, the profit on major books is even higher.

What do the numbers tell us? For some of us, they only bear out our worst paranoid fantasies that publishers are battening on the lifeblood of authors. These fantasies are fueled by the facts that publishers do not share their profit-and-loss projections with authors, conceal vital sales information when reporting royalties, and, because most publishers are owned by larger corporate entities, are not required to disclose financial information to stockholders or the public. One of my western writer clients says writers are like mushrooms: "They're fed a lot of horseshit and kept in the dark."

Others among us may realize that publishing is a tough, unpredictable, and treacherous business, and perhaps the people who play for such high stakes deserve a handsome profit for the risks they take and the capital they invest (though it must be said in all fairness that 15 or 20 percent is not exactly a windfall profit). I don't know the answer. But I can safely say that the profit-and-loss worksheets of most authors I know are a lot more depressing than anything I've seen from publishers.

CHAPTER 20

Pub Date

Few events in the life of a book are as thoroughly invested with magic and mystery as its publication date. Although the season, month, and day of publication are, as often as not, selected merely to satisfy the expediencies of a publisher's schedule, many authors and even some publishers assign cabalistic value to pub dates, and a great deal of myth and nonsense has come to surround the process. One hears such platitudes as, "January is a lousy month to bring out a book," or, "Nobody buys books in August," or "Can you believe they released my book on Friday the thirteenth?"

As some fifty thousand books are published annually, you may safely assume that a day does not go by without a book being officially launched somewhere. I know of no records correlating the success or failure of books with their pub dates, but I daresay that if someone were crazy enough to trace the fates of best-sellers back to the dates on which they were published, it would be demonstrated that successful books debut on just about every date on the calendar—including Friday the 13th. It would also be discovered, I'm sure, that just as many books flop as triumph whose pub dates are agonized over and deliberately selected for maximum impact.

A few words about the differences between hardcover and paperback distribution might be pertinent here. Hardcover books are for the most part shipped directly from publisher to bookstore (though the advent of powerful hardcover wholesalers and jobbers is changing this, it should be noted). Hardcovers can be, and are, shipped on any date, but traditionally they are categorized by season: spring and fall. Sometimes Christmas is designated a third "season." Hardcover publishers hold spring and fall sales conferences to introduce books scheduled for the following season, and they issue spring and fall catalogues. A hardcover published in July will probably be considered a spring book; one published in February, a fall book.

The rise of the paperback industry created a very different distribution rhythm. Until relatively recently, when the great bookstore chains made direct distribution of paperbacks a significant factor in the publishing industry, paperback books were carried only by the same distributors who stock magazines in newsstands and drugstores, and this form of distribution is still the dominant mode in the paperback industry. But because distribution of magazines follows a monthly cycle, the scheduling of paperback books became a monthly affair. Catalogues issued by mass market publishers are for the most part monthly, and, unlike their hardcover counterparts, paperback editors refer to pub dates by month, not by season. And while it is impractical to conduct a sales conference every month, paperback publishers do consult with sales staff and distributors on a monthly basis far more extensively than hardcover publishers do. The lingo of paperback distribution is closer to magazines, too: Hardcover books are *published*, but paperbacks are *released* or *issued*.

In an earlier era when novels and general nonfiction were affordable only by a wealthier segment of society, the summer was undoubtedly a dead time for booksellers as the carriage trade fled the cities for favorite rural watering spots. A book published in July or August could very well die, and it's easy to see where the notion arose that August publication is the kiss of death. In September the affluent returned to the city, presumably hungry for good books to read and mindful of the impending Christmas holiday, when books make excellent gifts. That is why fall has always been considered the best time to launch a book, and for the most part that remains true, because a book that goes on the best-seller list in the fall has a good chance of carrying into the Christmas buying season. And if January is considered a lousy time to publish, it's because bookstore owners are preoccupied with postholiday returns, budget deficits, and winter vacations to recover from the intense business of the previous few months.

Mass market publishing and marketing have smoothed out many of the hills and valleys of bookselling, making the business a year-round enterprise. The capital required to feed a mass market maw allows for no downtime. Every month must carry its share of the annual business, and every book, whatever its publication date, must be considered a source of maximum profit potential. "People used to say things like 'July is a good month for publishing but August is bad,' " Robert A. Gottlieb, former president of Alfred A. Knopf said recently in a *New York Times* article. "All those maxims are true until books come along that disprove them, then the opposite is true." Gottlieb added that Knopf publishes most of its books "at the first rational moment," and I would say that many of his colleagues do the same.

Some books definitely do have seasonal pertinence. Sports novels or nonfiction books come to mind, for they are often dependent on the start of playing seasons or tournaments. It makes common sense to bring a baseball book out in March and a football book in August. And sometimes there are excellent strategic reasons for publishing a book in a specific month. A publisher producing a gift book aimed at the Christmas market will schedule it for publication no later than October, because bookstores begin shutting their gates to new stock in November and cannot accommodate merchandise shipped after that. Science fiction publishers, too, are careful not to publish too late in the year any novel they feel might be a candidate for certain prestigious awards such as the Nebula, because they are afraid the judges will not have an opportunity to read it before the voting deadline.

The scheduling of books for publication on a specific calendar date is usually aimed more at gratifying whim or superstition—publisher's or author's—than at achieving any significant commercial advantage. It is flattering for an author to have his book published on his birthday, but from that day forward the book is on its own. It seems logical to bring out a biography of Lincoln on Lincoln's Birthday, or an account of the attack on Pearl Harbor on December 7, or a study of the John F. Kennedy assassination on November 22, for these dates possess a certain degree of promotional cachet. But that's as far as it goes. Some years ago a client of mine turned in a big Irish novel, and of course her publisher scheduled the book's pub date for St. Patrick's Day. We strongly urged the publisher to press the big Fifth Avenue bookstores such as B. Dalton, Waldenbooks, and Doubleday to put the book in their windows, because the annual St. Patrick's Day parade passes in front of every one of those stores. Imagine the demand that the parade will create, we argued. The bookstore people were not quite so optimistic, reasoning that the vast throngs lined up to watch the parade would have their *backs* to the store windows, and anyone with money in his pocket would probably be more inclined to buy a pin that said "Kiss me, I'm Irish" than a novel about Ireland. This proved quite correct.

As I compose this chapter, the number one nonfiction bestseller on most lists is *Fatherhood* by Bill Cosby. Its publication date was Father's Day. Is that why it's number one? Not at all. Leaving aside the fact that the *Bill Cosby Show* is a top-rated program on television, many factors of far greater significance than the book's pub date made it a runaway best-seller. It is not likely that a stampede of consumers bought the book for a one-day occasion, otherwise why is it still at the top of the best-seller lists many months later?

Many authors don't realize that books are shipped to the stores weeks, and sometimes even a month or more, before the official publication date, and although the stores are not supposed to put books on sale before the official pub date, this stricture is widely ignored. Many a book has gone onto the best-seller list before its pub date, and when you read an ad declaring that a book is in its "Third Big Printing Before Publication," you can now see how such a thing could come to pass. The Bill Cosby book was "pubbed," as we say in the trade, on Father's Day, yes, but it had been stocked in the stores long before then.

Quite clearly, a book's publication date is nowhere nearly as important as some other factors on which publishers spend a great deal of time and energy during scheduling meetings. Possibly the key one is what the competition is doing. If, for instance, Simon and Schuster knows that Crown is going to be publishing a new novel by Jean Auel in September, S&S might well think twice about scheduling its own fall leader around the same time. Information about the pub dates of major books by star authors is usually available from a variety of sources such as publishers' catalogues, *Publishers Weekly*, and the free exchange of information among friendly competitors. And occasionally, when the exchange of information is not so free, friendly competitors have been known to resort to subterfuge.

If, however, two lead books scheduled for the same time are not really competitive—a literary novel by Anne Tyler, say, versus an international thriller by Robert Ludlum—the publishers might not be afraid to go head to head, because two different audiences can support both books and simultaneously boost them onto the best-seller list.

Publishers may not be so gentlemanly if they get caught up in a race to be first out with a book on a hot subject. Dramatic news events such as Jean Harris's shooting of her lover, diet doctor Herman Tarnower, or the development of treatment for ailments or conditions (premenstrual syndrome dominated publishing one year, osteoporosis another), will occasion rivalries that are anything but friendly, for now the competing publishers are committing a great deal of capital to getting their books into the stores first. In 1985 two publishers, Doubleday and Atheneum, got involved in exactly such a high-stakes horse race with books about the trial of Frances Schreuder, a prominent patron of the arts who put her son up to murdering his grandfather—Schreuder's own father. Atheneum's book was originally scheduled to come out first, but Doubleday then slated its pub date for the month before Atheneum's, whereupon Atheneum retaliated by rescheduling its edition. Doubleday rescheduled, eventuating in publication of the two books, by Shana Alexander (*Nutcracker*, Doubleday) and Jonathan Coleman (*At Mother's Request*, Atheneum), one day apart. In this case, both books did well, but on many another occasion the second book across the line has suffered grievous losses.

You can see, then, that unlucky pub dates can occur on any given page of the calendar, and the circumstances attending the birth of your book are far more auspicious or inauspicious than the date. Any day is Friday the thirteenth for the author whose publisher goes bankrupt on his pub date, or the one who finds himself on pub date without a sponsoring editor because the one who originally acquired his book left six months ago to take another job, or the one whose pub date was unheralded by a single ad because the whole advertising budget for that month was allocated to a blockbuster on the same list.

But such misfortunes are not reserved to the lowly. Not long ago a superstar author reportedly blew a gasket because her publisher hadn't had the prescience to realize that another publisher had scheduled a book by an equally illustrious name for the same month as hers, and she dressed her publisher down in terms usually reserved for marine recruits.

CHAPTER 21

Great Expectations

If the discontent of authors could be likened to a pie, the largest slice by far would represent resentment about the failure of publishers to advertise, publicize, and promote their books. Although I'm fairly articulate when it comes to explaining to my clients why publishers do or don't do certain things, I'm all too often at a loss for an answer when they ask me such questions as, "Why would my publisher spend $25,000 to acquire my book and then only $1.25 to advertise it?" Or, "How could they spend $100,000 to advertise that dreadful piece of pornography and not a dime on my book about nuclear disarmament?" Or, "Why is my book the best kept secret since the Manhattan Project?"

We live in a world in which it is universally acknowledged that the most effective way to move merchandise is to hype it to consumers. In the publishing industry, however, most of the product goes un- or underadvertised, and even books that publishing people consider to be heavily pushed are ridiculously underboosted by the standards of most other business enterprises. A few years ago, I handled a book by a leading business executive, and one day I proudly announced to him that his publisher had decided to allocate $75,000 for advertising and publicity for his book. "Great!" he exclaimed. "And how much are they going to spend on the second day?" In his field, $75,000 could be thrown casually into a single-page ad in a magazine. Something is definitely out of whack here.

In defense against author complaints, publishers respond that writers cherish unrealistic expectations, that even modest promotional campaigns are too expensive, that many books sell themselves without any publicity whatsoever, that many investments in this sector are unproductive or actually counterproductive, and that authors are not always aware of the efforts their publishers make to promote their books.

I don't think it's unreasonable for authors to hope that their publishers will try to stimulate consumer interest in their books. Nor is it unrealistic to suggest that publishers might benefit as much as authors from the publicizing of their products. But after countless discussions with publishers on this issue (not all conducted sotto voce, you may rightly guess), I have to admit that it is more complicated than we may think. Before you rush to judgment, listen to what your publisher has to say.

• *Some types of books are going to sell whether we push them or not.* A great many routine paperbacks sell and sell well with little or no help from their publishers. The reason is that paperback publishers have learned that there is a hard-core audience for romance, science fiction, western, horror, and other genres. These readers will buy just about any book in their favorite category whether it is good, bad, or indifferent. In certain male sectors like action-adventure or traditional cowboy novels, for example, a paperback publisher can anticipate twenty-five thousand guaranteed customers, and he would have to work very hard to sell fewer copies than that.

But, you ask, don't publishers want to sell more than this minimum? You'll be surprised to learn that the answer is: not necessarily. The cost of stimulating sales beyond the minimum support level may not be balanced by the profits. Some publishers are content to take a small profit on each title, rather than risk a loss going for the bigger profit.

Paperback publishers have also discovered that popular authors will naturally separate from the pack as a result of such factors as word of mouth, good reviews, feature stories in the press, and consumer demand in bookstores and other points of purchase—all with little or no money spent to create that demand. When those sales figures begin drifting upward, a wise publisher will consider ways to elevate that author even further. At that point advertising and publicity may come into play. Which leads to a second truism that publishers hold dear:

• *Advertising can't make a book successful; it can only keep it successful.* The fate of most books is sealed long before they are released to the public. The critical period is when the sales staff solicits orders from bookstore buyers and distributors. The enthusiasm or lack of it will determine the print run, and if the support is feeble, as likely as not little or nothing will be spent to advertise. Nor will ads necessarily send buyers flocking to the stores, even assuming the publisher feels that ads are a wise investment. If, however, a book meets with high popular demand, publishers may spend money on advertising and publicity to reinforce that demand. A new book by a popular author will probably get advertised, even if it's a lousy book. A new book by an unknown will probably not get advertised, even if it's great. Which leads to the very next rule of thumb, to wit:

• *Very little midlist fiction benefits from heavy investment in advertising and promotion.* Publishers are, understandably, reluctant to invest a lot of money to push serious, literary, experimental, and first novels. With hardcover sales projected in the low thousands, and with no guarantee of book club or paperback reprint revenue to underwrite the cost of publishing such "midlist" books, publishers prefer to let them make their own way on the strength of free advertising such as reviews and feature stories or word-of-mouth praise, or low-cost advertising such as catalogue announcements, publicity releases, or house ads that tout many of the publisher's books at once. As we've seen, though, there is some reason to believe that even if publishers spent heavily on ads for midlist fiction, it wouldn't compel consumers to buy, because the authors' names are not familiar to most of them.

As for promoting the authors themselves, it almost never works for midlist fiction, and for a very simple reason: It is extremely hard to express effectively the virtues of a work of fiction on a radio or television program.

Those of you who write fiction will immediately grasp the problem if you'll pretend you've just been asked by a talk show host, "What's your novel about?" No matter how wonderful, beautiful, or profound your book may be in print form, it will sound like Dud City when you attempt to explain it. "My novel is about life and death, love and war in the South before, during, and after the Civil War. The scene I wrote about the burning of Atlanta is particularly vivid." "My novel uses farm animals as an allegory for the best and worst in human behavior." "This peg-legged captain has a fixation about a white whale . . ."

This is the stuff that catastrophic ratings are made of.

• *Star authors, as usual, are exempted from all of the above rules.* If midlist fiction is so hard to promote on talk shows, how come best-selling authors show up on them all the time? One reason is that the subjects of their novels may be discussed as if they were nonfiction. While the plot of a novel is impossible to summarize entertainingly and the characters are too complex to capture in a pithy one-liner, there is usually something in the subject itself that serves as an excellent launching pad for stimulating discussion. "Tell us who your drug-crazed starlet heroine is in real life . . ."

Even more significantly, in the world of best-sellers, people are often more interested in the authors than in the books themselves. Best-selling authors are celebrities like movie and sports stars. Publishers who promote them stress the charms of the writer as much as they do the charms of the writer's work. If you'll listen carefully when a star author appears on radio or television, you'll notice how superficially the book itself is discussed. Attention focuses on such questions as: "Where did the idea for your novel come from? Did anything unusual happen to you when you were researching your novel? How much money did you get for your book? Is it true you're: getting married, getting divorced, having a baby, having another baby, buying a yacht, buying a castle, buying a nation?" These are precisely the same questions that might be asked of a film star hyping his or her latest movie.

Best-selling authors are also exceptions to the rule that print advertising can't make books successful. While ads seldom make consumers visit a bookstore to buy a midlist novel, they will attract them in droves to purchase a new novel by Stephen King, Danielle Steele, John Jakes, or James Michener. Why?

Because these fans are predisposed to buy the books to begin with.

• *Nonfiction authors are easier to promote than novelists.* The subjects of many nonfiction books are, as we've seen, much more appropriate topics of conversation than the themes of novels. Nor must the author enjoy immense celebrity to qualify for an invitation to a talk show. An interesting subject about which you feel passionately and speak articulately is often good enough to score a hit on radio or television. Terrific buns, big bazooms, and cow eyes are not necessary (though I don't suppose they do any harm) to furnish an entertaining fifteen or twenty minute chat about the current state of bioengineering or the destiny of wildlife on Alaska's North Slope.

Although advertising, publicity, and promotion have become a way of life in modern book publishing, there are occasions when you have to wonder whether it's all going too far. A couple of contrasting anecdotes exemplify a world that seems to be wobbling far off its axis.

A while ago, a client phoned me and said, "There's an author I think you should meet. Your time will definitely not be wasted."

"What's her book about?" I asked. Not an illogical question for a literary agent to ask, you will admit.

"I'm not sure it matters," he replied.

The meaning of this cryptic utterance was made instantly clear when the author walked into my office. She was stunning.

Plunking her novel on my desk, she declared, "You don't have to read it. All I want you to do is make some appointments for me with some top editors. Preferably male. I'll pitch the book at them myself. Once they see me, I know they'll want to buy my book."

"Ah," I sighed, "if only that were the way to sell fiction. But I'm afraid it all starts with a good book. So give me an evening to read it."

She relinquished the manuscript and I read it in one night. It was not bad. But it certainly wasn't good enough in my opinion to merit the extraordinary departure from protocol that she was asking of me. A personal visit by her might have provided many editors as much diversion as it had done me. But I didn't believe it would sell her book. Call me a prig (I've been called everything else), but I declined to represent her on those terms. "Your beauty will be an asset after your book has been bought by a publisher, I told her, "but I seriously doubt if it will be before."

One of my colleagues had no such reservations, and he did sell the book (or, more accurately, the author) for a good deal of money to a publisher who brought the novel out with the author's photo on the front of the dust jacket. It was then that I realized that the publishing industry had moved even closer to show business than I'd dared to think.

Not long afterward, a journalist client of mine introduced me to a doctor with whom she hoped to collaborate on a book. The doctor had developed a technique for saving lives, during a certain medical procedure, that might otherwise be at high risk. The doctor was a quiet, congenial man who spoke articulately about his treatment, and I was deeply impressed by his dedication.

The two launched their collaboration, and it produced a superb presentation that glowed with the excitement of discovery and the power of the physician's devotion to his patients. I prepared several copies of the proposal and submitted it to half a dozen publishers. Within the week, they had all called to express keen interest. But they wanted to meet the doctor to assess his promotability.

Although our doctor was physically attractive and possessed a reassuring bedside manner in a one-on-one consultation with a patient, he admittedly did not have the charisma of a Robert Redford. But I felt he had charm enough; and more important, I felt that the significance of his message far outweighed the style of his delivery before a camera.

Boy, was I wrong.

"We are a highly promotion-driven house," the editors told me in subsequent phone calls, "and I'm sorry to say your doctor doesn't make it in that department. But his technique is fantastic. In fact, I'm going to send this friend of mine to see him . . ."

Luckily, one publisher decided to disregard all those other considerations and made a satisfactory offer. But it was a scary experience, and it made me wonder how many valuable medical techniques, how many life-saving cures and discoveries of past times, would have gone unpublicized because their creators flunked their auditions.

"I'm sorry about your Doctor Pasteur, Curtis, but his voice is too raspy and his delivery is pretty lackluster. Maybe a good media coach would turn him around . . ."

CHAPTER 22

Brand Names

Although I've learned never to take any boilerplate provisions of publishing contracts for granted, some items are so thoroughly integrated into the terrain of contractual language that even the most hawkeyed of agents sweeps over them with scarcely a glance. Things like a publisher's right to have your book translated into Braille free of charge or to pay no royalties on copies of books damaged by flood or fire—who would be so petty as to cavil with such articles of faith?

One provision that I never gave much thought to is the one prohibiting publishers from running commercial ads in books. The right to refuse the insertion of beer, cigarette, automobile, toothpaste, cosmetic, dog food, breakfast cereal, or feminine hygiene product ads in the pages of a book to which one has dedicated the last measure of one's creative devotion would seem to be both self-evident and inalienable.

Not long ago, however, as I was strolling through a publishing agreement my eye was arrested by this clause and I started to wonder. Whence was it derived? Are the conditions and attitudes that prevailed when it was created still valid? What's so terrible about running ads in books, anyway?

When I first entered the publishing business early in the 1960s the paperback revolution was in full swing, and among the innovations introduced at the time was the insertion of ads in paperbacks (other than ads for other books on the publishers' lists). Although a number of products were tried out, the ones I most vividly remember were cigarettes. There was debate on both Publishers' Row and Madison Avenue about propriety and economics, and I don't recall that I cared much either way; it was fine with me if people wanted to run ads in books, and fine with me if they didn't. The ads didn't inspire me to buy the product, but few ads do anyway. Nor did I find them a desecration of literature, mainly because the books they ran in were pretty much desecrations of literature already. Still, some authors did not like it, and others worried that the insertion of an ad for True Menthols in *The Attack of the Hydrangea People* today could lead to one for Desenex Foot Power in *War and Peace* tomorrow.

I doubt if such ethical considerations would have prevailed if the economics of carrying advertising in books were sound, but they apparently were not. In addition, the susceptibility of book buyers to such ads was not terribly high. Publishers and advertisers might, given enough time, have overcome these problems had not, the story goes, some publisher run some cigarette ads in a book about the dangers of smoking (the story may be apocryphal, but it's too good to resist telling it here). The incident pointed up the dire possibilities, and so it came to pass that many authors and agents demanded specific language in their contracts stipulating that no ads would be run in their books (except, as I said, for other books published by the publisher) without their express consent.

Ads in books are not very cost-effective ways of conveying a sales message. If the average distribution of a run-of-the-mill paperback original is fifty thousand copies (it's often less), of which perhaps half will be returned, you're talking about twenty-five thousand exposures of the ad, maybe a few more if the book is circulated beyond the original purchasers. That's not a great many exposures compared to the hundreds of thousands or millions an advertiser can get in national magazines, and its a pittance compared to the effectiveness of advertising on network television. But, you say, doesn't the advertiser pay less to run ads in books than in magazines or on television to compensate for the difference in exposures? He certainly does; so much less, in fact, as to make it scarcely worthwhile for the publisher to sell the space.

There are other problems as well. Despite the commercialization of the publishing industry, many publishers do have ethical compunctions about mingling ads with the texts of books, and although they may have few reservations about publishing books depicting human depravity in all its hideous glory, they draw the line at disposable razors and smokeless tobacco. You figure it out. Another problem is consumer resistance to ads in books. While most buyers of literature don't think twice about ads that appear in magazines, they find the same ads discomfiting in books. This may relate to the disposability of magazines; books are to keep, and book buyers may feel that their possessions are contaminated by ads.

The most serious of all objections has nothing to do with cost-effectiveness, ethics, or the proclivities of book buyers. It has to do with the U.S. Postal Service, for running ads in books jeopardizes the cheap rates the post office charges for books shipped via special fourth class. Today, routine shipments of books go this way, as opposed to the more expensive Parcel Post or third class rates, or truck or United Parcel Service. It's a (relatively) inexpensive rate and one that publishers continually lobby postal authorities to maintain. If, however, books begin carrying advertising, they cross the line into the territory occupied by magazines, thus running athwart of the postal authorities eager to collect the higher revenues generated by the mailing of periodical literature. If the profits from such advertising don't offset the higher postal expenses, the publishers will obviously have made an expensive mistake.

It may well be that the postal obstacle is fatal to any scheme for reviving the idea of running advertising in books. But if we accept the truism that where there's a will there's a way, then we may be able to find creative ways around the problem. First, however, authors have to acknowledge that advertising in books does not necessarily spell the twilight of western culture as we have known it. Perhaps they would have an easier time doing so if they thought there was something in it for themselves.

What's in it for publishers, we all know: money. Advertising defrays costs and enhances profits, worthy goals for any business. But authors do not benefit from advertising revenue, nor do I think many of them feel entitled to do so. But surely, if they consider the rates paid to contributing authors by such ad-rich publications as *The New Yorker* or *Playboy*, it should be clear to them that there is a distinct relationship. Without meaning to sound overly cynical, it's easier to imagine authors accepting ads in their books for disposable razors and smokeless tobacco if they're paid advances twice the size of those they're now getting. Maybe the time has come, then, for authors to rethink their hostility to the notion.

It may well be that, for the reasons I've given, it's an unfeasible one. Nevertheless, it does raise a related issue having to do with the relationship between book publishing and other commercial enterprises. You might call it brand-name sponsorship of books, and though our industry is awakening to its potential, there's still a lot of fuzzy thinking in this area.

Our society is heavily dependent on brand names for the selection of consumer goods, and the consumer of books is no different from the consumer of soap powder. Publishers are confronted by a serious problem in this respect, however, because when it comes to selecting books, the "brand name" of the publisher means nothing to the consumer. Oh sure, the average bookbuyer is probably more familiar with the names of Random House, Doubleday, and Simon and Schuster than he is with firms like M. Evans, W. W. Norton, or David Godine, but he does not *prefer* Random House books to Norton ones. The book buyer has no brand name loyalty, and damned little brand name recognition: I warrant 90 percent of all readers (except perhaps readers of romances, who seem to know their Silhouettes from their Loveswepts) cannot tell you the names of the publishers of the books they are currently reading. Readers who loved a recent Putnam book could not care less about Putnam books in general, and if the author moved to Viking, his readers would buy his Viking books as avidly as they bought his Putnam ones.

Readers, as I say, are as brand-name conscious as anybody else, but for them the brand names are favorite authors; authoritative titles, such as M.D., Ph.D., President, or Director; and brand names in other fields of endeavor, such as *The New York Times* (for, say, cookbooks) or the National Football League (for official player guides and statistical books). As far as the first two classifications are concerned, publishers already do as much as they can to acquire and promote popular authors and titled authorities. But I'm constantly surprised at how little advantage publishers have taken of the availability of brand-name companies to sponsor books—sponsor them, that is, the way product manufacturers sponsor radio and television programs. Yet, almost invariably, such sponsorship has resulted in big sales and often bestsellerdom. It's easy to understand why. The Procter and Gambles, General Foods, and Ford Motor Companies of the world are loaded with money and spend stupendous sums on advertising and promotion. The sums necessary to back a book and put it on the best-seller list are pathetically low compared to what must be spent to achieve consumer acceptance of some new product or model: We're talking about perhaps a hundred thousand dollars or a little more, the cost of one or two magazine ads for soap products or automobiles or cigarettes. For another thing, these companies are in a position to buy books—lots of them, for use as premiums given away or sold at high discount to purchasers of their products.

The dynamic is clearly seen in a phenomenon like the *Mary Kay Book of Cosmetics,* which sold hundreds of thousands of copies in hardcover at $19.95. Mary Kay is, of course, one of our leading manufacturers of cosmetics. Though I haven't read the book I doubt whether the advice it purveys is much different from what you can learn from any professional beautician. The difference is that nobody would buy a book by that beautician because she is not a "name."

Many writers are not names either, but may have wonderful ideas for books and superb expertise to bring to them. They will probably not get very far, however, because good ideas and extensive knowledge are unfortunately not enough to interest publishers in commissioning books. I cannot tell you how many worthy proposals are turned down annually by agents and publishers because the authors lack "credentials." When I see such proposals, I often suggest that the author try to link up with a brand-name company in that field and try to interest the firm in sponsoring his book.

The same principle might wed brand-name sponsors to whole lines of books. Cosmetic or fragrance manufacturers could be persuaded to back lines of romance novels, or a jeans manufacturer to lend its name to a line of western novels, for example.

There is gold mine potential in this area known as licensing, and, because it means more work for authors (and possibly lucrative deals for them if authors and their agents play their cards right), far more attention ought to be paid to bringing sponsoring companies onto the publishing scene.

Some purists will attack this notion as another form of subsidy publishing, and that, unquestionably, is what it is. But an industry subsidized by Marlboro cigarettes, Kellogg's corn flakes, and Alpo dog food is still preferable to the present system subsidized by authors.

CHAPTER 23

✿ ✿

Book Clubs

It recently occurred to me that in the years since I've been writing about the publishing industry, I've paid scant attention to book clubs. Perhaps that's because they are such solid fixtures in the lives of authors, agents, and publishers that we take them for granted, like enormous monuments that we no longer notice on our way to work every day. How impoverished our environment would be without book clubs can easily be grasped when you realize that some seven million Americans subscribe to them. And because changes in pricing, reader tastes, distribution, marketing, and other trends have drawn new attention to the functions of book clubs, this is a particularly good time to examine this phenomenon.

Book clubs are an outgrowth of attempts to reach a larger segment of the reading population than was then being served by bookstores. Experiments like department store book clubs (there were Macy's, Gimbel's, and Bloomingdale's clubs among others) and tie-ins of cheap editions of books with the sale of products (a tobacco company included miniature volumes of Shakespeare plays in its cigarette packs) inspired an enterprising merchandiser named Harry Scherman to found the Book-of-the-Month Club in 1926. He perceived that an enormous potential audience, particularly in rural areas, had inadequate access to bookstores in towns and cities. Mail order, which worked so successfully for many other products purveyed to rural people, ought to work with books, too, Scherman reasoned. But he put a twist on this concept that made it a dramatic departure from the Sears, Roebuck approach. It's called the "negative option," meaning that unless members expressly indicate that they do *not* want the latest selection, the club will assume they do want it and will send it to them. Scherman's insight into human nature was almost diabolically shrewd. Perhaps he didn't trust that members would buy books simply because they were good, and he counted on such human foibles as torpor, guilt, and confusion to make members default on their obligation to return their cards in time to prevent clubs from shipping selections to them.

Whatever the motives of Scherman and subsequent book club entrepreneurs, the clubs caught on fast and hard, sweeping the country and, in the process, revealing some serious flaws in the way that books in this country are distributed and promoted. One publisher observed that "the clubs advertised books extensively and nationally, sold them regularly to people who had previously been only occasional book buyers and, most importantly, fostered the habit of regular reading," according to John Tebbel in his excellent book about American publishing, *Between Covers*. Tebbel cites book clubs for professionals such as business people, engineers, and the like as particularly effective in reaching audiences that conventional bookstore marketing simply cannot touch.

Not unexpectedly, the creation of the clubs provoked a great outcry among retail bookstore owners, who felt gravely threatened by them, particularly when the Literary Guild added the wrinkle of offering books for prices below retail. Many retailers accused publishers who dealt with clubs of collaborating with the enemy. Harder to comprehend was the opposition by publishers, who after all did stand to profit from book club revenue. Their contention, however, was that book clubs represented an element of crass mercantilism and cynical exploitation of the hallowed spirit of literature (publishers believed the oddest things in those days!). *The Bookman* asserted that book club members were "too feeble-minded, too lazy, or too busy to make their own choices." But book clubs were an idea whose time had come, and after consolidating their gains during the Great Depression of the 1930s (reading being one of the few affordable pleasures of that grim era), they became the institution we revere today.

With few exceptions, the basic idea concocted by Scherman has not changed. A lot of other things have, however, forcing Book-of-the-Month Club and its imitators and competitors to take measures to keep up with changing times, tastes, and conditions.

One of these is the shrinking of rural America, making bookstores accessible to people in all but the remotest reaches of the nation. Fortunately for the clubs, accessibility of bookstores is not by any means the most important factor for potential book buyers. Indeed, urban members constitute a large portion of the clubs' memberships. A far more important element is price. Book clubs offer discounts on the list prices of books, starting at around 10 percent, and additionally offer free bonus books plus sign-up inducements such as free sets of books.

As long as a wide gap existed between bookstore and book club prices for books, clubs could hope to continue doing a healthy business. The critical test came when the paperback revolution took hold, making paperback originals and reprints available for prices far below those offered by clubs to their members. But the clubs came through the test unbowed, revealing how solidly the convenience factor figured in the thinking of book buyers.

Most recently, the clubs found themselves under intensive fire from their old enemies the bookstores following the explosive expansion of such chains as Waldenbooks and B. Dalton. Not only did these chains reach deeply into rural territories that had been big profit targets for book clubs, but they started discounting books at or below the prices offered by the clubs. And when you added postage and handling charges to the prices members paid for book club selections, the allure of the stores became very compelling. Fortunately for the clubs, the stores could not sustain the narrow profit margins generated by "deep discounting," and although discounts are still offered on certain books by chain stores, the threat to the clubs from that source seems to have been averted.

It would appear that no matter what weapons the enemies of book clubs throw at them, the clubs survive because they possess one advantage the stores cannot overcome: selectivity. For readers too busy or uncertain to sort out the welter of new books, clubs proffer the recommendations of a panel of experts who have screened the candidates and distilled the very best. Furthermore, many book clubs cater to specialized tastes. Book buyers interested in subjects ranging from dance to war, mysteries to science fiction, nostalgia to travel, sailing to nursing, business to computers can satisfy their predilections by joining clubs aimed at those specific interests.

Most book clubs make their selections in pretty much the same way. Publishers submit books at an early stage, in manuscript or proofs, accompanied by promotional material and any other information about book and author that the publisher may feel will make the book more attractive to club members. (On occasion, a book will be chosen by a club after publication.) The submission is assigned by the club's editorial board to a reader, hopefully one who will give it an informed and sympathetic reading. Recommended works are then circulated to the rest of the editorial committee and are discussed, rated, and voted on. The club then negotiates deals with publishers on the books they wish to acquire. The club either guarantees to purchase a quantity of copies of the publisher's edition or, if the club has its own printing facility, licenses the right to publish its own edition. In either case, most clubs pay an advance against a royalty, though some smaller clubs pay a flat fee for a fixed, one-time printing. After the deal is struck, the clubs solicit orders from their membership. Except for the clubs that do their own printing, most clubs earn their profit from the difference between the cost of copies purchased from publishers and the price received from subscribers.

Although most clubs allow members to pick and choose selections, the Reader's Digest Book Club operates by requiring its members to take each and every volume offered during their term of subscription. The RDBC selects several titles to go into each monthly release, then condenses and edits them for both length and taste. In keeping with *Reader's Digest*'s editorial policy, there are strictures against excessive sex and violence, hard-to-identify-with characters, and slow-moving or excessively philosophical, controversial, or experimental books.

Book clubs are a major source of book sales, the largest clubs reaching hundreds of thousands of subscribers, and one of them, the Reader's Digest, boasting approximately 1.5 million members. While condensation and/or expurgation of your book (and sharing of your royalties with companion authors in the same volume) may not thrill you, sale of your book to RDBC is a handsome score, with advances starting around $25,000.

For the biggest literary stars the advances paid by book clubs can be mind-boggling, such as the $1.75 million reportedly paid by the Literary Guild for James Michener's *The Covenant* after a bidding war with the Book-of-the-Month Club. BOMC's advance for a less-blockbusting main selection is still nothing to sniff at, around $80,000 on the average if there is bidding competition by other clubs. If, however, there are no bidders to bump up the action, book clubs may offer as little as they can get away with. In any event the advances paid by most clubs are usually below $10,000. Often, however, publishers can sell the same book to more than one club. Royalties usually range from 5 to 10 percent of the book club's price.

The money paid to publishers by book clubs is, with almost no exceptions, split equally between publisher and author, and in a great many cases the club income makes the difference between profit and loss for a publisher on a given book. Indeed, Nancy Evans, former head of Book-of-the-Month Club and now publisher of Doubleday Books, recently told a gathering of literary agents that she considers book clubs the saviors of midlist books. It can certainly be argued that in an era of increasing attention to frontlist books, book clubs keep a great many books in print far longer than publishers themselves are able to do.

Although the key interface with book clubs is the book publisher, agents often cultivate book club executives in order to give them early notice of publication deals on books that might be hot prospects for the clubs. Recently my agency performed the equivalent of passing a camel through the eye of a needle when we submitted an unsold manuscript directly to the Reader's Digest Book Club and secured a commitment from the Club to buy the book if we could find a publisher for it. We had failed up to then to sell this lovely family-type story that seemed to be too tame for the editors who had read it. But it was right up the RDBC's alley, and, armed with a five-figure book club offer, we easily attracted a publisher for the book. But this was a rare event and we just happened to have the right book in the right place at the right time.

It's hard to imagine authors failing to be delighted by book club sales, but there have been a few. Willa Cather's arm had to be twisted to accept book club selection of *Shadows on the Rock* because she considered it crass exploitation of her work (authors had the oddest ideas in those days, too!). More recently, a number of authors, notably Stephen King, have objected to book club acquisition of their books on the grounds that club sales cut into sales of hardcover and even of paperback editions of the same book, losing them both readers and money.

Their reasoning is by no means without merit. Take a big-name author such as King whose book is published by a hardcover-paperback company that pays him, we can assume, a full royalty on both editions of his book. Suppose the hardcover edition sells for $15 and the paperback for $5. One thousand copies of the hardcover edition might bring in about $2,000 in royalties. One thousand copies of the paperback edition might bring in about $500. Now, suppose 1,000 copies of the book club edition are sold at a 20 percent discount to subscribers, or $12. The royalty on those 1,000 copies will be about $900. But that money must be split 50–50 with the author's publisher, netting the author $450. Thus the book club's revenues are about 25 percent of what the author will get for the same number of copies sold in hardcover, and even a little lower than the royalties for the same number of paperback copies sold. Although it can be argued that the same thousand people who might buy the book through a book club wouldn't necessarily buy it in stores if it weren't carried by the club, you can nevertheless see how authors like King might view sales of their works to book clubs as losing propositions. The war between bookstores and book clubs still smolders, sixty years after the opening volley.

CHAPTER 24

The Book Stops Here

The bookstore buyer is the last link in the chain connecting author to reader. Or perhaps we should say he is the last obstacle between them, for as we track the life of a book from the time the author turns it in, we may well be put in mind of the upstream battle of a salmon against rapids, waterfalls, submerged rocks and trees, and a host of predators. Many perish before they reach the quiet headwaters, and most that make it are doomed as well. A book must struggle against all manner of challenges: the hazards of editorial judgment, the treacheries of corporate politics, the uncertainties of the economy, a host of human failings, and a congeries of unlucky or providential events.

The final, and perhaps most brutal, stretch in the obstacle course occurs when the publisher's sales representatives attempt to interest bookstore buyers in their forthcoming lists. These hardy men and women will have attended their publishers' sales conference, where scheduled books are introduced to them by the firms' editorial staffs. As we've seen, editors presenting their books accompany their pitches with pertinent information and sales aids: the author's track record, advertising and promotional plans, news of movie or magazine or foreign deals, anything, in short, that makes the book stand out from its partners on the publisher's list, or from the competition on the lists of other publishers. Then, bearing proofs, catalogues, covers or dust jackets, sales information, press kits, and novelty items such as buttons or bookmarks, the sales people make appointments to visit the buyers in their territories.

Before the advent of bookstore chains, these sales reps (or

"travellers," as they were then known) visited individual bookshops and pitched their lists to each store owner or purchasing manager. The dialogue between buyer and sales rep reflected their joint interest in matching consumer reading tastes with the current and past lists of titles offered by each publisher. Although bookstore chains have been around for a long time, until recently these were not a significant factor in buying patterns, and the relationship between sales rep and store buyer was a highly personal one emphasizing local values.

The rise of the chains has revolutionized every aspect of book merchandising, not the least of which is that special bond between publisher and bookseller. Today, of twenty-five hundred full-spectrum stores that carry trade books in any appreciable quality, about two thousand are controlled by Waldenbooks and Barnes and Noble/B. Dalton. The impact of this change cannot possibly be understated. The buying power of the chains is so highly concentrated and leveraged that even a modest order per store, multiplied by the number of stores in any given chain, can easily make the difference between success or failure for a given book; a larger order can put a book on the bestseller list or extend its stay on it for a long time. Indeed, some chains have their own best-seller lists on which publishers heavily rely in assessing sales activity of their books. To a disturbingly increasing degree, chain store buyers are being consulted by publishers about whether or not to acquire certain types of books, placing the buyer in effect on the editorial boards of some publishers.

The same power that can exalt a book can cast it down if the chain store buyers withhold their blessing. Thus, publishers are concentrating an ever-increasing portion of their time, energy, human and financial resources to currying favor with the chains at the expense of the independent bookstore. Not unexpectedly, this has resulted in the demise of the old-fashioned bookshop. These beloved emporia, with their casual atmosphere and librarylike hush, with the visual and tactile delights of wonderful and interesting books everywhere the eye settles, with the varied stock reflecting the eclectic tastes of both owner and clientele—these are yielding one by one to the march of progress represented by clean, tidy, bland, efficient, convenient chain store branches with their homogenized stock, distinctly unbookish sales staffs, and computerized record-keeping and purchasing programs. Individually owned shops cannot hope to compete with the discounted prices offered on frontlist books by the chains, nor can their low-volume turnover generate the kind of capital necessary to meet the rents in high-traffic urban and suburban shopping centers. Over the last few years an association of small booksellers in northern California litigated with a publisher, Avon Books, alleging that Avon offered preferential discounts to book chains, a practice that the small stores maintain is widespread through the publishing industry. The store owners simply did not have the funds to prosecute their suit to the bitter end and were compelled at length to settle, leaving the issue unresolved but guaranteeing that preferential discounting in favor of the chains will continue to drive nails into the coffins of the small bookstores.

The two largest chains are Waldenbooks, headquartered in Connecticut, and B. Dalton, formerly located in Minneapolis but now shifting its frontlist buying to New York after being acquired by another chain, Barnes and Noble. There are in addition many smaller chains ranging from a handful of branches to over a hundred. Although they differ from one another in buying policies and patterns, discounting practices, and many other respects, fundamentally all of the chains function in much the same way. Their buying staffs receive sales representatives of publishers or publishing groups and listen to their spiels about forthcoming titles. The buyers then consult their records and sales data, review the information and material furnished by the publisher, and, yes, they even read the books. After taking everything into consideration, the buyers put in their orders: some in large quantity, some in small. And sometimes, they may not buy any quantity at all.

How is business transacted in a typical buying office? Well, for one thing, you may believe that the publishers' reps talk fairly fast. Given the large size of many publishers' lists, salespeople have precious little time to give speeches. It has been estimated that they have between thirty and sixty seconds per title to get their message across. I suppose that if you divided the publisher's list precisely by the number of minutes granted to the rep for this interview, that estimate would be accurate. In fact, it doesn't quite work that way.

For one thing, there are some kinds of books that require little or no salesmanship: certain backlist books, for example. When the stock of Dr. Spock's *Baby and Child Care* or *The Random House Dictionary* falls below a certain number, it is usually reordered automatically. The latest novel in a long-running series like Nick Carter or Longarm may not call for extensive discussion. Some other types of book, such as most first novels, will seldom fetch large orders even if the sales rep talks himself blue in the face, unless it's something on the order of *Presumed Innocent* by Scott Turow or *The Hunt for Red October* by Tom Clancy. That is because the buying policies of the chain, or the parameters of the computer's purchasing program (about which more presently) simply prohibit a large order for first novels, and the experienced sales rep has learned to save his breath for pitching books for which there is more latitude—and potential for commissions. "Don't waste my time in the 'gimmes,' " one buyer is fond of saying. "Just tell me about your featured books." He is referring to such "product" as celebrity biographies, new books by best-selling authors, timely or controversial nonfiction books, and other books that the publisher believes will have "legs." On these the sales rep may soliloquize to his heart's content: He will invariably find an attentive listener.

What are the things that chain store buyers look and listen for when sales reps go into their routines? Bear in mind that salesmen are salesmen the world over, and whatever they are hawking there is usually a percentage of blarney mingled with the truth. Astute buyers have learned to detect it, and because they are powerful and have at their disposal the best information-gathering capability this side of the Russian embassy, wise sales reps seldom bluff, bullshit, or soft-pedal the truth. "Don't tell me my market," another buyer told me he frequently says to sales reps.

The thing buyers most want to hear is, how much is the publisher getting behind the big books on its next list? A sales rep will boast of enormous "in-house" enthusiasm for a book, may show the buyer a fancy bound proof specially printed to impress the book trade, may inundate the buyer with tie-in gimmicks of all sorts, may tender to the buyer an invitation to a publication party in a swank restaurant. Few of these inducements turn the buyer's head as much as a commitment by a publisher to advertising, publicity, and promotion. In particular, as one buyer reported to me, bookstore people are most impressed by plans for co-op advertising. As opposed to advertising that carries only the name of a book's publisher, co-op ads show the book's cover along with the name of the store: "Available at All XYZ Bookstores," such an ad might read. The cost of the ad is borne by both publisher and bookstore, and the publisher's commitment in hard dollars guarantees that the company will be getting strongly behind its product.

One of the most unsettling aspects of chain store buying practices is the use of computers to make decisions. As in so many other applications, the computer is both an invaluable tool and a frightening menace. It provides the book-buying office with highly detailed information about sales patterns on a book-by-book, author-by-author, store-by-store, region-by-region, publisher-by-publisher, basis, and the data are available instantly. Track records of previous books by any given author may be summoned by the touch of a finger or two on a computer keyboard, providing the buyer with all the input he needs to make his decision.

Some chains depend more heavily on computer data than others, and in many instances purchase orders are rigidly programmed: If we bought 10,000 copies of that author's last book, we cannot buy more than 10 percent more copies of his next one, so put us down for 11,000. It is here that the greatest danger to literature may lie, for obviously this slavish devotion to ordering programs simply does not take into account such critical factors as a buyer's common sense, his instincts, and his personal enthusiasms. Most of all, it does not take into account the quality of the book in question, for even if an author's book is a quantum leap in quality over its predecessor, the buyer who has not read it—or even one who has—may be compelled by his own computer program to order the same number he would if the book were no better than the last.

It was comforting for me to learn, as I prepared this chapter, that there are still buyers, even in chain store offices, who care about books and authors and maintain a personal rapport both with publishers and consumers. The best buyers recognize the computer for the tool it is, but understand that a time comes when you have to walk away from the green screen and go out among the customers.

Spencer Gale, Merchandise Manager for Doubleday Book Shops, believes that the vital information harvested by computers must be balanced by a humanistic approach to book ordering. "Computers don't read books and computers don't buy them," he told me. Doubleday Book Shops, with thirty-four stores at this writing, is much smaller than Dalton and Walden, and its buying staff is much smaller, too. Nevertheless, its four buyers are presented all of the books that the larger chains are shown. These buyers must of necessity have a broader range of interests than those of their specialist counterparts in the giant chain offices. The staff constantly discusses books with each other, creating a sense of teamwork that makes Doubleday Book Shops' batting average—its ratio of sales to purchases— possibly the highest in the industry. If one buyer says he just doesn't have a feel for a certain type of book or a specific author, he will defer to someone else in the office. One buyer for another store told me she conducts informal but highly accurate market surveys by showing new women's novels to her mother and highly touted young adult books to her teenage daughter. Good buyers look beyond their own predilections: "You are not buying for your taste alone," Doubleday Book Shops' Gale expressed it.

Nevertheless, one gets the uneasy feeling that the noose around the throats of all who love literature is tightening with each step toward the consolidation and computerization of the publishing industry. The acquisition of B. Dalton by Barnes and Noble and the chain's move to New York City forge another massive link binding seller and buyer together. The intimacy between the publishing and bookstore businesses is now all but visible and palpable. It may legitimately be wondered what use sales reps will be in the future if there no longer is any distance for the "traveller" to travel. A phone call, a lunch date, a stroll across town, and the fate of a book could be sealed even before its acquisition by a publisher.

CHAPTER 25

✿ ✿

1099 and All That

Every January, right after New Year's Day, the mails bring to my agency a flood of rectangular printed notices with the number 1099 printed on them, and with the arrival of each one I can feel the temperature of my blood rise. Misery loves company, and I want you to suffer with me. I am fairly certain that by the time you finish reading this chapter, your mood will be somewhere between deep depression and high dudgeon.

As any author who has signed a publishing contract knows, there is a line on the signature page of every such contract requesting the author's social security number or federal tax identification number. The reason publishers request this number is that federal regulations require it. At the end of every year, employers who do not withhold income tax and social security contributions from contract employees are obligated to report to the government the names, addresses, and social security or federal tax ID numbers of the recipients of such income, and to state the amount of money paid to them. In this way the Internal Revenue Service is able to match the income claimed by recipients with the sums that employers state they paid to them. Employers who do not report such payments or report them inaccurately may suffer penalties. Employees who do not report such income may suffer penalties, interest assessments, and possible prosecution for any of a number of statutory violations. The means by which this information is reported to the government is Form 1099. The employer fills the form out in triplicate. One copy goes to the IRS, one to the payee, and the third copy is retained for the employer's records.

Although this system brings us yet another step closer to an Orwellian future, I don't suppose any public-spirited taxpayer can argue with the principle that Uncle Sam has the right to know what taxable revenues are being paid to his citizens. In actuality, at least where publishers and authors are concerned, the system is hopelessly, disgracefully, dangerously screwed up. Authors are being taxed for money they do not receive, and the government is not receiving taxes it is owed. The agents, as usual, are caught in the middle. The situation is becoming critical, for, with the refinement of powerful computers, the IRS can be more assiduous in its pursuit of discrepancies, and when it focuses full attention on the tax returns of freelance authors, it's going to have a field day. And, because there is often a time lag between the "flagging" of such discrepancies by the IRS and the auditing of suspect returns, it may be years before you realize that you've been caught in a snare of Kafkaesque grotesqueness. By that time your records may be lost, destroyed, or fatally disfigured by mildew; and publishers or agents who might corroborate your claims may be long gone.

It starts with the checks your publisher pays to your agent on your contract. If, say, that sum was $10,000 last year, your publisher will issue a 1099 form to the IRS to that effect, specifying your name, address, and social security number. But—you did not receive that $10,000. Your agent did, and he or she deducted a commission. For argument's sake, let's say that that was 10 percent, or $1,000, meaning that you actually received a net of $9,000. Dumb beast that the IRS computer is, it only knows what your publisher told it, namely, that you were paid $10,000. And the computer will be waiting to see if you claim $10,000 of income. If you don't—if, say, you claim only $9,000—the computer will metaphorically scratch its head and wonder what happened to the other $1,000.

It is not your publisher's job to tell the IRS that that $1,000 was commission; and it is impracticable for your agent to do so. How, then, is the IRS going to know that that's what it was? I suppose you could report that you received $10,000 even though you did not, and claim deduction of $1,000 in agency commission even though you never actually paid it out of your pocket. The trouble with that solution is that if the government audits your tax return, it will find no proof—bills, cancelled checks—that you paid a commission to your agent, and the IRS might therefore invalidate your deduction of that commission as a business expense.

Our plot now takes an interesting turn, for in a great many instances, it is not the author's tax number that appears on publishing contacts and 1099 forms, but the agent's. Income tax that should be the author's responsibility is then levied upon his agent, and by the time the confusion is straightened out, the government will have lost track of the client to whom the money was actually paid, resulting in tax revenue lost. Straightening out the confusion can be a nightmare for the agent, too. Early in the 1970s, a few years after I had started my agency but before I incorporated it, a number of publishers issued 1099 forms bearing my social security number instead of my clients'. I did not make anything of it at the time, but years later the IRS invited me downtown to explain why I had failed to report something like $270,000 in income for a certain year. I checked my return for that year, scrupulously prepared by my accountant, and found not a penny out of place. The IRS auditor, however, produced a printout showing a $50,000 check to me here and a $25,000 check to me there, etc., paid by Macmillan, Simon and Schuster, Dell, and other publishers. It was clear that the government thought that I was the primary payee of those monies rather than the middleman for all but 10 percent of them. I now had to produce copies of contracts I had negotiated for my clients, cancelled checks, and letters from publishers certifying that the money they had sent me was not, to the best of their knowledge, kept by me but passed on to authors after deduction of commission. The IRS man was satisfied, but because I had accepted 1099s with my social security number on them for several years before incorporating, these summonses from the IRS became an annual ritual to which I looked forward with the same pleasant anticipation as intestinal surgery.

As if the situation weren't confusing enough, many agents themselves send 1099s to their clients. They do so on the advice of their accountants or attorneys, even though agents are not really "payers" of money to authors; they are agents for the "payees," that is, for their client-authors. Nevertheless, they do send these forms out, reporting the net sums (after commission) that they remitted to their clients in the previous year. This simply helps to turn an ungodly mess into a nightmare, for *now the Internal Revenue Service will have on file two 1099s for the same transaction*! One will be from the publisher stipulating the gross amount paid to you, the other from your agent stipulating the net amount. Thus, on that $10,000 check your publisher sent to your agent, the government will show on its records a total of $19,000: the publisher's $10,000 and your agent's $9,000.

Obviously, there is no solution to this dilemma, for, like a beanbag, if you squeeze it at the ends it will pop out at the center, and if you squeeze it at the center it will pop out at the ends. Either the government, the author, or the agent will be victimized. The closest thing to an ideal system that I can think of might be structured along the following lines:

1. Publishing contracts would bear only the author's social security number or federal tax identification number, never the agent's.

2. Publishers would continue to send 1099 forms to authors and agents stating the gross sum remitted to each author in the past year.

3. Agents would not send out 1099s to clients, but would upon the client's request issue a statement describing the gross amounts collected for the author from each publisher, the amounts of commission and expenses deducted, and the net sums remitted.

4. Authors would keep accurate records of income remitted by their agents. If challenged, their records would match their agents' item for item.

This system would not prevent the discrepancies I've described, for there would still be a gap between the sums stated on your publisher's 1099 forms and those reported in your tax returns. But at least, when your friendly IRS auditor invites you to his office for a little talkie, you could produce detailed and accurate documentation of gross versus net revenue, and in all likelihood the matter would be dropped.

If not, then I suggest you bring a copy of this chapter to your tax fraud trial. It won't get you off scot-free, but it might at least cause the judge to mitigate your sentence.

CHAPTER 26

Audits

Most book publishers' contracts have provisions granting authors the right to examine the books and records of their publishers under certain conditions: i.e., the examination must take place on the premises of the publisher during normal business hours; no more than two audits may be conducted in any given year; an audit must be commenced within a reasonable time after the issuance of the royalty statement in question; the records on any given book shall not be examined more than once; the publisher is not required to keep records on a book for more than a certain period of time, etc.

Although, I am told by one accountant, examinations of publishers' accounts are on the rise, invariably these have been conducted by authors with lucrative contracts. I can say with certainty that the vast majority of authors has only the vaguest notion of what is involved in an audit. Perhaps we can rectify that problem here. Harder to rectify is the somewhat bovine attitude on the part of many authors that their contracts are too small to merit auditing, and the royalties to be liberated by an examination of a publisher's books would not be worth the cost, which can run to a thousand dollars a day or more.

These assumptions are not necessarily correct. While a publisher's profits from midlist and category books are indisputably smaller than those from best-sellers, the *total* profits from the former can be immense by virtue of the fact that there are so many more of them on publishers' lists than there are best-sellers. And because most best-sellers are by established big-name authors, the huge royalties they earn are usually paid in advance, giving publishers little leeway to reserve royalties, whereas publishers commonly hold at least half the royalties collected on midlist and category books for which modest advances are paid.

If collective audits of such routine books can be undertaken, thus spreading the cost per author, they may well yield a surprisingly good return on the authors' investment in an accounting firm. More important, such group audits keep publishers honest by exposing questionable accounting practices. It is therefore heartening to note that some author and agent organizations are sponsoring such group audits or making funds available for them. Because your book, or books similar to yours, may be spotlighted by an audit, you might like to tag along with the C. P. A. for a visit to a publisher's ledgers.

Before we embark, we ought to discuss just what gives us the right to audit a publisher, anyway. As I said at the outset, many publishers grant that right in the boilerplate language of their contracts. Certainly, every author or agent negotiating a book contract should insist on an audit provision. But if it is absent from a contract through oversight or design, or if a publisher refuses to grant that right to an author, does that necessarily rule out the possibility of an audit? Not according to the attorneys and accountants I have spoken to. They maintain that any licensor whose contract calls for royalties is entitled to examine the statements and supporting data of the licensee. Therefore, whether your contracts stipulate that right or not—indeed, even if you've been so foolish as to waive that right—your publisher cannot legally prohibit you from auditing his books. He can make it damned hard: He can postpone and stall, he can "misplace" and "lose" documents, he can subject your accountant to unpleasant conditions, a monastic cell with a hard chair, rickety table, and one flickering taper. But he must, ultimately, let your accountant go over the books.

Within recent memory there were some shady publishers who did that sort of thing, but happily they were driven out of business by their legitimate competitors. Today, while some publishers are frugal with their hospitality toward accountants, many shrug and say, "Come on in, we have nothing to hide."

Assuming your publisher is cooperative, the first step is for the accounting firm to make an appointment. The accountants will have examined the author's contract and all royalty statements from publication date to the present and will use these as the jumping-off place for their investigation. They will then request the printer's affidavits stating how many copies of the book were run off, along with information about damaged or destroyed copies. They will, of course, expect affidavits for all printings of the book. If there has been more than one printing, the accountants will want to know if the cover price of the book was raised.

Then the accountants will examine the records pertaining to distribution of the books, either to wholesalers or directly to book chains. The number of copies distributed plus the number of copies left in the warehouse plus the number of copies damaged, destroyed, or given away free should add up to the number of copies printed. If they don't, suspicion will certainly be aroused that the publisher printed copies he has not reported.

The next critical source of information is copies returned. In hardcover publishing, the books themselves are returned to the publisher for credit, and counting these, while tedious, is not as stupefying a task as counting returned paperbacks, for the dimensions of hardcover printings and distributions are nowhere near those of paperback. In paperback publishing, however, returns are usually effected simply by stripping the covers off the bound books and returning the covers to the publisher's warehouse, saving the substantial cost of shipping whole books back whence they came.

Obviously, the job of hand-counting paperback covers, which even for a modest-sized publisher number in the hundreds of thousands each month, is impossible to do by hand. Some paperback houses handle the problem by printing product codes, those black and white coded bars similar to those you see on canned and packaged goods at your grocery store, on the backs of their book covers. The stripped covers are fed through machines that read the codes and compute title, author, list price, number of copies returned, and other data. Unfortunately, not all companies possess such up-to-date hardware. How then do they do it? The old-fashioned way: They stack the covers up, count the number of covers in one or two inches, and multiply by the number of inches in the stack. If this sounds antediluvian, blame it on the system that makes books one of the few consumer products that are fully returnable for credit.

We now have all the information we need: number of copies printed, number of copies distributed, and number of copies returned. But there is still a gap between what the author feels is owing him and the actual amount of royalties he has been paid. That gap is the royalty on the number of copies the publisher has reserved against returns. As most authors now know, publishers create such reserves in order to give credit to distributors and stores that might return copies of books in the future. The reserve is determined by the executives who run the publishing company, and while it is to be hoped that these individuals will base their judgments on experience, reasonable evaluations of market conditions, and common sense, the existence of this tempting pool of undisbursed money has a tendency to cloud executive judgment, particularly in the pressure cooker of corporate bottom-line expectations.

Here, then, is the answer to the commonly asked question, Is it possible for print, distribution, and return figures to be falsified? The answer is, not without enormous difficulty, for it is neither safe nor practical to do so. For that to happen, the entire publishing organization—the clerks who document the printing and distribution information and count the returned covers, the bookkeeping and accounting departments of the publishing company, and the staffs of the printer and distributor—would have to be in on the conspiracy and sworn to secrecy. That is plainly preposterous: There simply isn't enough profit in the publishing business to make such wide-scale corruption worthwhile.

It is also completely unnecessary, because the same results are achieved by the decision of a handful of publishing officers to fix reserves against returns at an excessively high level. And it's all perfectly up-and-up from the publisher's viewpoint, because the establishment of reserves is a business judgment that may be argued but cannot be cited as fraudulent—unless one takes the position that the entire system is a license for publishers to earn interest at the expense of authors.

No, my observation is that print, distribution, and return

information are not falsified, at least not in a way that could be described as deliberate and systematic. It would be closer to the truth to say that publishing bookkeeping is subject to the same goofs as the bookkeeping of any other industry. And though it may seem that the errors always fall in favor of publishers, the accountants I've spoken to state that as many fall in the authors' favor. Thanks in good measure to the consignment method of selling books, publishing bookkeeping is far, far more complex than it has to be, and that makes it a breeding ground for error. Let me cite a couple of examples that suggest that publishers are not so much wicked as they are clumsy.

A couple of years ago my agency conducted an audit of a paperback publisher's books. Five of my clients were represented. The accountant determined that the books of four out of the five had excessively high reserves, and got money released to them. But in examining the records of the fifth author, he discovered that she had been paid twice for the same shipment of books, meaning that she had collected $5,000 too much in royalties. The publisher therefore deducted this $5,000 from royalties owing her on another book This author was not in a good mood after the audit, you may be sure. But the incident did demonstrate that the errors don't always benefit the publisher.

In another audit, the accountant discovered a disparity between the number of copies of a certain book distributed and the numbers returned or reserved for return. At length the clues led him to the discovery that this book had been used in a boxed set with books by two other authors. But while each individual book had its own accounting number, a number corresponding to each specific author, the boxed set had its own accounting number, a number corresponding to nobody. Since this obviously meant that there was no author, no author received the royalties earned on the boxed set! The comptroller of the publishing company was triply mortified, for not only did his firm have to pay my client the royalties due on his book in the boxed set, it had to pay the other two authors as well. The toll was $33,000.

One of the standard provisions of every audit clause in book contracts is that if errors of more than a certain amount, usually 10 percent of the sum stipulated in the publisher's royalty statement, are found by auditors, the publisher pays for the cost of the audit. Such a provision might make it tempting for authors who feel shortchanged by their publishers to hire an accountant, figuring the accountant will certainly be successful in detecting an excessive reserve against returns and get it at least 10 percent of that reserve released. Thus the publisher would be required to pay for the audit, right?

Wrong. A high reserve against returns is not an error. It's merely—in the publisher's eyes at least—a judgment call, a prediction or anticipation that a certain number of copies will be returned. Anybody contemplating an audit of his publisher's records should therefore be prepared not to recoup his accountant's fees from the publisher. Released royalties might defray or pay for the audit, but the publisher will stoutly maintain that no *bookkeeping* error was made.

Is there some alternative to hiring an accountant to find out whether your publisher is giving honest weight? Well, if you can prevail on your publishers to furnish you with information about the number of copies printed, distributed, and returned, you need nothing but a pencil and paper and a grade-school math education to figure out whether you have collected everything that is due you, and what the reserve against returns is. Then it's simply a matter of arguing with your publisher over the propriety of holding so much reserve money, or holding it for such a long time. The problem is getting that information: If publishers wanted you to have it, they'd put it up front routinely in their royalty statements. With persistence, however, you or your agent or your lawyer will be able to secure the information.

After reviewing it, however, you may feel in your bones or have other reason to believe that the figures furnished to you are incorrect, that your publisher printed or distributed more copies than he's told you, or took in fewer returns. You will then have to hire a professional accountant to examine the publisher's books, as the job is too complex and time consuming for untrained individuals. This is especially true if there is reprint, book club, foreign translation, and other subsidiary rights revenue, another very common source of bookkeeping errors among publishers but one that space prohibits me from analyzing here in detail.

Some powerful agents are able to build into book contracts provisions requiring publishers to furnish details of printing, distribution, returns, and reserves against returns in royalty statements, or copies of contracts and statements from sub-licensees such as book clubs and reprinters. For most agents and authors, however, it is futile to attempt to make publishers comply with such demands. This can only be achieved by collective action on the part of a determined, organized, and fearless cadre of professional writers or agents.

CHAPTER 27

Never the Twain

Most authors have a simplistic notion about how books are marketed and sold to the movies. Their impression is that their literary agent, operating alone or with a Hollywood co-agent, submits a book to producers until he finds one who likes it enough to make an offer, the same way that book agents submit manuscripts to publishers. In truth the process is maddeningly complicated and confused and can daunt many otherwise sophisticated New York literary agents. And while some agents have better movie and television track records than others, none has formulated a single and satisfying solution to the challenge of efficiently finding the right producer for movie or television adaptations of books.

The film business is by no means a monolithic industry where purchases are made by only a handful of companies. Completely to the contrary, the world we know under the umbrella term "Hollywood" is kaleidoscopically fragmented. Countless producers, bankrollers, screenwriters, actors and actresses, directors, agents, studio and network executives, and coattail riders scramble endlessly to assemble "packages" that will stay still long enough to get a property purchased, developed, produced, and released.

The New York literary agent, faced with this jumble of elements and claims, is all too often at a loss to know with any certainty what is genuine and what is dross, particularly because, as one learns after even brief exposure, the lingua franca of the movie business is insincerity. Unlike the publishing business, where if somebody says he owns the rights to a book you may be fairly certain he's telling the truth, Hollywood swarms with people selling things they do not own. I call it the Hollywood Hustle, and I can name on the knuckles of one finger the people out there who do not practice it in some form. Suppose you want to make a movie, and the only things you need are a book, a screenwriter, a director, a cast, a distributor, and $20 million. You start the ball rolling by, let's say, asking the agent of a famous movie star if the star would be interested in a certain book if he could put a deal together for it. Of course, the agent is going to say maybe. That's good enough for you. You now go to a screenwriter, show him the book, and ask him if he'd like to adapt it, and of course, the screenwriter is going to say, sure, why not, if the price is right, who have you got to star in the movie. And you say, you're negotiating with this star. And if you have just enough of a track record so that anyone bothering to check your background doesn't reveal a complete fraud, and if you talk fast and knowledgeably, you just may be able to line up enough interested parties so that one or two actually sign. You can then make the rounds clutching that contract and get the others to sign as well. Congratulations! You've just gotten full screen credit as a producer!

The reason it's hard for a New York agent, even one possessed of highly sensitive baloney detectors, to sort out the truth is that the movie and television businesses are characterized by an ever-shifting flow of power, capital, and influence, and it is labor enough to keep up with the scramble of musical chairs in the publishing field, let alone that of movies and television. New York agents respond in any of a number of ways: They employ a movie and television specialist to operate out of their New York City offices; they engage independent specialists based in New York City; or they engage West Coast movie agencies.

It would seem that the last choice is far and away the best solution. That may have been so ten or twenty years ago, but I do not believe it is necessarily so today.

When I first came into publishing, the movie industry was still something of a definable, organic entity. A handful of powerful studios controlled the assembly of movie packages, and the three networks controlled television programming. And because the field was more orderly, the role of the West Coast agent was, too. West Coast agents did in fact do for movie rights what East Coast agents do for book rights: They offered novels or original screenplays to movie producers and studio story departments, negotiated deals, took a commission, and remitted payment to the author or the author's literary agent.

As the 1960s and 1970s progressed, however, and the unified studio system gave way to one based on independent producers, artists, and sources of finance, the West Coast agents' approach shifted. They began accepting "talent," such as producers, directors, and actors, for representation. These clients sought the agents' help in negotiating their fees and acquiring literary or screenplay properties that they could produce, direct, or star in. Quite clearly, these agents were sailing into uncharted and very dangerous waters, for they no longer represented sellers only; they now also represented buyers as well, and in a growing number of instances they represented both the buyer and the seller of the same property or service. This is clearly a conflict of interest, because representation of buyer and seller makes it impossible for an agency to handle a negotiation at, as the legal phrase is, arm's length.

The creature emerging from this broth was the agent-packager, a breed that assembles movie and television deals out of client-components within each agency's own client list. The dilemma of which client to take the commission from—the buyer or the seller—was resolved by creating a "packaging fee" that is negotiated off the top of the total money available to finance the package deal. The net money after deduction of the packaging fee is then distributed according to the formula negotiated by the agent-packager with each client.

Students of power dynamics will realize that the distribution of these net monies, including those paid to authors for the rights to their literary properties, may be manipulated if not arbitrarily assigned by a shrewd agent (and West Coast agents are nothing if not shrewd). Indeed, students of power dynamics will realize that the function of the West Coast agent-packagers is identical to that of the old-time movie studios, with the exception that the agent-packagers do not actually distribute movies or air the television programs they package. To put it succinctly, the West Coast agent no longer represents the seller vis-à-vis the buyer; he *is* the buyer!

The reverence in which these powerful West Coast agents are held may be illustrated by the story about the Hollywood screenwriter who returned home from the studio at an unexpectedly early hour of the afternoon. He entered his bedroom to discover his startled wife in a state of deshabille, hair tousled, makeup smeared. The bed was a jumble of sheets and had obviously been used for something other than sleeping.

"Okay," he demanded. "Who was it?"

Caught dead to rights, his wife could only drop her eyes and confess. "It was your agent."

"My agent!" gasped the writer. "My *agent* came to my *home*?"

The New York literary agent surveying the West Coast scene sees arrayed before him a growing number of agent-packager-producers, and in due time it may dawn on him that these outfits are in competition with each other. Each West Coast agency has its own client list out of which the components for a deal are selected, and although those agencies do work out deals with one another in order to obtain the services of each other's clients, it can safely be stated that the desirable route is to cull the package entirely out of the agency's own stable.

What this means for authors and their New York literary agents is that West Coast agents are no longer as capable of thoroughly covering the movie and television markets as they used to be. If you or your agent engage a West Coast agent to sell movie or television rights to your book or story, you should be aware that that agent may not be accepting the mandate with, to use another legal phrase, clean hands.

About ten years ago, when I started to recognize how these agencies were evolving, I half-jokingly suggested to the head of one of them that if he was interested in handling my clients' properties, he ought to option them. He did not get the joke and regarded the suggestion with horror. "But look," I reasoned. "When you consider that your agency behaves in every way like a producer, doesn't it make sense for me to make you pay for the exclusive right to package a film out of my clients' material?" Of course, he refused even to consider it. But, interestingly, in the last year a number of West Coast agencies have been exploring this very concept, optioning books and stories in order to buy their firms the time to put together deals.

Perhaps the answer is to submit your book to more than one West Coast agency at a time? No, I'm afraid that's *not* the answer. The key to movie and television deals is distribution, which is controlled by the studios in the case of motion pictures and the networks in the case of television, and if two or three or four West Coast agencies bring the same projects to the same studios or networks, there will be chaos. For if a studio or network gives the green light to the development of a project, which agent-packager will they give it to?

Another reason New York agents don't always like to turn their properties over to West Coast agencies is that it means splitting a commission with them. New York agents charge 15 percent commissions on movie and television deals on the average. If they let a West Coast agency make a deal for them, they'll have to give that agency at least half of their commission, and maybe more than half: Some West Coast agents feel that because they do most of the work on such deals, they should get a higher percentage of the commission.

While many New York agents reason that 5 percent or 7½ percent of something is better than 15 percent of nothing, the big numbers paid for movie and television rights can make an agent excusably greedy, and many therefore try to handle those rights themselves. It is not an easy task, for they must keep up with ever-changing industry buying patterns, personnel changes, news, and gossip, and in the movie business even more than in books, timing is critically important: You have to be there with the right property at the right time, and know the right person to call. Frequent trips to California may be necessary to meet and deal with the movers and shakers out there.

The fact that the movie studios, networks, and many major producers have New York offices, story departments, and scouts makes it seem easier for a New York literary agent to conduct movie and television business in Manhattan. To a degree that is true, but not to a sufficient degree. The New York offices of West Coast firms are good for expediting the submission of literary properties (and they're great for extending screening invitations to literary agents), but almost none has the authority to purchase or negotiate. Furthermore, it is not always desirable to give early looks at upcoming hot properties to New York scouts and story departments. In fact, it is often important not to let them get their hands on those properties. There is only a small number of studios and networks, and if they all "pass" on a property—turn it down—it will effectively be dead. A commonly held view of the people who read and screen literary properties for studios and networks is that they are not notable for their vision and imagination, and that they operate on the bureaucratic principle that it is safer to say no than yes.

Many New York agents therefore feel that it is much better to offer their properties to producers who can visualize a work's cinematic values and who have at their command the financing and industry connections to put together an impressive package that they can bring to studio and network brass. But which producers to offer those properties to? Aye, my friends, there's the rub, and it brings us right back to the desirability of going through West Coast agencies.

There simply doesn't seem to be a happy answer, and perhaps the best that can be said for agents on the opposite coast is what is often said about people of the opposite sex: You can't live with 'em, and you can't live without 'em.

CHAPTER 28

Books into Movies

It's often said that They're Not Making Movies the way they used to. That's a matter of opinion (it happens to be mine), but if it's true, the decline can be attributed to the fact that they're not adapting books the way they used to. Since the golden age of filmmaking in the 1930s, the ratio of theatrical films based on books to those made from original screenplays has been steadily shifting to the latter. Today the odds that your novel will be made into a movie are distressingly low, even if your novel becomes a best-seller.

I can't believe there are fewer adaptable books today than there have been in the past. Why, then, aren't they making books into movies anymore?

One reason facetiously offered by book people is that nobody in Hollywood reads. Relying on my own experience, I'd have to say that's untrue. What is probably closer to the mark is that movie people don't have a lot of time to read, but then, neither do book people. Most of us are so busy reading manuscripts for business that we can't spare a moment to read for pleasure. While I, like so many of my colleagues, can read three or four book-length manuscripts in one evening, I have been plodding through a published biography, at a rate of a few pages a week, for over two years; it's taking me longer to read that book than it took the author to write it!

At any rate, what little reading time movie people have is usually spent reading screenplays. Books are synopsized for them by readers, and only if a reader's recommendation makes the book sound as if it has strong movie potential will a producer read the book itself. And sometimes not even then.

The downward trend in film adaptations follows the decline of the studio system and the corresponding rise of one revolving around independent producers. Under the old arrangement, all-powerful studios acquired best-sellers and other literary properties and adapted them for producers, directors, and stars belonging to the studio "family." The studios were self-contained entities possessing financing, production facilities, and distribution capability, the three elements essential to making commercial films. After World War II, however, producers, writers, actors, and others challenged the studios in a bid for more artistic independence and a bigger piece of the profit pie. They succeeded to a degree in weakening the studios' absolute power and control, but at a high cost: the loss of efficiency. Today's producers cannot simply scoop up all the talent they need from one studio pool, but instead have to assemble "packages" out of a fiendishly complex and far-flung tangle of artists, agents, lawyers, unions, guilds, financiers, smaller distributors and other elements.

This radical change has taken its toll on adaptations of books. Let's see how.

The hardest part of getting a movie made is raising the money. It is easier to raise a sunken treasure galleon than to raise money for a movie. These days a film budgeted at $5 million is considered a home movie, but it's still a lot of money, and anyone furnishing it to a filmmaker expects either an excessive participation in profits or an excessive say in the way the movie is made, both of which are abhorrent to a producer. Studios are not disposed to back films until all elements of the package are in place, or at least a "bankable" star or director has made a commitment.

In short, few independent producers have any money. Not long ago—fifteen or twenty years—we used to see a number of outright purchases of books for movies. Though an outright purchase doesn't guarantee a movie will be made, the size of the outlay, often hundreds of thousands of dollars, certainly guaranteed an earnest effort would be made to recoup the investment. Today, one seldom hears about outright sales. Everything is optioned. When independent producers start piecing together a movie deal, the item on which they least want to spend what little money they possess is the book; for them, the key item is the screenplay.

The screenplay opens the doors to securing financing by stimulating the interest of stars and their agents, and then to assembling the rest of the elements. Once these all come together and the money has been put up to make the film, the author can be paid. Until then the author is in effect asked to subsidize the writing of the screenplay by being moderate in his asking price for the option. In many cases authors are asked to give producers a free or nominal option against a big purchase price and share of the profits. These strangely unbalanced deals—often options of a few hundred dollars against purchase prices of hundreds of thousands—result from the fact that the option money has to come out of the producer's own pocket, whereas the purchase money comes out of someone else's.

Although there is a lot of activity in options of books for the movies, it can be argued that the option system is actually harmful to a book's chances of being made into a movie. Options are usually purchased in six- or twelve-month increments, but are renewable at the producer's option for several more six- or twelve-month periods with the payment of additional option money. The process can tie up a book for eighteen months, two years, or longer while the producer frantically tries to juggle screenplay, financing, distribution, director, and stars in the hopes of getting them to sign a contract. Nobody wants to sign a contract until he has a guarantee. The financiers may want a distribution commitment before they fork over their money; the director may want a particular star to agree to appear in the film; the star may want a terrific screenplay; the screenplay writer may want a huge fee; the studio may want the book to be on the best-seller list.

Since the odds against everyone signing are so high, it's likely that when the option or renewal lapses, your book will have been shopped all over the movie business. Though you'll then have an opportunity to market the rights again and pursue those who might have been interested in your book a year or two ago, the book will probably have the smell of death clinging to it, and you'll be unable to revive it.

Clearly, it's a lot cheaper and easier for a modestly heeled producer to option or commission an original screenplay than to get involved with books. But with the kinds of movies that are pulling in big bucks at the box office these days, it may reasonably be asked, What do producers need books for, anyway? So many of these films are youth-oriented, exploitive, devoid of ideas, predictably plotted, action-packed, and populated with stick-figure characters. A producer contemplating making one of these teenagers' fantasy films is certainly not going to seek those values in books. Indeed, he would have to search far and wide to find books bad enough to make into today's hit movies.

Interestingly, the one area in the entertainment industry where books are still welcome, and in fact welcome as never before, is television, and the immense appetite of the networks and cable companies does not threaten to diminish in the foreseeable future. Publishers' lists are combed furiously by producers seeking movie-of-the-week or miniseries candidates, and because of network commitments to air scores of these films annually the search has become intensely competitive. Most of the properties optioned or acquired are novels, but television producers, unlike theatrical film producers, plunder short stories, articles, and nonfiction books as well as novels in their quest for adaptable material.

Ironically, the quality of television movies now often exceeds that of many theatrical films. Once characterized as a vast wasteland, television has discovered ideas and begun to develop them into vehicles that are often intelligent, sensitive, moving, and controversial, touching on themes that the movies used to portray but seldom do any more. Out-of-wedlock children, incest, senility, child abuse, drug addiction, kidnapping, and physical disability are some of the themes that have been woven into recent original television movies, and few who have watched them can claim that they are inferior to most theatrical films made today or that they are not the equal of many made in the past.

From the viewpoint of the author with a book to sell, this change is of major importance, for it no longer is smart to disdain television deals while holding out for a theatrical one. It is likelier than an option will be exercised for a TV movie than for a theatrical one, and the price gap between the two media has begun to close. And, from the viewpoint of pride of authorship, the chances are better than ever that an author's vision will be preserved intact in a television adaptation. For all these reasons I recommend that if you or your agent are approached by producers interested in adapting your work for television, and the terms are comparable to what you might get from a movie-movie producer, don't hesitate to make that deal.

Here are some other suggestions for improving your chances of making a movie or television sale in today's market.

• *Prepare an extremely brief—no more than two pages—synopsis of your book to show to interested producers.* It should of course be a highly compressed summary of the theme, story, and characters, and should read like a jacket blurb except that the emphasis should be on the cinematic values rather than the literary ones. Potential buyers will want to see the manuscript, proof, or printed copy anyway, but if they have time to read nothing else they will read your summary, and a well-written one will enable them to visualize the film the way you yourself visualize it.

• *Give no free options, even of a few weeks' duration.* Inevitably you will be approached by would-be producers claiming they know exactly the right studio or network executive who will buy your book, and all they need is a couple of weeks to make a deal, and could you let them have just this one shot free of charge because by the time the papers are drawn up it will be too late, etc. Most agents who have dealt with movie and television people have heard this line before and shut the door on it; they've learned that people don't respect properties they get for nothing. An investment in an option guarantees a certain amount of commitment and responsibility. You don't have to draw up a complete movie contract for such a modest deal, but a deal memorandum synopsizing the highlights of the negotiation such as option price, purchase price, profit percentages if any, duration of option and renewals, reserved rights, credits, and so forth, is a must.

As for that claim that the producer needs only a few weeks, don't believe it. Everything in the movie business takes six times longer than you would imagine it should. I have seldom seen a movie option exercised after six months, and indeed have seen producers dig themselves into an awful hole by paying too much money for too brief an option, necessitating their renewing the option for too much money again for yet another brief option. The author who finds himself in the position of dealing with such a producer enjoys the rare pleasure of being in the driver's seat, so if someone wants a short option, give it to him, but make him pay for it.

• *Renewals of a producer's option on your work should be more expensive than the original option and should not be deductible from the purchase price of the rights.* The initial option is usually applicable against the purchase price, but thereafter the producer is in effect paying rent on your property. If you allow him to deduct renewal fees from the purchase price, he is in effect not renting your property but buying it from you in installments, and relatively painless installments at that. You'll want that lump sum due upon exercise of the option to hang over the producer's head like some ominous cloud. And, by making renewals more expensive than the original option, you are telling the producer that tying your property up for such a long time is an inconvenience, and one that is not mitigated by the money he's paying you to extend your option.

• *If you option your book before publication, try to negotiate the deal in such a way that the option expires around your publication date and is not renewable beyond that date.* Your property will probably never be hotter to movie people than before it's published, when it will not have been exposed to the entire industry or shopped all over town. Thus anyone taking an option before publication is getting your work at its ripest moment. If, by the time the book is published, your producer has not been able to make a deal, his option should expire, and expire without hope of renewal. If your book then goes on to get good reviews and/or hits the best-seller list, you have a second lease on life.

CHAPTER 29

Take This Job and Shove It

Most writers dream of leaving their day jobs (some have night jobs as well) and launching careers as full-time free-lancers. In their eagerness to realize that goal, many of them quit as soon as they've made a few sales. This decision invariably turns out to be ill-advised if not catastrophic after the author discovers that he did not properly reckon the cost of independence, project the size and flow of earnings, or prepare himself psychologically. Even an author lucky enough to strike it rich on his first book should use the utmost restraint before quitting his job to become a writer. By the time he realizes he doesn't know what to write for an encore, he may have raised his lifestyle to an unsupportably high plateau.

The questions of whether and when writers should go full-time are among the most common and vexing that agents have to deal with, and if an agent ever had a notion to play God, here is his opportunity. The responsibility for this decision is awesome and demands ten times the prudence required to advise authors about such matters as selecting the right publisher for their books. The number of factors is large and their complexity intimidating. It's the kind of decision that should be reviewed with a great many people to collect as much input as possible.

An excellent idea is to make a list of pluses and minuses, what you stand to gain and what to lose. Often the right choice will jump out at you when you review this list. The secret is to make sure you have enumerated all the factors. Then you must be brutally honest with yourself. You do not want to subject yourself and your family to needless suffering because you erred on the side of wishful thinking when you drew up your scenario.

My first rule of thumb is to determine whether you have enough work lined up *under contract* to guarantee employment for one to two years, for that probably means you have reached a level of skill and reliability your publisher can count on. I seldom permit an author to include in his expectations income that is not absolutely guaranteed: royalties, foreign rights sales, movie deals, and the like, unless there is a solid history of such windfalls in his track record. If you've never sold British rights to your previous books, if you only *hope* your next book will earn royalties, if your father-in-law *thinks* your book is a natu-ral for the movies, I toss these items out of the equation, because they are only fodder for self-delusion and disappointment.

I do, however, include in the equation the renewal of current contracts after you have fulfilled them, particularly if you are a genre writer. If you have a three-book contract in an ongoing series, I tend to consider it a likelihood that you'll be given another contract at the expiration of this one. If you're an established mainstream writer with three or four books under your belt and a potful of good ideas for new ones, I'm disposed to take for granted that you'll land a new contract when you complete your present book.

The renewal of contracts means money payable on signature of those agreements, so that when you look down the road for money to be earned after fulfillment of your present commit-ments, you should be able to count on income from new deals. It is also reasonable to figure that you'll get more money per book than you're getting now, because it's likely the publisher will feel you're a better writer and there'll be more of a sales record to justify raises. There is also a tendency among publish-ers to give raises to their regular writers if for no other reasons than inflation, longevity, loyalty, faith in the future, and hu-mane motivations. You have to ask for these raises, but there's a good chance that if you don't push it too hard, your publisher will give you a little more the next time around just because you're a nice person. You *have* been a nice person, haven't you?

Another important factor I weigh when discussing with authors the decision to go full-time is increased productivity.

At present, because you're only able to devote an hour or two to your writing in the evenings, and maybe twice that much on the weekends, you are not capable of turning out more than two books, say, per year. But if you launch a full-time writing career, you may be able to double or triple your annual output, meaning double or triple the revenue. There is also, I've observed, a tendency for writers to improve the quality of their work after they become full-timers, because they're exercising their skills to a greater degree, and (domestic distractions notwithstanding) their concentration increases. And if you do become a better, faster writer, the prospects for raises in pay from your publishers become even better. The process, in due time, becomes self-perpetuating.

Having painted the future in broad, and slightly rose-tinted, strokes, it's time to focus on the hard realities of budgeting your money after you make The Big Move. Get out that legal pad and set up two columns, Income and Expenditures. So far, so good. Unfortunately, that's about the only straightforward thing about setting up a budget, because when you start to analyze each item, you quickly see that simple concepts and definitions are elusive.

When you work for The Man, you most likely receive a regular paycheck from which certain mandatory deductions are withheld. Among these are federal and state income taxes, sometimes municipal ones as well. Social security contributions are also compulsory. Then there may also be deductions for disability insurance, worker's compensation, medical insurance, union dues, stock option purchases, pension contributions, and donations to the boss's pet charity. Your net take-home income has been 20, 40, even 50 percent or more of your gross salary.

When you become a full-time writer, however, you suddenly find yourself in the position of "taking home" a "paycheck" from which nothing (except commissions, if you have an agent) has been deducted. At first glance that's great. At second and third glances, you realize that the heavy burden of responsibility for many of those obligations, formerly taken care of by your boss, now rests on your own shoulders. You will have to set aside enough money to pay income taxes, social security, and other taxes such as unincorporated business taxes, occupancy taxes on your business property (your office, that is); medical and/or disability insurance premiums; pension contributions (you may now qualify for a Keogh Plan savings account); and whatever other "benefits" you wish to continue enjoying as carryovers from your erstwhile job. So, the $50,000 per annum that you project taking home when you go full-time may translate into $25,000 of disposable income after you set aside all the obligations your employer used to pay on your behalf.

To your projections of income from your writing, add income from your spouse's job if any; investment dividends and savings interest; and other sources of guaranteed revenue such as teaching, lecturing, or consulting income. And you must not rule out your savings as a potential source of income. Because delays are more the rule than the exception in the publishing game, it is entirely possible that you will have to tap the principal in your savings account, or liquidate a long-term investment, in order to tide yourself over between checks.

Because many major expenses are payable quarterly (such as estimated federal taxes), semiannually, or even annually, you might consider opening a savings account for those obligations only. You can then earn a little interest on the money you have set aside to pay those bills. Needless to say, you must never invest that money in speculative ventures like hot stock market tips or the fourth race at Santa Anita. Why did I say "Needless to say" if it was needless to say it? Because I know of a number of authors who gambled their mortgage or tax money on such things, and lost it (of course). Naturally, they ended up hitting their agents for advances.

When you try to tote up the "expenditures" side of your projections, you once again discover that nothing is as simple as it seemed to be when your boss took care of things. You will immediately see how costly medical insurance is, particularly when you are no longer participating in a group health care plan. The social security rate for self-employed people is higher than for those in "respectable" jobs (writing has not been a respectable job for twenty-five years).

And then there are those bennies and perks you took for granted when you worked for that company. If you had an expense account, you will now have to absorb that part of the benefit that was formerly spent on yourself, in particular travel and entertainment. No longer can you charge the firm for your spouse's meal when you take clients or customers to dinner; no longer can you bill your boss for mileage incurred on that side visit to Disneyland during your business trip to Los Angeles. And because current tax law permits you to deduct only 80 percent of legitimate entertainment expenses, you've also lost the 20 percent your company absorbed in tax on the undeductible part. Say good-bye to the free use of the postal machine when you mailed off your personal bills; to the telephone from which you called your publisher, your agent, your kid in college, your mother in Florida; to the photocopying machine on which you ran off copies of your manuscript after everyone had gone home; and to the office typewriter, word processor, computer, coffee maker. Say good-bye to the paid vacation. You want a vacation, you now can take fifty-two weeks a year if you want, only you have to pay for them out of your own pocket. Say good-bye to sick days on salary. Say good-bye to the company car and the company jet and the company dining room. Buy your own car and jet and dining room.

I am not saying there aren't also many hidden benefits to leaving your job for a full-time writing career. But somehow, the savings on carfare or on the expensive wardrobe you're retiring in favor of the free-lancer's uniform of jeans and T-shirts don't seem to balance the hidden costs. And not everybody fervently believes that getting to see more of one's spouse or kids is a hidden benefit.

The biggest challenge to the newly independent is the large lump-sum payments due with unforgiving regularity throughout the year. Among these, as I've said, are quarterly estimated federal income and social security taxes, but there are also state and local taxes and estimates and medical insurance premiums. This is not to mention those other lump sums you have to pay whether you are self-employed or not, such as automobile and home insurance, private school tuition, summer camp fees, repair contracts on major appliances, and the like. And these all have a way of going up. Add to them the cost of occasional but inevitable contingencies, the kind that always seem to rear their heads hours after your warranties expire and moments after you have served notice to your boss of your intention to leave his employ: washing machines giving up the ghost, television picture tubes burning out, automobile engines seizing, wisdom teeth impacting.

Aside from being fiscally unprepared to deal with these aggravations, you may not be emotionally able to cope with them. This is by far the graver problem, for while you can often juggle your accounts or hustle up some money to cover short-term deficits, it is much, much harder to find the psychological resources for dealing with that condition of perpetual anxiety about money that is the lot of most free-lance people.

The truth is that not everybody is constitutionally cut out to work for him- or herself. There are those who are incapable of preparing a budget or of staying within its rigid boundaries. There are those who cannot handle the loneliness of free lancing and the loss of the social support that comes from working with others. There are those who lack self-discipline, those who, after years of punching in and out at a time clock, reporting to boss or supervisor, adhering to rules and regulations and work orders, are at a loss to structure their own time. There are those who cannot set short- and long-term goals or keep to them. There are those who cannot live with the distractions of full-time domesticity. There are those who go to pieces at the prospect of drawing on their savings or selling off an investment to cover an unexpected expense. There are those who indulge their newfound freedom by tackling that Great American Novel they've always dreamed of, instead of doing the commercial projects that have to be done to keep their finances on a steady course.

Having tried the free-lance life for several years in my twenties, I can testify to having flunked most of the above tests. Though I did produce a goodly number of books during that period, and earned a decent living, I found the loneliness and isolation very hard to bear, and the budgeting of money impossible. I had some savings salted away, but having been raised to think of drawing money out of savings as tantamount to filing for bankruptcy, I suffered woefully. Every month, when the time came to pay my bills, I developed all sorts of neurasthenic symptoms ranging from vapors to hysterical pregnancy.

So, be as candid with yourself as you can be when you contemplate making this critical career decision, and ask your spouse, your best friend, your accountant, your attorney, your shrink, and your agent to be so, too. If they vote yes, then all you'll need is a ream of paper, a pair of jeans, and a few T-shirts, and you're in business.

Oh yes—don't forget $100,000 worth of book contracts!

CHAPTER 30

Breakout Books

From time to time a writer bursts upon the literary scene with a first novel of astonishing accomplishment, and the world gasps as if witnessing the genesis of a supernova out of a hitherto undetected star. Critics poring over the author's pedigree for clues to his development usually find only such banal biographical facts as that he was a reporter for his high school yearbook or a bridge columnist for some obscure midwestern newspaper. But this author had apparently been struck to his knees by a sublime inspiration and spewed the work out of his soul in one volcanic eruption. One thinks of *Catch-22, The Naked and the Dead, Gone with the Wind,* or *Raintree County.* In some cases the author never again rises to the height of his first book, and in not a few the author never writes another book at all. But that first book is enough to make the author's name a household one forever after.

Professional writers often greet such events with mixed emotions. On the one hand they cannot help but join in the outpouring of adulation. On the other, if they are honest with themselves they will probably confess to intense envy. For, this . . . this *amateur* has somehow hit a grand slam home run on his very first time at bat, has achieved in one stroke something that most writers may never achieve in their lifetime, or may achieve only after decades of struggle and sacrifice: a Breakout Novel.

It is always instructive to examine a society's underlying assumptions, and it seems to me that the Big Breakout has become an article of faith for everybody involved in the world of books, from publisher to critic to consumer. What disturbs me is that it has also become an article of faith for writers. But before I elaborate on that statement, let's see if we can define a breakout book.

Implicit in the term is that there is something to break out from. In many cases it is a body of work in a genre, such as romance, science fiction, mystery, or western. Or it may simply be what is opprobriously termed the midlist, that purgatorial place between success and failure occupied by books that are good but not good enough, bad but not that bad, promising, interesting, nice, pleasant, okay, and a lot of other less-than-hyperbolic adjectives, books that are profitable enough to tantalize or not unprofitable enough to discourage.

The world of genre and midlist books is populated by writers whose fates are still being fashioned by the gods. Some of them will remain in their comfortable niches forever, content with nonhyperbolic work and relieved that there is always a buyer for their books. Others will hang in long enough to see their books hailed as venerable classics, probably after it is too late for them to appreciate it. Still others will drop—or be driven—out. And others still will break—or be broken—out.

The breakout process occurs in a number of ways. An influential critic "discovers" an author and proclaims his greatness to the world. This happened with William Kennedy (*Ironweed*) and John Irving (*The World According to Garp*). Thriller writer John D. MacDonald awoke one Sunday morning after toiling for decades to find his latest Travis McGee detective novel hailed on the front page of the influential *New York Times Book Review*. Or perhaps an army of loyal readers will storm the bookstores and cast a favorite into the pantheon by popular acclaim, as happened to Alice Walker and *The Color Purple*. Sometimes reading tastes veer unpredictably, exalting a cult figure into the mainstream, such as John Barth whose *The Sotweed Factor* was a college classic for a generation but until recently a well-kept secret from mass audiences.

And finally there is the author who, by dint of Herculean effort, catapults himself (with the help of a substantial capital investment by his publisher) into the front rank with a work that shatters the mold of his former creations. It is this type that most publishing people mean when they talk about breaking out. So let's look at it a little more closely.

The breakout book marks a departure in quantity and quality. Often it is actually, physically, larger than previous works. Genre paperbacks range from fifty thousand to one hundred thousand words, generally speaking, and midlist hardcover fiction is seldom longer than, say, eighty-five thousand words. In order to justify the higher price that publishers charge for lead fiction, they look for works of at least one hundred thousand words, and in many cases the books run far longer. Recent best-sellers by John Jakes, James Michener, James Clavell, and other denizens of best-seller list summits, are over one thousand printed hardcover pages long, extending to as much as half a million words between covers. Although these works can't be defined as breakout books, since the authors have long and successful track records, they do illustrate the difference between best-selling authors, who are encouraged to write thick books, and midlist authors who are importuned to keep the length down. Although you may be able to break out with a gemlike Slim Little Volume, the tendency is definitely toward heft, for heft is equated, for better or worse, with importance.

Naturally, I don't mean merely padding a hundred-thousand-word novel with fifty or a hundred thousand more words. The plot must be proportionately more complex, the time span longer, the characters more numerous and treated in greater depth, the *mise en scène* more elaborate, the details of time and place portrayed with greater attention. And even with all these elements, unless the author has breathed life into the work, it will not fly.

It's hard to say just what it is that makes the difference. It's not necessarily the writing, for horribly written books are exalted onto the best-seller lists all the time, and if you've been a bad writer all your life, it's not likely your breakout book will be better written than anything else you've ever done.

But there is certainly a departure in quality that marks the breakout book. Publishing people sometimes refer to it as the author "finding his voice," meaning that he has fused a large, original, worthy subject and well-honed skills with the flame of inspiration and love.

202 / RICHARD CURTIS

And so, while the book may belong in a superficial sense to a category, it will amalgamate traditional category elements and formulas with that unique viewpoint, theme, style, passion— with that "voice"—to create something entirely new and grand and wonderful. The whole will be larger than its parts, so that it is not merely a super-romance or a super-mystery, a super-western or a super-science fiction novel. In a sense it will be a new genre. For example, occult and horror fiction were here long before Stephen King, but he transmuted the genre and stamped his name on it, as did Louis L'Amour with westerns, Georgette Heyer with period romances, Danielle Steele with contemporary romances, and Ray Bradbury and Arthur C. Clarke and Robert Heinlein with science fiction.

Implicit in the breakout event is the sense that the author's metamorphosis is permanent, and that henceforth he or she may be counted on to produce a consistent body of work in the same vein as the book that broke out. Reading the work of today's best-selling authors, you get a strong impression that they're not merely striving to repeat a winning combination, but rather have discovered their true identities in their books. James Michener with his geographical sagas, Harold Robbins and Judith Krantz and Barbara Taylor Bradford with their sex-and-power fantasies of the super-rich, John Jakes with his American historicals mingling fictional and factual characters, Sidney Sheldon with his tales of lust and vengeance—you might well wonder if in these instances soul, style, and story have not been blended into one entity.

As I'm drifting treacherously close to the metaphysical, let me bring you back to earth with a simple definition: You know an author has broken out when publishers start commissioning imitations, referring to the authors as if they were registered brand names. "I want a western family saga à la Louis L'Amour's Sacketts, or maybe a little sexier like Janet Dailey's Calders," one might hear at the luncheon table. Or, "I'm looking for a writer to do England the way John Jakes has done America." Or, "Do you have a client who can portray Madison Avenue the way Judith Krantz did Rodeo Drive?"

The Big Breakout requires, of course, the complete commitment of the publisher. But though you might think publishers are dying to push a ton of chips behind anything faintly resembling a breakout book, in truth they feel rather ambivalent about the process. For one thing, obviously, it costs an awful lot of money, and the premature launch of an unripened author, or a misjudgment about the breakoutability of a book, can create catastrophic losses and profound embarrassment followed by the sound of rolling heads. Publishers often therefore err on the side of caution, preferring to launch their breakout campaign only after the "numbers" on previous books by that author are immense, rather than hype somebody who has not built a broad audience. But by the time the publisher reaches the conclusion that the author's moment has come, the author may be gone: His agent will have found a publisher that wasn't so ambivalent.

I've also observed that publishers, who like all bureaucrats love pigeonholes, sometimes tend to keep a good author down because he's so productive where he is. An author who, let's say, delivers books in a genre series punctually and ably, and requires little or no editing, is so highly valued that publishers will stubbornly resist his blandishments to let him try something larger. Thus a potential breaker-out is smothered precisely *because* of his talent and competence! And you thought *authors* were weird?

From time to time, readers will actually be ahead of a publisher in the creation of a breakout. Publishers sometimes underestimate an author's popularity and the demand for his work. In due time, the groundswell of demand for an author will be felt in a publisher's office thanks to reports by the salesmen out in the field, and if the publisher is smart he'll ship as many copies of the next book as the traffic will bear. But if he is not alert, he'll lose the author to a house that is. This happened when thriller writer Dick Francis switched from Harper and Row to Putnam, where he now enjoys best-selling hardcover sales of every new book. Putnam knew the potential was there and detected the clamor that Francis's previous publisher failed to hear.

I sometimes wonder whether writers shouldn't step back and question whether breaking out is all it's cracked up to be. While success has been a goal in all ages, I don't think I am romanticizing the past in stating that the pressure to succeed has never been more intense for writers than it is now. Thirty years ago when I came into this business, there was among writers some sense that a life of quiet literary accomplishment book after book, the appreciation of a small but discriminating audience, and an income sufficient to support a middle-class lifestyle were worthy ideals. It was joy enough to be read; the heart swelled to see somebody reading one's book on the subway or to come across it in a library (remember libraries?).

Today such goals seem not merely unattainable to most writers, but inconceivable. Although the shift in thinking has been evolutionary, for many writers the realization impacted in the late 1960s and early 1970s, when a series of blockbusters starting with *The Godfather* altered our thinking. No longer was it enough for a book to be read: it had to be experienced by the Global Village, had to become an international mass market multimedia event, in order for the author to feel fulfilled. Such feelings are promulgated and perpetuated by publishers and the press in the form of the Blockbuster mentality, adding to the conviction most writers today have that they are faced with but two options: Go for the jackpot or become a janitor. The anxiety generated by these forces is enormous. Authors no onger feel that they have time to patiently develop craftsmanship, to build an audience, to attract the attention of critics—in short, to become professional writers. Instead they feel they must come roaring off the blocks with a spectacular work.

Although the apprenticeship opportunities for writers today are not the same as they were a decade or two ago, there are still many places where an author may develop his work and confidence without succumbing to the undertow of the break-out maelstrom. There are nonfiction, genre fiction, journalism, and other formats in which talent can be nurtured and a Minimum Daily Requirement of money earned in the process. And let's not forget one other option available to writers: They don't have to publish. Many writers have learned their craft merely by turning out work after work, learning from them, and putting them in a drawer.

Section Four

Sins of Commission

CHAPTER 31

Publishing Spoken Here

I've often thought that one of the critical roles literary agents play is that of translator. We perform the task on several levels. The most obvious and fundamental is explaining the nomenclature of publishing to the uninitiated author. The writer who sells his first book to a publisher and reads his first contract is plunged into a sea of words that may be totally unfamiliar to him, or that are used in a totally unfamiliar way. "Force majeure," "net proceeds," "matching option," "warranty," "discount"—these need to be defined for the novice author. There are many difficult concepts to be grasped, such as "advance sale," "midlist," "fair use," "reserve against returns," "pass-through," and "hard-soft deals." The language has its own slang, too, and our initiate hears bewildering references to who handles the "sub-rights," what is the tentative "pub date," and what happens when the book is "o.p.'d."

Agents patiently try to demystify these terms, but it may take many years of experience before our clients are completely at ease with them. It may well be true that what distinguishes professional authors from their amateur brothers and sisters is that the pros have undergone this linguistic rite of passage, and are now able to sling around "pre-empts," "first proceeds," and "escalators" with the best of 'em.

But there is another, and profoundly more important, job for the agent-translator to perform beyond explaining to his clients the terminology of the book industry. I'm talking about using language to forge and strengthen the bonds between authors and publishers. For, while the goals of both may ultimately be

identical, they are usually achievable only after many conflict-
ing viewpoints and interests have been reconciled. Sometimes
those conflicts become intense, and if allowed to go unresolved
can cause serious if not fatal breakdowns in the relationship.
An agent, standing between these potential adversaries, must
find common ground for them to stand on, else all—including
his commission—is lost. And though their differences may be
genuine, sometimes they are semantic, and if an agent can
pinpoint and settle the linguistic problems, perhaps the more
substantive ones will not seem quite so insuperable. Although
it's a stimulating challenge, not all of us enjoy sticking our
heads up in this no-man's land.

It might be reasonable to assume that authors, being creative
types, are more sensitive than editors. I am by no means
convinced that this assumption is warranted. Editors do of
course work for corporations, which are generally not thought
of as being particularly responsive to human emotional needs.
But it is unfair to equate the characters of those who work for
large companies with the characters of the companies themselves. In point of fact, editors (as well as other publishing
people) are as sensitive as everybody else, including writers.
Their first response when pinched is to say "Ouch!" and, when
insulted, to feel the same outrage, humiliation, or depression
that the rest of us feel. The difference is that while authors
compensate for their pain in a solitary fashion (such as becoming paranoid), editors are often able to find consolation in the
anonymity and shared responsibility—what might be called the
collective insensitivity—of their companies.

You must not think, however, that editors cannot be seriously wounded. And it is important to know that fact, because
a hurt editor (or art director or royalty bookkeeper) may not
want to work as hard for an author who has irked him or her as
for one who has been supportive, tolerant, and forgiving. This
is not to say that editors are so thin-skinned they fold the first
time someone criticizes them. But I do know that if an author
or agent injures an editor's feelings seriously enough, it can
undercut his or her initiative, and that may eventually redound
to an author's detriment. Some years ago I phoned a bookkeeper who had been verbally abused by an author a few

months earlier. This author was owed another check, and I wanted to know where it was. "Funny thing about that check," she said, deadpan, "it keeps falling to the bottom of my pile."

It is therefore vital that editors and their colleagues in other departments of publishing companies be handled with a certain degree of diplomacy, and it is in the language of that diplomacy that most agents are adept. We have learned that "a soft answer turneth away wrath." And most of the time, we are able to rephrase or paraphrase the blunt demands, the raw needs, the hard feelings, the hostile remarks, of our clients into gracious packages of civility that convey everything the author intended without damaging the fragile sensibilities of the person at whom they are directed.

I've been keeping some notes about discussions recently conducted with editors and am happy to offer herewith a few examples of this process in action. Some of them are tongue in cheek, others are deliberately exaggerated. Still others will sound stilted, and that is because, unfortunately, that is the way I speak.

Let's take one of the commonest problems in our business, that of getting editors to make up their minds about submissions. Editors are burdened with a great many tasks that curtail their reading time. They may be inundated with manuscripts to read. They may be on the fence about a submission and wish to postpone a decision for a while. They may be soliciting opinions or sales estimates from colleagues in their company. They have many legitimate reasons for taking a long time to read submissions.

At the same time, some editors seem to have a considerably dimmer sense of the passage of time than people in other fields, such as airline management or television programming. So, one of the first lessons one learns in the agenting profession is how to translate an editor's promises about time. "I'll read it overnight" too often means, "I'll get around to it in a week." "I'll read it in a week" means, "I'll be back to you in a month." And "I'll read it in a month" may well mean that the manuscript is lost.

In order to reasonably hold editors to their promised schedules, agents use the elegant phraseology of coercion. "As I'm loath to keep manuscripts out of circulation," I might say or write, "may I trouble you for a decision?" If this fails to yield a reply, I might escalate to something more pointed, like "My client is getting restless," or, "I'm under some pressure to determine where we stand."

Sometimes a humorous approach is in order. I'm a great believer in the power of teasing to accomplish that which solemnity cannot, and I'm not above a little sarcasm under the appropriate circumstances: "When I submitted that manuscript to you, the oceans were two inches lower." Or, "It's hard to believe a new century is just a decade away. I wonder if I'll have heard from you about that book by then."

If an editor has sat on a submission for an unconscionably long time, I will invariably get a phone call from my client saying, "You tell that sonofabitch that if we don't have a decision by Friday, I'm personally gonna come down there and rearrange his prefrontal lobes with an ax haft!"

Justified though that ultimatum may be, it is couched in language this is terminally infelicitous. By the time I'm through modifying it, it may sound something closer to this: "As you don't seem able to make up your mind, suppose we say that if I haven't heard from you by Friday, I'll put another copy of the manuscript into play elsewhere, and you may take as much time thereafter as you wish. If you eventually decide you want to buy it, I'll be glad to discuss terms with you—as long as I haven't sold it someone else." And sometimes I'll put a finer point on my message with this veiled warning: "Do let me know when your work load is down to a more reasonable size so that I can resume submitting books to you."

I'm certain that you must be saying to yourself, "How is an editor going to get these messages if the agent pussyfoots around that way?" The answer is, editors get these messages loudly and clearly, for unless one is incredibly dense, he will have little doubt that a knife has been placed against his throat.

Another common problem for agents is, of course, overdue checks. Authors are remarkably articulate when it comes to expressing the discomforts of financial deprivation and to depicting the character and ancestry of those who conspire to keep them in that condition. Unfortunately, most editors would go through the roof if exposed to the authors' invective. Enter the honey-tongued agent, and though that agent might love nothing better than to say, "Pay up our we'll vaporize you," it's more likely he or she will say something a bit more subdued. Perhaps a subtle form of extortion: "It would be to your advantage to remit payment promptly so as to avoid scheduling delays." In plain English, this informs the editor that unless his company ponies up the dough, the agent isn't going to deliver certain manuscripts that the publisher desperately needs to put into production. Because a late manuscript can wreck a production schedule at fearful cost to a publisher, the wise editor will undoubtedly give the check-processing machinery an extra-hard spin when he gets a message like that from an agent.

I can think of lots of other ways that agents refine the harsh language of their clients without sacrificing effectiveness. For instance, though we may be thinking, "My client just turned in a real turkey," what we are telling an editor is that, "My client thought you might like to see a first draft of his book before he starts polishing it."

Or, "My client is going to sue your ass into Rice Krispie-sized pieces" becomes, "My client is contemplating contacting his attorney, at which point the matter will be outside of my control."

Or, "My client thinks your editor is so incompetent, he couldn't spell cat if you spotted him the C and the T!" becomes, "I'm not certain that the author's and editor's views about the book are entirely compatible."

"My client is so upset he's taking big bites out of his living room sofa" translates into, "My client is finding it hard to understand why . . ."

"You'll use that cover on my client's book over his dead body!" may be altered to, "My client is pretty determined."

Here's a brief glossary of other agently euphemisms commonly employed when tempers start to overheat:

• You: "I'm thoroughly disgusted with those people."
Agent: "My client is somewhat disenchanted."
• You: If I had that editor's throat in my hands . . ."
Agent: "I'm not sure my client is completely comfortable working with you."
• You: "They're lying and cheating."

Agent: "My client feels he may have detected some discrepancies."
• You: "What a crummy deal!"
Agent: "Some of the terms leave something to be desired."
• You: "I wouldn't sell another book to that butcher if he were the last editor on earth."
Agent: "Let's have lunch."

The transmutation of hurtful language works the other way around, too, so that when we have to tell a client that his publishers hate his book so much they want to manure a cornfield with it, we may say something like, "It didn't live up to their expectations," or, "They found it lacking in certain respects." Or an editor's remark to the effect that a certain author couldn't write his way out of a trash can liner becomes, "They don't feel you've reached your potential quite yet."

Here are a few others.
• Editor: "This material is simply lousy."
Agent: "Your editor is disappointed."
• Editor: "What language is your client writing in, anyway?"
Agent: "Your editor pointed out some obscure passages."
• Editor: "Your client is the rudest person I've ever had the misfortune to work with."
Agent: "Your editor seems to have overreacted to what he perceives as a slight."
•Editor: "Is your client crazy, or what?"
Agent: "I'm not sure your editor appreciates your eccentricities."

Of course, not all agents approach matters as delicately as this. Some of us are in fact quite plainspoken, and even the most tactful among us realizes that there are unavoidable occasions when we must unsheath a steel fist from the velvet glove. Still, it is gratifying to know that—at least when it comes to the language—one may still find reminders of the time when publishing was a profession for civilized ladies and gentlemen.

CHAPTER 32

When To

Okay, hotshot, we all know you're smarter than your agent. At least, that's what you're always telling your friends. So let's see how well you can do second-guessing him or her in a few hypothetical situations. For every correct answer, you get a free power lunch in the Grill Room of the Four Seasons with any publisher of your choice; for every one you get wrong, same prize but you treat.

• Your client has had twelve genre novels published in paperback. They've sold about fifty thousand copies each. She thinks the time has come to be published in hardcover. You tell her:

   a) She's absolutely right and you're getting on the phone at once.
   b) She should write another dozen paperbacks that sell fifty thousand copies each, then you'll move her.
   c) Wait till her paperbacks start selling in the hundreds of thousands of copies each.
   d) She's crazy to want to be published in hardcover.

• Your client has just turned in the manuscript of a book that has good film possibilities. The time to start contacting producers is:

   a) When the book is in bound proofs.
   b) When finished copies come off the presses.
   c) When the book starts getting good reviews.
   d) Yesterday.

• You recently sold a client's first novel to a publisher for
five thousand dollars. The client has an idea for a new novel
that he thinks has big money potential, and he wants a much
bigger advance. The best time to ask for it is:

a) Now.
b) Six months from now.
c) Around the time the first novel is published.
d) A year after the first novel has been published.

•••••

In case you haven't noticed, all the questions in this quiz
have to do with timing. Few authors realize it, but one of the
most important reasons for hiring agents is that they have a
superior sense of timing. "Timing is everything" might almost
be called the agent's motto. The most successful agents are
those who understand that there is a season to push and a
season to ease up, a season to fight and a season to turn the
back, a season to watch and wait and a season to strike.
Sometimes the moment presents itself on a platter; sometimes
it has to be worked with brute force like steel on a smithy's
anvil. And there are times when, for all an agent's scheming,
for all his exertions, for all his manipulations, he simply cannot
make the thing happen. (That's usually a signal for me to go
shopping.)

Most authors are impatient. It's a forgivable character trait,
for it often goes hand in hand with ambition. But because
authors cannot possibly be as objective about the progress of
their careers as their agents are, their impatience can make
them their own worst enemies. A goodly part of an agent's day
is spent restraining authors.

Although we usually associate timing with the moment when
an agent pulls off some million-dollar coup, many of its applications are far more prosaic. A couple of years ago a literary
agent wrote a piece for *Publishers Weekly* complaining about
rude editors who do not return agents' phone calls. Her broadside elicited a chorus of cheers from fellow agents, and from
writers who'd had similarly unpleasant experiences.

I had a different reaction, though. Her article made me
wonder whether the telephone is not greatly overused by agents,

and whether there are many occasions when a note would do instead of a call. This is particularly true in the conduct of routine business such as inquiries about submissions, contracts, and checks. Editors are usually harried with paperwork, urgent business, and other phone calls, and so there is an odds-on probability that a scribbled note taken down during a phone call will presently be buried beneath the day's alluvial deposit of letters, internal memos, manuscripts, catalogues, contracts, and junk mail. I've noticed, however, that editors seem to place more significance upon written inquiries, and they move on them more promptly. More importantly, underuse of the phone by an agent may motivate editors to take his calls when he really needs to get through. If an editor doesn't want to talk to an agent because the editor thinks the agent is calling about that overdue check, when actually the agent is calling to pitch a hot new property, a vital opportunity will have been missed for both of them.

The preceding is not a particularly glamorous example of timing, but in the last analysis it's the daily employment of wise timing that makes a good agent effective.

But then there is that dramatic application that makes an agent feel he's been waiting all his life to yank the ripcord, and the decisive moment has come. Not long ago a fellow agent called me for consultation on a particularly delicate timing problem involving a star author. This author had a very big book scheduled for publication about nine months from that time, but because he was very unhappy with his publisher, he had asked his agent to seek another one. His agent had done so and lined up a terrific deal. In order to get out of his option with his current publisher, the author merely had to submit an outline and reject whatever was offered. *When* to do that—that was the problem.

The new publisher was pressing the agent to finalize their deal. Publishers get very nervous about leaving big offers open for too long: Agents have been known to use those offers to solicit even higher ones. Despite the possibility that the offer would be withdrawn, the agent was dragging his heels. By breaking with the current publisher too early, the agent could demoralize the sales people and cause the company to pull

some of its advertising and promotional money from the upcoming book: A publisher that is losing an author may not
work as hard for him as one that looks forward to a long
association.

What did I advise my colleague to do? I'll let you brood
about it for a minute or two in the security of your armchair,
but remember that in this real-life situation, millions of dollars,
the agent's relationship with his client, the agent's relationship
with two publishers, the fate of a book on which the author had
spent a year, the fate of many books to come, and a lot of egos
and reputations were on the line. Perhaps you would understand it better if you got out of your armchair and read the rest
of this chapter while standing on a rickety stool with a hang-
man's noose around your neck.

Although I have tried to demystify the publishing business
for you, I have to confess that the instincts governing the sense
of timing, including my own, are wonderfully and impenetrably
mysterious to me. I am fairly certain that they are of a piece
with artistic inspiration. Most of the time, if you ask me to
articulate the reasons why I chose a certain moment to demand
a dramatic raise in an author's pay, or to go from a book-by-
book arrangement to a multibook package deal, or to move a
client out of paperback originals and into hardcover, I can
express them fairly coherently. But then there are those inexpli-
cable revelations, blazing across the mind when one least ex-
pects it, that illuminate a situation with dazzling clarity and put
one in touch with some very profound impulses.

I take pride in handling most business matters expeditiously,
but occasionally something will come along that I frankly don't
know what to do about. It will sit on my desk glowering at me,
mocking me, demanding attention but eluding solution. I gaze
back at it, mutter an oath, but am paralyzed with uncertainty.
You might call the condition agent's block. The client, the
publisher, are pressing for a decision. I offer feeble excuses that
sound very much like procrastination or, worse, timidity. In
truth, I'm simply waiting for the green light to go on in my
brain. Inevitably it switches on, but when I least anticipate it,
such as awaking from a nap or feeding my kid a snack. The
answer is suddenly printed in bright headlines before me, and

what was so difficult suddenly becomes ridiculously easy. The time, at last, has come.

Lest I start to sound as if agenting is a variety of religious experience, however, let me let you in on a little secret. Some of the things agents do that authors think are brilliantly timed are in truth matters of dumb luck. An author writes a book and I sell it to precisely the right editor and it goes on to become a best-seller. I would love for you to think that I selected that editor the way a handicapper selects a winning horse. And perhaps I did. But sometimes, finding the perfect editor for a book is a matter of who is not out to lunch, in a meeting, or in the bathroom when an agent starts making phone calls.

Now, about that quiz.

Situation Number 1: The paperback author who wants to be published in hardcover. Despite the evidence that you can make a much better living writing original paperbacks than you can hardcover books, most authors feel an uneasy sense of illegitimacy about paperbacks. And it is true that hardcover books have a better chance of being reviewed (negatively as well as favorably, don't forget) and selling to the movies. But if an author's paperbacks are selling in routine numbers, as in this example, the time may not be propitious for the leap into hardcover, for the author hasn't built an audience prepared to follow her into the more prestigious and expensive format. On many occasions a premature debut in hardcover can be catastrophic and the author may forever lose the opportunity to be published in boards again.

Situation Number 2: What is the best time to start soliciting movie rights to a book with promising film potential? The answer is, immediately if not sooner. Movie and television people need to feel they are getting in on something hot. By the time a book is published it will have been circulated among all the key studios, networks, and producers owing to Hollywood's highly efficient system for obtaining early looks at anything that sounds interesting. "A published book," the late producer David Susskind once said to me, "is very dead meat." There are of course exceptions to this rule, and examples of books made into successful movies decades after publication. But if you have a hot movie property, there's not a moment to lose. And remember, it's a good idea to prepare a brief synopsis of the book, highlighting its cinematic qualities, to accompany the submission for those in Hollywood who don't have time, or don't know how, to read.

Situation Number 3: When is it appropriate to ask for a higher advance? The answer is, it's always appropriate to *ask*, but not always appropriate to expect. For new authors, the period of time between the sale of the first novel and publication is an extremely perilous one. Assuming an author is of average productivity, he will have ideas, outlines, or even completed manuscripts of new works long before that first book has been published. *Until* that first book has been published, however, the publisher will have no basis for calculating the value of the author's work and will therefore resist offering him more than a token raise in price. Indeed, because publishers don't formulate a clear picture of a book's sales for about a year after publication, owing to the time it takes for unsold copies to be returned, it may be two or three years from the time you sell your first book before you are justified in requesting prices bigger than starting pay. So if you answered (d) on the quiz you may have been closest to the truth.

You can't, of course, afford to sit around for several years waiting for the results on your first book, so there are several strategies for bridging the gap. One is to become more prolific (including writing books under pseudonyms for other publishers if your first publisher can't absorb your entire output). Another is to write your second, third, and even fourth novel on speculation rather than trying to line up contracts for them on the basis of outlines or portions-and-outlines. As I've said before, publishers are able to make much faster judgments about finished books than partial ones, and usually pay higher prices.

Finally, we return to the quandary of the agent torn between responsibility for his client's forthcoming book and eagerness to nail down a deal with another publisher before that publisher backed out. The situation was, as I pointed out, quite treacherous, but I advised the agent to wait until the very last moment, a few weeks before publication of the book, before informing the current publishers that they weren't going to get the author's next book. By that time the advertising was set, the author's tour locked in, the books were in the stores, and the publishers were committed to doing everything possible to make it a success and recover their investment.

As for the publishers threatening to withdraw their offer if the agent delayed, the agent visited the head of the company and persuaded him to leave his offer on the table. "Look," said my friend, "you have my word of honor that I will not use your offer to seek other bids. I cannot afford to offend a rich and powerful publisher like you. Please bear in mind that if we announce the author's decision too soon, the other publisher may pull its advertising and promotion and their book will flop. And that will make it much harder for you to sell the author's next book." Happily, the publisher saw the wisdom of this argument and held his offer open. It all worked out happily, even for the publisher who lost the big-name author. Oh, the publisher was sore for a few weeks, but then the agent phoned him and told him that another client was unhappy with *her* publisher and wanted to move to another house. "Interested?" he asked. Of course he was interested!

Now, that's what I call an agent with an exquisite sense of timing.

CHAPTER 33

Is Life Too Short?

In the last chapter we discussed one of the most important qualities a literary agent can bring to his job: good timing. I've been thinking about another virtue that most good agents possess, and that's patience. If timing is the art of When To, patience might be said to be the art of When Not To. In many cases, that means when not to knock your head against a wall, when not to wring a client's throat, or when not to hop in a taxi, race over to a publisher's office, and trash his desk.

Although some people are born patient, for most of us it's an acquired quality. We attain it only with experience, and it may be the only significant benefit of aging.

If you are constitutionally incapable of practicing patience, you are definitely not cut out to become a literary agent. Despite the appearance of furious activity, and notwithstanding such timesaving innovations as multiple submissions, word processors, laser printers, high-speed presses, overnight mail, instant books, and quickie releases, the truth is that just about anything of importance that happens in our industry happens slowly. Good books are written at a snail's pace, submissions take ages, negotiations drag on, money flows like cold lard, and the building of an author's career from first sale to best-selling masterpiece is about as dramatic as watching a lake evaporate. Difficult publishers test our patience, as do difficult authors. If agents seem to have a higher per-capita ratio of weekend homes than other professionals, have pity on them: They must have a place to go to chop wood, bay at the moon, and otherwise relieve the strain of holding their natural impulses in check during the other five days a week.

I do not own a weekend home, but I do have a set of molars that have been ground down close to the nerve endings from restraining the desire to commit a variety of felonies in order to make things move faster. Behind a demeanor that one of my clients once described as "judicious" seethes a cauldron of emotions, energy, grievances, and heroic fantasies. I smile, I speak moderately, I behave politely, I move deliberately. I polish my buckler and hone my sword, my ear cocked for the call to arms. It may come in the form of a letter, a phone call, an offer, an opportunity, an insult. But I am ready for action (see "When To"). Meanwhile, I wait.

I wait, for instance, for you to finish your book. Because my agency does a lot of business in paperback original series, I have to wait only a month or two for many books. For most mainstream ones, however, I have to wait nine months, a year, or longer. The potential in these books presses heavily upon my consciousness; I'm dying to wheel and deal. But with few exceptions there is little to be done to convert that potential until the manuscript has been turned in. However much I am dying to go into action with that book, I cannot advance the calendar by one day, the clock by one minute. I grind my teeth and wait.

I wait for publishers to make up their minds about my submissions. Decisions on manuscripts can be forced by means of the auction, and when agents have to move fast they can elicit decisions virtually overnight. But most material does not command that kind of attention. The more conventional approach of one submission at a time, or at best two or three simultaneously, is what is usually called for. Like most agencies, we have a reminder calendar and regularly write or phone publishers prodding them to keep the property in question at the top of the pile.

Despite every measure taken to make editors respond to submissions promptly, it is unrealistic to expect decisions in less than six weeks, and quite realistic to expect none in less than three months. If a work isn't placed on the first or second round of submissions, therefore, a year or more can pass with relatively few submissions to show for all the investment of time. So we wait.

We wait to make deals. Deals can be struck in a matter of minutes. But many negotiations take days, weeks, or even months to unfold. With the evolution of publishing from an individual entrepreneurial enterprise to a bureaucratized corporate one, seldom do agents end up negotiating with the principals of a publishing company. Instead we take up terms with editors, who refer them to superior officers or editorial boards. Several weeks may pass if the appropriate executives are not available to formulate offers or counteroffers. Often, figures have to be worked up by a variety of departments to help the company determine its negotiating strategy. During which time, we wait.

We wait for contracts. The people who work in the contract departments of most publishing houses are among the most professional in our industry. Nevertheless, it is seldom possible for them to produce contracts for signature in less than six or eight weeks. Earlier, we saw a typical scenario: After the editor reaches agreement with the author or agent, he prepares a deal memo summarizing the terms of the contract, for approval by the head of the company. After approval has been rendered, the deal memo goes to the contract department where it serves as the basis for the formal agreement. This agreement is reviewed by the acquiring editor and an officer of the company, then returned to the contract department for issuance to the author or agent. After signed contracts are returned to the publisher, they are circulated for signature and a voucher is issued directing the accounts payable department to prepare the check. We now wait for the check.

We wait a long time for the check because in many cases the accounts payable department is not in the same building or even the same state as the contracts department. After receiving the voucher from the contracts department, accounts payable prepares a check that must be reviewed and signed by the controller or other officer of the company. It is then forwarded to the contracts department to be issued with the contracts, or sent to the payee directly from the accounts payable office.

If form follows function, publishers could not conceive of a better structure for attenuating the time it takes to release money. Even with all hands working at maximum efficiency—not a very desirable state, you must realize, when there is interest to be earned—I figure two to three months is now the industry average for payout from the time check vouchers are issued. Agents who have managed to map and penetrate the system can keep things moving with phone calls to various departments along the paperwork routes goading delinquent clerks to press on with their tasks. Nevertheless, we wait. We wait for books to be published.

Well, you get the idea: Just about everything concerning publishing is a test of an agent's patience. Everything, that is, but the publishers themselves. I don't mean publishing companies; I mean the owners. They simply aren't trying our patience the way they used to.

Only a few decades ago, the industry was still populated by men and women who had started, or perhaps inherited, the companies that bore their names. These were fascinating, entertaining, charming, eccentric, crazy, exasperating, wonderful characters, entrepreneurs who loved books and authors. These individuals were to be cultivated, handled, flattered, humored, and feared. With the transformation of publishing to the corporate mode, the founders have been eased out or squeezed out and replaced by a more cautious, subdued, controlled type, systems-oriented and often trained more extensively in business management than in literature. In a great many ways our industry is better run under the new breed. The old companies were often operated by people who understood books better than they did business, or who loved money too much and drained their companies of capital. Either way, the older publishers were vulnerable when the business climate cooled down, and most of them either succumbed or sold out to better-heeled competitors or predatory conglomerates.

The loss of these characters can be likened to the disappearance of rugged individualists when our frontier gave way to the taming influence of more civilized and cultivated settlers. The old breed of publisher could be maddening to authors and agents, but its passing is one of the most lamentable aspects of the evolution of our industry since the end of World War II. Our workplace is simply a lot less fun.

I have no such complaint against authors, however. Although modern authors are more sophisticated about business than their brothers and sisters of yore, they are still highly individualistic, and I have observed no diminution in the number of writers who try their agents' patience. One of my colleagues has created, with tongue somewhat in cheek I suspect, an index for rating his clients; he calls it the PITA factor. PITA stands for Pain In The Ass. He assigns his client a rating from 1 to 10, depending on such factors as how often they ask him for advances, how many times they call him at home at six on Sunday mornings, how many editors they insult, and in general how much maintenance they require beyond routine care and feeding. Their PITA factor is then divided into the commissions realized on their sales. Applying his criteria, an author who earns only $1,000 annually in commissions but who is a model client with a PITA Factor of 1 is as valuable to his agent as one who earns $10,000 commission but is a raving lunatic meriting 10 on the PITA scale. "Life," says my friend, "is too short to have to deal with pains in the ass."

Well, I don't know. As I said at the beginning of this article, if you do feel that way, the literary agent's trade is not for you and you should go into something less aggravating, like commodity trading or hospital emergency room administration. When it comes to dealing with artists, irritating behavior comes with the territory. And, far more important, think of what *they* have to put up with. With the rare exception of the author whose first book stuns the critics, sweeps the public off its feet, and soars to the top of the best-seller list (and even then, it probably took the author ten years to write it), most success for writers is won only after decades of economic struggle, mental anguish, crushing obscurity, and the consumption of murderous doses of pride. They spend a lifetime practicing patience, and if they do not always practice it very well, if they are difficult when they're starting out, difficult when they begin to make it, and difficult when they finally arrive, a larger degree of tolerance is called for on the part of those who serve them, particularly if they've never tried that life themselves. A PITA scale that does not factor in the emotional satisfactions of midwifing an author's first book, of nurturing his career as he gains in skill and confidence and stretches to grasp his vision, and of attending his graduation ceremony featuring smashing reviews and sales by the trainload, requires some serious rethinking.

Life is not too short if an agent's patience is rewarded with such satisfactions as these.

CHAPTER 34

To Fee? Or Not to Fee?

To fee? Or not to fee? That is the question.

And for many literary agents, reading fees are a hot question indeed. In the eyes of many writers, publishers, and even other agents, the charging of fees for agents to review the work of aspiring writers is unethical at the very least. Some feel it is downright fraudulent.

There is a lot of evidence to support the detractors of this practice, I regret to say. But fee reading also satisfies some very important needs, and if rendered ethically and responsibly it can create opportunities for developing writers that are no longer available to them through traditional channels. Let's examine the conditions and problems confronting literary agents that often give rise to the necessity of charging fees.

Until the post–World War II era, the responsibility for discovering new writers belonged almost entirely to publishers. Although literary agents have existed since the nineteenth century, their emergence as a decisive force in the publishing process had not yet commenced, and authors almost invariably submitted their work directly to publishers. As the number of would-be authors was not overwhelming, publishers were able to sort through submissions in a relatively reasonable time. And though the ratio of unsuitable to suitable submissions was undoubtedly as high as it is today, the lower volume of manuscripts made it economical for publishers to retain editors on staff whose task was to find good material in what has come, lamentably, to be called the "slush pile." In short, the profits realized from successful books pulled out of the slush pile outweighed the cost of reading the rest of the material.

All of this changed as the century wore on. The publishing business became more competitive and expensive, forcing publishers to look harder and harder at their bottom lines. One of the items that didn't fare very well under scrutiny was the cost of reading slush. The chances of finding a best-seller there were about as good as discovering a diamond tiara in a corn flakes box. About eight or ten years ago, Viking Press vigorously publicized its discovery in the slush pile of Judith Guest's *Ordinary People,* a big best-seller that was then made into an enormously successful movie. But it was the first unsolicited novel bought by the company in twenty-seven years!

How many editors had worked how many hours at how much salary to haul that prize fish out of the sea of submissions? A little number-crunching might suggest some answers. I have it on the authority of several editors that unsolicited submissions received by the average publishing company number some ten thousand or more annually. If you figure that a reasonably intelligent editor can read between five and ten of these a day (assuming he or she has nothing else to do but read), he or she will be able to polish off approximately one to two thousand submissions in a year. Even assuming the higher figure, it means that a minimum of five editors is required just to read so-called over-the-transom submissions.

Starting salaries in publishing these days are approximately $15,000 annually; with fringe benefits and employer contributions to social security, it's probably closer to $20,000. Thus, the cost of retaining a staff strictly to read slush is at least $100,000 per year, not counting the cost of handling and postage for rejected material. Or the cost of the time that senior editors spend reading those manuscripts that may be recommended by the slush pile editors. All things considered, it probably costs upward of $150,000 for a publisher to keep its doors open to unsolicited material—and that's every year. It would probably cost that much to publish works that are discovered there. And then there's a little matter of making a profit. In brief, a publisher would probably have to sell close to half a million dollars' worth of books discovered in its slush pile in order to justify the existence of a well-managed program dedicated to finding good books there. That's every year, chum.

Clearly, the game is not worth the candle; at least, not when publishers know that it is infinitely more cost-effective to acquire material from literary agents.

As the twentieth century progressed, agents grew more and more influential, and publishers increasingly relied on them for quality material. In due time, trade publishers began to neglect their slush piles, and ultimately, most of them abandoned them altogether. Today, most large trade publishers return unsolicited manuscripts unread or scarcely glanced at. Some houses, however, particularly paperback ones that publish a lot of genre material, do manage to read unsolicited books, at least books that seem at first glance to have merit. But, at a cost of between $25 and $40 per manuscript, which is the going rate for outside readers, the toll can be high. One editor told me his monthly nut for outside readers runs well over $1,000.

Publishers that refuse to read slush generally return manuscripts with printed notices stating that the firm reviews only submissions made by literary agents. In effect, agents have become the slush pile readers for the publishing industry. In certain respects, this task is not as burdensome for agents as it is for publishers, for agents' slush piles are excellent sources of potential new clients. Publishers offer narrower windows of opportunity to authors than agents do. A publisher seeks books to fill its own list only, but an agent seeks them to fill many lists. An author submitting a novel to a publisher that publishes only nonfiction will be wasting that publisher's time. But if he sends that same novel to a literary agent he won't necessarily waste that agent's time, because the agent knows of lots of houses that do publish fiction.

In another respect, the shift in responsibility for discovering and developing new talent has placed a heavy burden on agents, for along with the benefits go the expenses. After all, if it is costly for publishers to maintain a staff to read slush, isn't it equally costly for agents to do the same thing?

As a matter of fact it is. Indeed, it could well be argued that it is more costly, because agents work on a much lower profit margin than publishers do. The average literary agency is staffed by two to five people including the boss. It is well nigh impossible for them to read manuscripts during the day when the phones are constantly ringing. That means taking reading home.

Reading at home is the cross that everyone in the publishing industry must bear, though it often intrudes on our evening and weekend (and vacation!) leisure time. For agents, however, that leisure time is usually occupied with reading manuscripts, contracts, and correspondence relating to our professional clients. It is difficult, and for some agents impossible, to devote quality time to the work of new authors.

Every agency that lists itself in the industry's directories receives a large quantity of unsolicited submissions from hopeful writers. I don't think my own agency is exceptional in this respect: On any given day, we receive between fifteen and twenty-five solicitations from unpublished or unestablished writers. The task of screening their queries, outlines, and partial and complete manuscripts takes my staff the better part of a morning. As you might expect, the material breaks down in the proportions of 5 percent interesting, 10 or 15 percent marginal, and the rest clearly unsuitable. (I hasten to add, unsuitable for us, but not necessarily unsuitable for other agencies.)

That means that I and/or my associates must find a way to seriously review ten submissions or more per week, excluding work by our regular clients. How much can I read without jeopardizing the interests of those clients? How much can I ask my employees to read beyond their normal burden of homework before they demand additional compensation? How can I ask outside free-lancers to read manuscripts free of charge?

And that's just reading: What about replying? While much of the stuff we send back doesn't call for extensive analysis, many agents feel that it would be rude if not cruel to return it without a few lines of explanation, criticism, encouragement, or consolation. And if the material is above average, a thoughtful letter is certainly in order. Where is one to find the time, or the money to pay for that time?

I am not telling you all this because I want you to feel sorry for agents (*that* will be the day!), but because it's important for everyone connected with publishing and literature to realize that the economics of slush are as inexorable for agents as they are for publishers. We are faced with the dilemma of either coldbloodedly returning this material unread and thus making it even harder for promising authors to get a hearing; or devoting serious attention to new authors at the expense of our clients' interests, to say nothing of our own.

For many agents, the solution is reading fees. These fees are designed to compensate agents, their employees, and their outside readers for the time they must invest in reviewing the work of new authors and cultivating the better ones.

Of course, for anyone interested simply in getting a manuscript criticized, there are a great many reading services that do not, and do not claim to, perform agenting tasks. The quality of their services and the fees they charge vary widely. One can, though, often come away with a helpful analysis of one's manuscript and perhaps improve the quality of one's writing skills, as long as it's understood that the reading service cannot place the work with publishers.

It is when reading services are combined with agenting capabilities that some troubling moral issues arise. If a manuscript reading is offered with the implicit promise that the work will be offered to publishers, or if an agent accepts reading fees without offering anything by way of constructive criticism, authors will justifiably feel that they are being ripped off. Most agents can judge the quality of a manuscript within the first few pages, and critics of literary agency reading fee services feel that if the agent were honest, he or she would simply return the manuscript with the fee and a brief note stating that the work lacks merit or is unsalable.

It's hard to argue with these criticisms, but some agents who charge fees justify them on the grounds that they never mislead authors about the unpublishability of submissions; that the quality of their evaluations is high, and many authors genuinely benefit from them; and that from time to time, salable works and talented authors are discovered in agents' slush piles. I myself know of a number of books discovered in agents' slush piles that went on to get sold, initiating successful writing careers for their authors. And I can cite many authors who feel they profited immensely from literary criticism and marketing expertise for which they paid fees to agents.

Unfortunately, the taint of fraud still hovers over the business of reading fees, making even the most ethically and responsibly run services suspect. Some years ago, I started a program dedicated to discovering new authors, the cost of which was to be defrayed by reading fees. Although my intentions were completely honest, and we did indeed find and sell some excellent books, it was impossible to separate opinion about our service from the unethical reputation that characterized other fee-reading operations, and ultimately I decided to discontinue the program.

But I still wonder whether, handled properly, a fee system might not provide one way of keeping stocked the literary breeding grounds that have been drying up in the shifting sands of modern publishing. It would mean, of course, that an effective means of regulating these activities, for setting guidelines and policing abusive practices, would have to be devised. I don't have any answers, but before we brand all reading fee services as crooked, we ought to make some constructive attempts to make them work.

CHAPTER 35

Extraordinary Expenses

This chapter is dedicated to those clients who cock their eyebrows over deductions for expenses on checks my agency sends to them. I am in fact fairly sure they do more than cock eyebrows when they open the envelopes. I suspect they kick their cats, pound their desks, and bark at their spouses and children before composing temperate inquiries to me about the nature and size of the sums subtracted from their checks.

I know that this is a common reaction among clients of most other agencies, too, so let's talk about the out-of-pocket expenses that agents charge to their authors.

Among the commonest classes of such expenses are long-distance telephone calls; telegrams and international cables; photocopy of manuscripts and documents; messenger pickup and delivery of urgently awaited manuscripts, contracts, and checks; special delivery and overnight mail charges; purchases of extra copies of authors' books for exploitation of subsidiary rights; international postal charges for submissions of books to foreign agents and publishers; and loans to authors.

These are a perpetual source of friction between agents and authors, and the policies on charged expenses differ from agent to agent. The reactions to them differ from author to author, too. Some will resignedly accept a deduction of hundreds of dollars, others will fight like trapped beasts over a dollar that they feel has been improperly ascribed. But if these charges are a source of irritation to authors, you should be aware that they are not much fun for agents, either. The bookkeeping on them is complex, energy intensive, time consuming, and thankless. It

232

is also an absolute necessity. Looking at it positively, "extraordinary" expenses help us to make extraordinary deals, move properties and money faster, and serve our clients more effectively. Or, looking at it from a negative viewpoint, extraordinary expenses would sap an agent's profit if they weren't charged off to clients. While the debits may not be huge for any individual author, in the aggregate they can be so high that they could force an agency out of business if they were not paid out of author income.

Many a session of literary agents' organization meetings has been devoted to questions of what are appropriate deductions, how costs can be reduced, and how to get publishers to pick up some expenses that are currently laid on the shoulders of authors, and I assure you we take these matters very seriously. Never think that, since it's not our own money we're spending, we're unconcerned with holding costs down. Most agents lay the money out on behalf of their clients, and although they ultimately recover it from money flowing to those clients, they no sooner collect it from one client than they must lay it out for another. So we are always out of pocket in that respect, and so it may fairly be said that it *is* our money, and the less we can get away with spending, the less, you may be sure, we will spend.

Because the headaches surrounding this issue are intense, some agents have raised their basic commissions in exchange for the assumption of all extraordinary expenses. Authors selecting an agent will want to weigh the value of extraordinary expenses against the value of that additional commission—all other factors being equal in the choosing of an agent, of course.

The conflicts surrounding these expenses arise over the definition of what is a "normal cost of doing business" for an agent. It would be impossible for an agent to do normal business without making long-distance phone calls, making photocopies of manuscripts, or purchasing extra copies of books for servicing subsidiary rights. Yet the agent justifies charging some or all of such outlays to clients on the grounds that they are expenses the authors would have paid if they were operating on their own without an agent. A reasonable author, for example, faced with a choice of making a photocopy of his manuscript in response to an inquiry from a movie producer, or waiting until his book is published nine or twelve months later, wouldn't hesitate to opt for the former. But he *could* wait. His decision not to incurs an extraordinary expense for him. If he has an agent, his agent makes those decisions for him and advances the money to pay for the additional costs.

The line between ordinary and extraordinary expenses can get fuzzy, though. When I started my agency I charged clients for long-distance phone calls. It was easy to keep records of such calls when I had only a handful of clients; it was something to do while watching New York Giant football games. But as my firm grew larger the task of poring over multi-page phone bills became intensely agonizing, particularly because the years of my company's rapidest growth coincided with the period when the Giants were playing awful football, so that by the time I'd finished the task of charging calls to authors I was fit to kill. Add to this the grousing of clients about being charged for what they contended was undeniably a normal cost of doing business and I was obliged to drop such charges except for international phone calls. With domestic phone bills running between $500 and $1,000 a month currently, I look back at my decision with pangs of wistfulness, but that's the way it goes, I guess.

Let's go over some other types of expense.

Telegrams and international cables. With the tremendous advances in telephone technology plus the advent of mailgrams, the necessity and cost of domestic telegrams have declined sharply. But mailgrams and telegrams are vital for furnishing written confirmation of deals when urgency is called for. Agents use mailgrams for other purposes, occasionally, such as publication day congratulations. (I recently heard a story about an agent charging a client for such a mailgram, but I strongly suspect it was a bookkeeping goof.) International cables, telexes, faxes, and phone calls are an absolute necessity in this age of high-powered international electronic negotiations, but even when they are cheap they are expensive. Yet, no author would want to risk blowing a deal by insisting that his agent convey decisions and information via old-fashioned airmail.

Photocopy. The photocopying machine has been a prime

factor in the transformation of the publishing industry into the high-powered business it is today, creating the immediate accessibility to material that makes for more dynamic book auctions and early sales of subsidiary rights. The process has also added to the burden of expense for author, publisher, and agent, and that burden upon even the smallest of agencies is tremendous. In New York City a price of 10¢ a page is standard, with discounts offered for high-volume jobs. An agent must usually make at least one photocopy of any manuscript that he believes has subsidiary rights potential, so that he can make more copies from that one as the need arises. If a book has any sub rights potential at all he will probably need half a dozen copies to service first serial submissions and to hit movie producers and foreign publishers eager for an early look. Figuring six copies of a three-hundred-page manuscript at 8¢ a page, that's more than $150 for the job, including tax.

At any given time in the life of even a modest-sized agency there may be between five and ten such literary properties in circulation, an outlay of $1,000 or $1,500. I invite authors who think they can make their own copies cheaper to do so by all means, bearing in mind the cost of shipping those copies to their agents, the inconvenience of arranging for their own photocopying, and the time lost in getting sub rights submissions in the works while the agent awaits the arrival of the copies shipped by his client.

By the way, an intermediate stage between manuscript and printed book is bound, uncorrected proofs, and agents frequently use these for subsidiary rights submissions. They cost about ten dollars a set on the average.

Messengers. Like most other businesses in New York City, the publishing industry runs at a breakneck pace, and while routine submissions, contracts, and checks are sent by ordinary mail or United Parcel Service, a day seldom passes in the life of a literary agency when some exigency or another doesn't require the use of a messenger, and sometimes the sheer importance of a project or deal demands use of a messenger to deliver a long-awaited manuscript or pick up a huge contract or check. The same exigencies demand the employment of special delivery or overnight express mail. Seldom do authors complain about these expenses as long as their agents use common sense in incurring them on their behalf.

In New York City, messenger services charge by the zone for routine errands, with one-zone deliveries and pickups starting at about $7. Parcels that are too weighty or bulky to go by bicycle (the standard messenger conveyance) must be picked up by van at extra charge. If you figure two or three calls daily for a messenger at a small to medium-sized agency (the largest agencies employ their own messengers rather than outside services), that comes to $400 or $500 a month. Overnight mail charges start at $10 or $12.

Next come *book purchases*. Although agents utilize manuscripts or proofs to exploit subsidiary rights to key books, much of the time we can wait until the book comes off the presses before offering those rights. Authors are entitled to a certain number of free copies, but anything beyond that must be bought, usually in hard cash, by the author or agent at a courtesy discount of 40 or 50 percent. If an agent is to do a thorough job of covering potential subsidiary rights markets—and sometimes the demand for a book extends over decades—he's going to need between twenty and fifty copies of a book. In the foreign market there are about a dozen key language territories, and in some cases the agent or his subagent partner in those territories will want to submit a book to more than one publisher at a time. Furthermore, after buying the rights to a book, a foreign publisher will usually request between two and five extra copies for translation, production, cover art, and other purposes.

If the book in question is a paperback original, the cost of buying extra copies is not excessive, but in the case of hardcovers the cost can be awesome. A $15 book discounted by 40 percent is $9, and thirty copies will set you back close to $300 including shipping costs. Publishers refuse to charge most such purchases to authors' royalties as they once did because so many books fail to earn out their advances and the publisher is thus left absorbing the cost of book purchases. So they demand cash on the barrelhead before processing book orders, and most agents cannot count on their clients to afford them or pay promptly. In any given month, therefore, an agency of any dimension will have to shell out $1,000 or more for book purchases. I try, when I negotiate contracts, to raise the number of free authors' copies to the maximum I can get away with.

Then there's the *cost of marketing books overseas*. Whenever possible—that is, in cases of routine submissions—agents use surface mail to submit books overseas. It may take months for books thus submitted to reach their destination, but when you hear how much it costs to airmail a book you may well decide the tradeoff between cost and time is an acceptable one. A hardcover book costs about $5 to ship by boat; by plane it costs $15 on the average. Now, if the book is important or timely, if the author is eager to see results, or if there are guaranteed sales awaiting the delivery of a book, it is penny wise and pound foolish to send books via surface mail, but if you have as many fingers and toes as I have you'll have figured out that that's about $300 in postage to service a book via airmail. If the book is hot, an agent may even airmail a copy of the manuscript. The cost is so obscene it will nauseate you and I will not sully these pages by uttering it here. I try to remind authors that the cost of foreign submissions is easily wiped out by just one foreign sale, but they have a tendency to overlook this when they get a check with $200 or $300 deducted for foreign postage.

Advances. You may not think that loans to authors should legitimately be classified as extraordinary expenses, but I suspect you would feel differently if you were sitting at my desk poring over that particular column in my ledgers. I can't speak for other agencies, but for mine, despite every effort to harden our hearts to pleas for advances, these "quick" loans to authors represent a larger debit than all the others that I have listed combined. An author who recently joined our agency told me he'd chosen me over two competitors because, "Another client of yours told me you were a sucker for a hard-luck story."

I suppose I am. At this writing, I have succumbed to the following hard-luck stories: (1) My Wife Just Left Me And Cleaned Out Our Account ($1,500); (2) The Hurricane Damaged My Roof And When The Engineer Inspected It He Discovered Extensive Termite Damage ($2,500); (3) I Have To Go Into The Hospital For Diagnosis But They Require Prepayment ($500); (4) It's Christmas . . . ($750); (5) It's The End Of The

Month . . . ($650); (6) The Internal Revenue Service . . . ($1,250).

Most of these advances will be recovered within a month or two out of monies soon payable to my agency, but then, as surely as rent is due monthly and taxes quarterly, I will be besieged by a new wave of requests, so that the balance of unrecovered advances seldom drops below $7,500–$10,000—which the clients are getting at a most attractive interest rate: 0 percent.

If robotlike efficiency were the goal I could slash many of these extraordinary costs to the bone. I could submit all manuscripts by fourth class mail; send checks and contracts to clients by routine mail; require clients to run off their own photocopies; submit books to foreign publishers via banana boat; and slam my teller's window to even the most abject appeals for loans. I would then take the savings and plunk them down on a Jaguar XJ6.

But then I start thinking, and at length I say to myself, How ridiculous it is to prefer the thrill of pushing a gorgeous piece of automotive engineering to the max on an open highway over the pleasure of hustling my tail off to cover a monthly out-of-pocket deficit of fifteen or twenty thousand dollars. But hell, a man's entitled to daydream, isn't he?

CHAPTER 36

Good News About Death

Owing to a number of death threats I've received from paperback publishers, I was stirred by a letter from a reader urging me to write about the problems writers face when their agents die. I have, of course, written about terminating your relationship with your agent, but that advice was predicated on his being alive. My omission is forgivable. Nobody likes to think about death, especially agents. Writers at least have an opportunity to immortalize themselves through their books. But what do agents have to be remembered by—their deals? Somehow the tribute "He Negotiated the Sweetest Option Clause in the Industry" on an agent's tombstone doesn't have the lilt guaranteed to inspire pilgrimages to his grave.

In fact, his survivors and former clients might be inspired to shake their fists over his poor moldering body if he made inadequate provisions for the operation of his business in the event of his demise. Among the prizes of my publishing horror-story collection are those about authors whose money was tied up for years while their late agent's estate underwent probate.

These disturbing tales vividly point up the need for agents, while they are still vital and compos mentis (if anyone consciously choosing to become an agent may be said to be compos mentis), to determine exactly how their estate administrators or business partners or employees will handle their business, especially cash flow in and out of their agency, until the formalities of probate are concluded. For, despite the remark by one publisher that the only good agent is a dead agent, the worst living agent in the world is better than the best dead one if the latter's passing creates a lot of aggravation for his clients. But much of it can be avoided by candid discussion of these matters between author and agent, and by some simple contractual measures in cases where the agent hasn't made appropriate privisions.

So let's look death squarely in the eye and utter the unutterable: Sooner or later your agent, like everybody else, has got to meet his maker. Despite the image of invulnerability and immortality agents try to project in order to intimidate publishers and reassure clients, actuarial statistics indicate that their track record in escaping the Grim Reaper is no better than anybody else's. And while autopsies do reveal some physiological characteristics unique to literary agents, such as overdeveloped spleens, ossified hearts, jaded palates, and a circulatory system of iced water, there are no indications of divine creation. This means that they are fallible just like you, and like you they don't pay as much concern as they should to the practical consequences of their death. But as the practical consequences of your agent's death may be to drive you close to bankruptcy, it's best for you to raise questions now while his body is still warm; if you choose to avoid the subject, you may be casting yourself to the treacherous winds of state probate law.

Let's talk about that law.

Although it differs from state to state, it is almost universally true that an individual's assets are frozen as soon as the authorities learn about his demise. This information is communicated to those authorities in a variety of ways: death certificates issued by doctors and hospitals, newspaper obituaries, cemetery and funeral home records, and voluntary reports by estate executors, next of kin, etc. As soon as the authorities have been informed, they are required to order the immediate freezing of all known bank accounts belonging to the deceased and the sealing of his personal safe deposit box. Except for insurance settlements and whatever liquid assets (cash, jewelry) may be converted for the use of the survivors, no funds are available to settle claims until the deceased's estate has been probated.

Entire court systems exist in every state for the probating of estates. The purpose of this procedure is to insure the proper settlement of claims on those estates. If the deceased made out a will, it must be reviewed to make certain it was properly executed; heirs must be located, signatures of the deceased and witnesses confirmed, and claims by heirs, legatees, and creditors examined. Even when the process proceeds without a hitch, it can take months and months. If the will is challenged, the delay may be even longer. We're talking about years, folks. *And*—if the deceased left no will at all, requiring the appointment of a public administrator to sift through the deceased's affairs—well, you don't want to know about it.

This procedure applies equally to rich and poor, male and female, mighty and humble, to people of every race and creed, to industrial magnates, ditchdiggers, doctors, lawyers, Indian chiefs—and literary agents. Unless your agent is incorporated, it doesn't matter whether he has a thousand able people working for him, the best law firm in the country, and the most sympathetic survivors you could ever ask for: You will not immediately be able to get your hands on the money owing to you by your publisher.

Within days after your agent's death his agency checking account will be frozen, and whatever balance is in it will remain in it. Whatever funds are receivable by him, such as your advances and royalties, will go undisbursed while his estate is probated. Do you see a horror story shaping up? Wait—it gets worse.

You (or your lawyer, or the new agent you hired after three minutes of mourning for your last one) pay a visit to your publishers. You talk about your late agent. "Terrible thing," you say, clucking your tongue.

"Terrible," your publisher replies, but clucklessly.

Now you get down to business. "You know, royalty time is coming and you guys are going to owe me all this money. Those idiot lawyers for the estate are giving me a hard time about probate. So how about you paying the royalties directly to me, or to my new agent. If you want to go on paying the commission to the estate, fine, but the rest should go to me. Any problem with that?"

Your publisher's eyes are all sympathy, but his palms are turned up in a gesture of helplessness. "It's not that easy.

We've referred the matter to Legal, and you know how *they* are."

"No," you reply through clenched teeth. "How *are* they?"

"Uh, very technical," says your editor.

What your editor means is that in the absence of clear-cut legal instructions, Legal can and will do nothing. And there's a lot about your agent's death that is not clear-cut. Did you have an agreement with him spelling out what commissions he was to take on your money? How can anyone be sure he didn't advance you money or incur some charges against your account (like that $435 in manuscript photocopy charges for that auction that flopped) that must be recovered? About the only things that are clear-cut are the contracts your agent negotiated with your publishers irrevocably requiring them to pay all your money to *him*! Legal cannot take the risk that the estate will sue your publishers for paying you money that rightfully belonged to your agent. The only thing Legal can do is point you in the direction of the bathroom so you don't whoops all over their carpet.

If your agent was incorporated you can breathe a big sigh of relief. Among the many reasons corporations exist is to furnish uninterrupted operation of the firm should the principal officer die. When a corporation is created, stock is issued. If it's issued to just the owner or a small number of people it's called a "closely held" corporation; or the stock can be issued or sold to a great many people. Either way, the principle is the same: The corporation is a business entity with a life of its own. Even if the corporation consists of just one person, the corporation survives his or her death. The corporate bylaws and minutes provide for the administration of the firm by other appointed officers or ones appointed by the heirs to the deceased's estate. The stock in the company is part of that estate, but no matter how horrendous the battle over the deceased's will may be, or even if he or she didn't make one out at all, the fiduciary function of the corporation cannot be interrupted. Of course, if it *was* a one-person operation there may be a lot of delay and confusion while your situation is being sorted out, whereas in a larger company there are usually other employees familiar with your account who can fill the breach left by your late agent and provide immediate continuity. But whether the corporation is great or tiny, its accounts cannot be frozen. Corporate law allows the firm to carry on while the late owner's estate is being settled.

Why then, you may ask, don't all agents incorporate? The reason is that it doesn't pay to do so if their revenues are modest. The start-up and administrative costs of a corporation are considerable, and the rule of thumb is that unless your firm is earning $100,000 annually or more (which, for an agent, means upward of $700,000 in sales depending on whether he charges 10 or 15 percent commission), it's not worth incorporating. I don't know exactly how many literary agents are currently incorporated, but a quick stroll through the pages of *Literary Market Place,* the directory of the publishing trade, suggests that at least half the listed agents are not incorporated.

If your agent is among these, what can you do to avoid the dreadful problems I've described? After consulting with a number of lawyers I would like to make a suggestion that will probably not endear either you or me to your agent but may rescue your money from the clutches of state probate law. And that is for you to ask your agent to sign a letter (with the signature notarized) directing your publishers, in the event of his death, to thereupon pay your net share of monies after commission directly to you and to pay only the agent's commission (10 percent, 15 percent, or whatever) to the agency or its legal heirs or assigns. I don't know whether such a letter will stick with all your publishers, and it's impossible to predict whether it might be disputed by your late agent's estate, but it beats the scenario I described earlier. Speak to your lawyer about drafting such a letter, which might either be a To Whom It May Concern document or a letter addressed to each specific publisher who publishes you.

You might also ask your agent what, if any, provisions he has made for the operation of his company in the event of his death, and whether his employees or heirs are sufficiently familiar with his business to administer it after he's gone. It may be that he has given the matter some thought and decided— even provided in his will—to sell or assign his "agency of record" to some other agent with whom he feels his clients will be compatible should he die. It may even be possible for him to structure a sale or assignment to that other agent that is triggered by your agent's death, as a means of avoiding tie-up of cash flow during probate. It's certainly worth exploring, given the alternative.

Even if your agent is incorporated, it's desirable to discuss candidly the measures he has taken against the possibility of his demise. Can his colleagues or employees take over the company? Can his spouse or other heirs? Does he contemplate liquidation of his firm or sale to another agency? Does he carry insurance naming the corporation as beneficiary to furnish it with operating cash during the transition period?

The questions we've raised here are important enough to be factors in choosing and remaining with an agent. For, while every literary agent hopes to live to a ripe age and die in bed, his flesh is heir to the same afflictions that strike so many others down before their time, to say nothing of muggers and crazed taxi drivers. Should your agent succumb to any of these, you will not want his tortured spirit to roam the earth forever howling over the colossal foul-ups and bad will he created by not planning ahead.

Section Five

Manners and Morals

CHAPTER 37

Courtesy

In a column I wrote several years ago, I observed that there seems to be a tendency for some authors to drink more than they should at publishing luncheons to allay their nervousness. This occasioned a call from one of my clients. "It's fine for you so sit there pontificating," he grumbled, "but couldn't you give us some constructive advice about how to behave when we go out with editors, so we're not so damned nervous?"

The fellow was absolutely right, and he helped me realize that authors are often understandably uncertain as to how to behave in their dealings with editors. I believe there are two reasons why. The first is that they may not be aware of some of the psychological forces influencing their behavior. The second is that they may not clearly understand the system of manners and protocol that governs the editorial world. It's a kind of dance—more of a minuet than a reel—with set, stylized steps, and postures that authors, editors, and agents are required to perform.

Three pairings constitute what might be called the Editorial Triangle: author and editor, author and agent, and agent and editor. The dynamics of the triangle might best be understood in terms of dependencies. Each party is dependent on the other two in some fashion. The author is the supply side, the editor the demand side, and the agent the merchant negotiating between supply and demand. Together the three form a miniature closed society revolving around the cash crop known as Books.

While you would think that the weight of dependency would be pretty much equally distributed among the three, it's obvious that the burden is carried by the author. Authors do not have the extensive social support system that many editors and agents do; they are often isolated from the marketplace by physical distance; and they rely heavily on the largesse of their publishers and the competence of their agents for financial and emotional sustenance. It's perfectly natural, then, for authors to set their publishers and agents up as mother figures, and while I have no degree in psychology it stands to reason that anyone as dependent as authors are on the twin breasts of publisher and agent is going to have a highly developed sucking response. Put a glass in their hands under the tense circumstances of a publishing luncheon or cocktail party and you'll see it in action.

So much for why authors get bombed at publishing luncheons.

Every society creates rules to prevent anarchy, and the society of author-publisher-agent is no exception. Of course, the more civilized the society, the subtler its rules and the more sophisticated its sanctions for reinforcing them. The publishing business certainly fits the description of a civilized society, comprised as it is of well-educated, literate individuals operating in highly organized (sometimes, anyway) corporate organizations and dealing in the extremely sophisticated activity of translating ideas into merchandise.

Actually, if you step far enough away from the sophistication of the publishing process you will see that it still boils down to a matter of seller, buyer, and broker struggling primitively with one another for dominance. Anyone who has lived in or studied the publishing anthill for any length of time can testify that there is as much plundering, treachery, rapine, and bopping on the head as may be found in the most aboriginal of civilizations. The only difference is that we prefer not to call these things by their names, as it sullies our self-image. I remember an editor describing the dapper, distinguished head of one of our most illustrious publishing companies: "Oh, he stabs you in the back like everyone else—it just takes you two weeks to realize you're dead."

In publishing, the rules governing behavior are codified into a system of protocol and etiquette called courtesy. Courtesy is not always easy to define because editors, authors, and agents each have their own code and the three don't always harmonize. For instance, some agents feel there is nothing wrong with not telling an editor they are submitting the same manuscript to other publishers. From an editor's viewpoint, however, that is a discourtesy, for if an editor knows he is one of several considering a submission he will behave differently than he will if he thinks he is the exclusive recipient of the manuscript.

Editors may balk at discovering that an author has taken on a project for another publisher while under contract with them. Even though the author may not be breaching his contract (some contracts prohibit authors from working on any other book until the contracted book is completed), and even though the author completes the first book satisfactorily and on time, and even though the author took on the second project because the advance on the first was inadequate for him to live on while writing it—the editor may nevertheless feel that the author has discourteously affronted the monogamous spirit of the author-editor relationship.

Despite the quaintness of the word, then, a breach of courtesy can be a grave offense that leads to strained or even ruptured relations between an author and publisher or agent and publisher. I recall with a shiver how, as a tyro in the publishing business, I committed such a gaffe against the late and great Macmillan editor Peter Ritner, a blunt and bearish man who brooked no nonsense from green upstarts. It happened in a swank restaurant at the height of the luncheon hour. I told him I had been speaking to another publisher about his author. "That," Ritner boomed at me in his awesome operatic baritone, "was most discourteous of you, sir." All that night I tossed in bed listening for the stomp on the stairs of Macmillan editorial assistants coming to frog-march me off to interrogation.

Space limitations prohibit me from enumerating all the points of protocol and etiquette that prevail in the editorial world, even if I knew what they were. Many of them are the same rules of the road that regulate other forms of social intercourse. Others are unique to our business. Until you feel completely comfortable in that world, until you know the players and are able to bend or break the rules with impunity the following ten commandments ought to keep you out of the more serious forms of trouble.

1. *Keep your big mouth shut.* When speaking to agents and editors, refrain from criticizing other agents and editors. You must never assume that the person you are talking to cherishes the same poor opinion of someone that you do. Many is the time I've listened to prospective clients complaining that this editor was a jerk and that publisher was a fool and this agent was a crowning idiot, and I've found myself thinking, "What's wrong with this guy?"

If you've had a bad experience, say as little as you can, and if you can't be charitable, perhaps it's best to say nothing at all. Lord knows, people in our business understand when you tell them you toured Chicago and Denver and there were no books in the stores, or your publisher originally promised you a 25,000-copy printing but ended up ordering only 7,500 copies. But for you to say, "My editor just sat there and did nothing, and my agent was too busy going to cocktail parties" may reflect worse on yourself than on those you so harshly judge, however deserving of criticism they may be.

2. *Don't be overly chummy with editors.* Whether or not you have an agent, be restrained in your dealings with editors. It is more important for them to respect your work than to like or love you. You must never forget that editors work for corporations dedicated to making a profit, and as often as not that profit is made at the expense of authors. However tight you and your editor may be, the time must inevitably come when you will want something he cannot give you, and he will want something you cannot give him. In the resulting negotiation, the closer your friendship, the harder it will be for you to hold out for the best terms. Your editor may care deeply about you, but his corporation cares deeply about its bottom line, and few editors will stake their job for the sake of an author.

From the viewpoint of an agent, the biggest discourtesy imaginable is for an editor to take advantage of an author's vulnerability. That's why many agents take strenuous measures to keep authors and editors apart and to funnel all communications through their agency. Many agents resist giving out their clients' phone numbers to editors or allowing any direct exposure of authors to publishing personnel. They are acting out of concern that editors may take advantage of authors if given the opportunity.

My own view is that a certain amount of contact is both necessary and desirable, and as long as authors are aware of the pitfalls of such contact, and keep their agents apprised of all developments, things cannot go too far wrong.

3. *Keep your big mouth shut.* Think before you speak. The things you tell an editor may not have the effect you intended, and in fact may have the opposite one. The editor who granted you a nine-month delivery date on your book may not be delighted to learn that you'll be finishing it four months ahead of schedule. He may in fact be appalled that a project as demanding as that one will take so little of your time, upset that you're not doing your research or that you're writing too fast or that the manuscript will come in too short. Better simply to say, "Don't worry, you'll get your book on time." If you do think you're going to finish it early and your editor thinks he would like to get it on an earlier list, you can say you'll try to turn it in sooner.

Volunteer as little information as possible, and try to think things through from an editor's viewpoint. *Should* you be telling your editor you don't want any more money this year? *Should* you be telling your editor you weren't terribly happy with the first draft but you're sure the final one will be fine? *Should* you be telling your editor you had to take on another writing project to make ends meet?

Authors volunteer all sorts of information because they feel the editor is their friend. But if you'll try to project yourself into the mind of your editor, or better yet of his boss, you might find yourself biting your tongue a little more often.

4. *Go through your agent for everything.* If you do have an agent, centralize all dealings through him or her. Contracts, submissions, delivered manuscripts should all be sent to your agent no matter how convenient it is for you simply to send the material directly to your editor. Aside from observing the procedural proprieties by doing things this way, you keep your publishers on notice that you prefer for them to deal with your agent rather than with you. Even your correspondence with

your editor should be sent to your agent for review and forwarding. That way your agent may pick up on some things you probably shouldn't be telling your editor. And if that sounds like censorship, it's better than committing a blunder that might injure your relations with your publisher.

5. *Keep your big mouth shut.* If you have an agent, he will brief you before you go into a meeting with an editor. Listen very carefully to what he has to say. A good agent will background you not merely on your immediate business with your editor but on such things as the state of your publisher ("They're hot right now," or "They're hungry, they haven't had a big book in three seasons"), the position of your editor ("He just joined the firm and he has to bring some good books in fast," or "He has no clout over there"), and other tidbits that will help you get a fix on conditions at your publishing house. Your agent will also tell you what to say and, perhaps more important, what not to say. And if he tells you not to say something, then for crying out loud don't say it, or leave it for your agent to explain. Your agent undoubtedly has good reasons for withholding certain information from your publisher, and those reasons may not always be clear to you. There may be undercurrents in his relationship with your editor that have nothing to do with you, or your agent may know something that you don't. He may be conducting negotiations with your editor for other authors besides you (there *are* other authors besides you, you know), and his dealings on your book may be part of a larger strategy. If your agent accompanies you to a meeting or luncheon, watch him so he can signal you with his eyes. Or sit beside him so he can signal you with a swift kick in the shins.

6. *Report everything to your agent.* In due time you may have direct contact with your editor and other staff members of your publisher concerning a variety of matters. Your editors may feel there's no point in bothering your agent about small stuff, so they contact you directly. In most cases the business at hand will be routine, and requests will be innocent. But they can develop into problems if the author isn't alert or fails to discuss developments with his agent. Those routine queries about your manuscript by your copy editor can develop into a request for a rewrite. The nice young lady who calls asking you to name

some dates when you're free for promotional appearances may end up bullying you to accept a time that is inconvenient to you. I'm not saying it will happen every time, but it has happened in the past, and it can happen to you if you don't keep your agent *au courant*.

7. *Keep your big mouth shut.* When you're out with an editor, don't contradict your agent or question his handling of your work. And don't tolerate your editor's questioning of your agent's handling of your work. Publishers often have a vested interest in dividing authors and agents, and anything you inadvertently do to help them promote such divisions can only rebound to your discredit and disadvantage.

8. *Don't play your agent and editor off against each other.* In your eagerness to please everybody, you may end up defeating yourself. On many occasions, for instance, an author and editor may have a friendship that long predates the relationship between author and literary agent. The introduction of the agent into that bond creates instabilities that may result in jealousy, tension, and even hostility, and the author sometimes fosters these emotions without realizing it, for it is, after all, highly gratifying to have two people fighting over you. How often has a client said to me, "That S.O.B. Joe down at Feemster House has been taking advantage of our friendship for years, so on that next contract I want you to wring every dollar out of him that you can." Then, a moment later, he'll add, "But go easy on the guy, okay? I mean, he and I are old friends."

Experienced agents are sensitive to the dynamics of friendships between authors and editors and don't barge into the middle of them like a crazed water buffalo. If, however, your agent does feel he has to be firm or tough with your old buddy, don't interfere. That, after all, is what you hired him for.

9. *Keep your big mouth shut.* Don't spread rumors or gossip, however knowledgeable it makes you look. For, in the long run, it makes you look like, well, a gossip. Because this *is* a gossipy industry, discretion is a highly prized virtue, and one that far outlasts the pleasures of spreading the Hot Scoop about somebody. And because this is also a small industry, gossip has a way of turning on its disseminators. As in any small town, you never know who is a friend, ally, relative, or business associate

of whom. Rumors are traced to their sources with far more ease than you would imagine. Don't be a source: You don't need enemies.

10. And finally—*Keep your big mouth shut*. When in doubt, err on the side of silence. Let your work and your agent speak for you. Whenever you feel that impulse to say something that you suspect may be out of line, consider that you really have only two choices; Count to ten and call your agent, or count to twenty and call your agent.

Don't make your agent's job harder by putting him into the position of having to apologize for you or explain away some indiscreet things you may have said. "God!" an agent friend of mine once burst out. "My job would be so easy if it weren't for authors!"

Although we tend to lose sight of the fact, writing is still a profession. Behave professionally. As a wise person once said, the best way to save face is to keep the bottom half of it closed.

CHAPTER 38

Pet Peeves

From time to time I will get a phone call from a publisher who has read one of my columns. "There you go again," he'll complain. "Every month you take publishers to task for something. If it isn't late payments, it's lousy royalty statements. If it isn't lousy royalty statements, it's acceptability. How about a break? Why don't you write about all the terrible things authors do to publishers?"

"Like what?" I'll ask.

"Like delivering manuscripts flagrantly late. Or buying authors' copies of their books and not paying for them."

Now, I am nothing if not fair and am perfectly willing to be convinced that the rotten things authors do are at least as rotten as the rotten things publishers do. But after half an hour of intense soul-searching (it is a waste of time to search an agent's soul longer than that), I have concluded that it just ain't so.

I have, however, compiled a list of pet peeves about authors accumulated over many years of association with them. I know that many of my publishing colleagues share my attitudes, so I trust that my complaints will not sound mean-spirited. And while I offer them to you with a light heart, some of them may be irritating enough to your agent or publisher to take the keen edge off your relationship with them. So, if you are a perpetrator of a few of the transgressions described below, I urge you to mend your wicked ways forthwith.

I must say right off the bat that among the things authors do that upset me, delivering manuscripts late is not one of them, at least most of the time. Lateness is the medium in which agents live. We breathe late manuscripts and eat late checks and drink late contracts. And lateness in a creative person is certainly more understandable and forgivable than it is in a business organization. I have never known an author to be deliberately late with a book, but I have known many a publisher to be deliberately late with a check. (Oops! There I go again!)

What kills me is authors who don't *tell* me they're going to be late. Publishers schedule books many months in advance, and in most cases are able to pull a book out of the schedule if given sufficient notice. In most cases, too, a publisher will grant the author a reasonable extension of the delivery date. If, however, out of embarrassment or some other reason (such as a moon-lighting gig the agent doesn't know about), an author doesn't level with his agent, he will not only get himself into trouble, but his agent as well. An agent who knows the truth can go to bat for his client, make excuses, concoct a fib. But if an agent sincerely assures an editor that a book will be turned in in June because that's what his client told him, when the client knew all the time that there wasn't a chance in hell that he could make the deadline, the agent's credibility will be damaged.

I make very few inflexible rules for my clients, but this is one of them: No matter how embarrassing your reasons may be, I insist that you tell me the truth so that I can make proper excuses for you. (I, of course, have never lied on behalf of a client. What kind of agent would I be if I lied on behalf of a client?)

Lying to your agent is a mortal sin, but authors commit many venial ones as well, and oddly enough, it is the latter variety that drive me absolutely up the wall.

Take authors who misspell "Foreword," for instance. I strongly feel that anybody who turns in a manuscript containing a "Forward" deserves automatic shredding of his script plus the first three fingers of his right hand. You would think I would not have to explain to professionals who make their livings with words that a foreword is a *fore-word*, a *word* that comes *before* the main text. But as the Forward-to-Foreword ratio on manuscripts submitted to my agency is about one to three, I can see that the correct spelling cannot be stressed enough. (I hesitate, however, to criticize writers for not knowing the difference between a foreword, a preface, and an introduction, since I don't understand it either.)

The Forward-Foreword offense is part of a larger conspiracy to send me to an early grave. I am referring to authors who don't copyread their manuscripts before submitting them. An occasional, random typo is one thing, but when I realize that the author never bothered to reread his manuscript or have it reviewed by a good speller, a murderous rage comes over me and I am compelled to steal into the night to overturn garbage cans and scratch automobile fenders with my ring. Don't authors understand, I growl at alley cats as I kick them, that today's literary marketplace is so intensely competitive that a poorly spelled manuscript can lose somebody a sale?

A subspecies of the above-mentioned type misspells critical words and names, and misspells them consistently, focusing a glaring light on its own carelessness. I remember a biblical novel in which the word "pharaoh" was spelled "pharoah" throughout, and in a book that long, that's a lot of pharoahs. I have often wondered why, if the word is pronounced *fay-ro*, lexicographers have chosen to place the *a* before the *o*. In fact, what is an *a* doing in the second syllable at all? Such speculations do not mitigate one's intense annoyance at having to correct such errors over and over again in saga-length manuscripts.

Speaking of repetitious errors, I'm reminded of those authors who type the title of their book at the top of every page of manuscript. I don't know where this quaint custom arose. I suppose it has its origins in the paranoiac fantasy that part of a manuscript will inadvertently be separated from the rest in a publisher's office.

Against this remote possibility must be weighed the not so remote one that the title you type on every page of your manuscript will be a lousy one. Like many publishing people I am a fanatical believer in the importance of titles: A good or bad one can significantly affect the fate of a book. All too often I'll get a good book with a bad title, and after kicking alternate titles around the author and I will agree on a new one. I'll then prepare a new title page only to discover that the discarded title appears on every page of the manuscript. Now what? I must now either go out with a badly titled book or have the entire manuscript retyped just to knock the offending title off every page. Luckily, the advent of word processing makes it easier to run off a slightly modified manuscript. But not everybody has a word processor. So, do us both a favor and put your name—and only your name—at the top of every page.

Mention of word processors reminds me that many agents and editors find it disconcerting to read dot matrix printouts. I recommend letter-quality printers, but I've discovered that a cheap and fast way to correct the dot matrix problem is to make a photocopy of the original: The copy comes out darker and makes the dots disappear. Also, many authors use poor-grade, thin, gray, anemic printout paper, which makes the manuscript look flimsy and insignificant.

On occasion an author will send me a book printed out in uncut, accordion form. I ask myself what terrible thing I did to this person that he should avenge himself on me so cruelly. Am I supposed to read his manuscript standing up, or to unfold it on my living room floor and creep down the room on my hands and knees? Am I expected to separate each page at the perforation after completing it? I think it's time that writers understood something about literary agents: Their standard reading posture is supine, head elevated sufficiently to glance at a baseball game on television. Now that I've revealed this tightly guarded secret, perhaps you'll be more considerate and instruct your printer to separate the pages of your manuscript.

One author used a poor printer that made all lower-case *g*'s look like *s*'s and *s*'s look like *g*'s, so that words like "kissing" came out "kiggins" and "giggles" looked like "sissleg." I developed severe eyestrain after three pages and was certifiably brain-dead after fifteen.

These may sound like the querulous whinings of an excessively fastidious man, but most responsible agents feel it's better to catch problems in their offices than risk irritating editors, who, all other things being equal, might choose the clean manuscript over one requiring any editorial work.

No amount of work will rectify the manuscript that smells of tobacco smoke, however. Every once in a while I will open a manuscript box to be greeted with a gust of vile, fetid air. "This manuscript stinks," I will comment to an assistant, "and I haven't even begun it." Heavy smokers don't realize that their habit imparts the same odor to typing paper that it does to clothing and hair.

Occasionally I come across intriguing items nestled in the leaves of a manuscript, notably hair. Although the appearance of a long female hair may stimulate pleasant fantasies for me as I leaf through somebody's book, not all agents and editors respond quite so benignly, particularly if the hair is not human. So please, authors, fumigate and groom your manuscripts before posting them to your agents and editors.

And when you do post them, may I ask you not to have them bound or specially boxed or wrapped? Just a loose manuscript in a typing paper box wrapped and taped securely enough to get safely through the postal system. There seems to be a law of nature that the quality of a manuscript declines in inverse proportion to the elaborateness of its package. When I receive a manuscript bound by brass screws with a plastic embossed cover, lovingly wrapped in chamois cloth, set in a velvet-lined cedar box, shrink-wrapped, packed in turn in a fireproof strong-box secured with iron bands, I am prepared to stake my career on the likelihood that this book is one colossal dud.

There is a particularly lukewarm place in my heart for foreign authors who are obliged to use typing paper of different dimensions—approximately one half inch too long and a quarter inch too narrow—from the standard American 8½ by 11 inches. I realize how chauvinistic it must sound to deplore the paper that was probably good enough for Thomas Mann, Jean-Paul Sartre, and Graham Greene, but because agents usually place manuscripts in submission boxes to protect them and present them attractively, it drives us crazy to get a misshapen manuscript from the Continent requiring Procrustean measures to package the submission.

Authors who submit their only copy of a manuscript are, to say the least, an intense source of curiosity to me. They brazenly challenge the immutable law causing such manuscripts to get lost in the mails. The advent of cheap photocopy services has stimulated a rise in lost manuscripts, for authors who used to type an original and carbon now type an original only and bring it to a photocopy shop, where another immutable law causes it to get mixed up with somebody's master's thesis. Again, the development of word processors will eventually make the question of lost manuscripts academic, but until then I urge you not to forsake the reliable carbon set. (When I was a free-lance writer I rented a safe deposit box and regularly brought carbon copies of works in progress to store there. It was when I realized that storage costs for the carbons exceeded revenue earned from the originals that I decided to start a new career as a literary agent.)

Then there are the authors who administer tests to their agents. Some try a cute trick of turning one page in their manuscript upside down. If the agent returns the manuscript with that one page still upside down, it proves he didn't read the manuscript page for page. There are authors who quiz their agents about specific scenes and characters. A typical dialogue might sound like this:

AUTHOR: Did you like my book?
AGENT: Oh, yes, loved it, loved it.
AUTHOR: Great. What did you think of my character Pflonk?
AGENT: Pflonk? Terrific character. Nicely developed.
AUTHOR: Hah! Gotcha! There was no such character in my book!

I assure you that when it comes to an important book your agent reads your manuscript carefully. With so much riding on it, he has to. But most agents I know don't have time to read their clients' work page for page, nor do they need to in order to get a sense of its quality, organization, and pace. In fact, they don't even need to in order to sell it. With certain kinds of material, such as books in a series, a light once-over is enough to satisfy your agent that all is in order and the work follows the original outline.

Plainly, the evil that authors do may be categorized as Class B Misdemeanors punishable by groans, rolling eyes, sighs of frustration, and indulgent smiles. I would like to think that you are as tolerant of your agent's foibles. Agents do have them. (I know this only from talking to authors). There is one extremely successful agent who likes to boast he's never read anything he's sold. And there's another who, every time he makes a big deal for a client, gloats, "That will pay for a new set of radials for my Corvette," or, "Now I can put that new wing on my house."

I consider myself truly fortunate in not being possessed of any personality traits that irritate others. Well, maybe one or two. All right, maybe a few more than that. Okay, okay, so I'm riddled with them. But at least I know how to spell Foreword.

Chapter 39

This Sporting Life

If you're a sporting type you don't necessarily have to travel to Las Vegas or Atlantic City to find exciting action. It's right here on Publishers' Row. Behind the doors of every publisher and literary agency you'll find enough off-track gambling to satisfy the most reckless plunger. And while it's not, at first glance, as heady as chemin de fer or baccarat, the stakes are often just as high and the suspense as nerve-racking.

All business decisions are gambles to a degree. That is why one important Roman patron goddess of business was Fortuna, the same deity who presided over the fates of gamblers. Fortuna was depicted as blind, undoubtedly furnishing our language with the term "blind luck." However much the prudent business person attempts to minimize risk, however extensive the safeguards, warranties, disclaimers, escape clauses, and statistical precedents insuring the success of any business venture, there is always Blind Luck lurking just out of view, concocting some preposterous scenario, an unheard-of disaster, a combination of events that defies all odds, a random occurrence that mocks human intelligence and humbles the mightiest among us.

The risks essayed by publishing people may not be as glamorous or dramatic as those of, say, folks in the oil business, but the processes of evaluating information and acting on it are essentially similar. In fact, the analogy may be very apt, because in both fields you will find two distinct types. On the one hand, there is the wildcatter who risks everything on a hunch. On the other is the cautious investor who sinks wells over known and extensive oil pools that have been mapped and measured by geological experts. The wildcatter, risking all, walks away either a millionaire or a pauper; the conservative investor may spend nine dollars to make ten, but his return is as close to guaranteed as anything Dame Fortuna can deliver.

I have a tendency to romanticize the past and suspect I may be doing so when I say that it seems to me that publishers of an earlier era in our history took more risks. But from what I have read about our industry, and what I remember about the time when I entered it, publishers were disposed to gamble more than today's breed. This may be due to the fact that their companies were more independent than present ones are, and the founders of earlier publishing houses relied more heavily on their own taste and judgment rather than on the input of editorial committees, the pressures exerted by conglomerate managers and hierarchs, and the unsettling influence of book-store chains. There are still some wildcatters in the publishing business if you know where to look, but I'll stand by my opinion that today's publishers conduct their business more conservatively than their forebears.

These publishers assess reading trends the way insurance companies assess actuarial data. They seek proven authors wherever possible, or make unproven authors prove themselves with extensive samples of their work. They do, of course, publish their share of first novels, midlist books, and works of serious literature, but their lists are amply weighted in the direction of books by or about stars, books that fit safe formulas or follow fads, books developed with a view to making a sure profit. The phrase "downside risk" is frequently heard in the board meetings of today's publishing companies as the officers contemplate worst cases and invent catastrophic scenarios designed to chasten adventurous editors. They are reminded that only one book out of ten makes a solid profit for the company, and only five out of ten earn back costs and overhead. The resulting books are, predictably, seldom imaginative. The recent spate of publishing mergers and acquisitions and attempted mergers and acquisitions focused on companies with large backlists, like Harper and Row, Doubleday, and Harcourt Brace Jovanovich. Backlist houses generate a great deal of guaranteed and easily harvested revenue to balance potential losses from gambles hazarded on best-sellers.

On any given day in the publishing industry, you can find countless numbers of people weighing odds and placing bets. The most common center of this activity is acquisition of books. The purchase of even a midlist novel is far more of a risky business than most authors think. Authors complain, Why can't a rich company like Simon and Schuster or Random House take a chance on my novel for seventy-five hundred lousy dollars? But that amount is just a fraction of the cost of publishing a book. The expense of manufacturing, distributing, advertising, and selling it, plus the publisher's overhead expenses covering rent, staff payroll, office maintenance, utilities, and the like, may bring the investment to ten times or more the advance that the firm paid the author for the rights to his book. Thus, as the fate of your manuscript is being weighed by a publisher, all those costs are being assessed against the projected revenue from book sales and subsidiary income.

If acquisition of a midlist book is as fraught with risk as this, what kind of gamble must a blockbuster be? Interestingly enough, in some respects it's probably less of one. A literary novel by an unknown writer is far more dependent on the vagaries of reviewers, word of mouth, and luck than is the latest novel by a best-selling author. Looking at the numbers on that author, a publisher can pretty much guarantee a minimum sale on the new book that justifies a huge offer, however good or bad that new book may be. When the bidding for James Clavell's *Whirlwind* came to rest at $5 million, with the hardcover-paperback prize going to William Morrow and Avon, Tom McCormack, publisher of St. Martin's Press, wrote an article demonstrating how safe an investment $5 million actually was in light of Clavell's illustrious sales history.

Nevertheless, when the bidding for a big book or author gets frenzied, publishers can sometimes lose their heads in precisely the way that bidders at an art auction do. Then such unwonted and dangerous emotions as lust, greed, and vanity cloud the normal equability of a publisher's mind and you end up with one of those headline-making deals that elicits comments from people in the trade, at lunches for months afterward, that "they'll never earn that advance back in a million years." Sometimes publishers deliberately overpay to acquire a coveted author. That author's books may become a loss leader to make some kind of statement to the publishing industry, to authors and agents, and to the press. At other times, publishers overpay or seem to overpay because they genuinely believe they can earn their investment back. Some years ago, an agent conducted what is known as a blind auction on a very commercial first novel. Unlike the usual publishing auction where publishers are informed of each other's bids and allowed to raise theirs until top dollar is reached, in a blind auction each publisher must make one offer and one offer only, and that one must be his best. The auction was won for a price reported at $850,000; the next highest bidder came in for something like $250,000! Had the top bidder overpaid? In fact, the high price they paid stimulated a Herculean effort to recoup it, and I am reliably told that the investment was indeed recouped. So, one publisher's crazy gamble may prove to be another's shrewd investment.

Another form of legalized gambling conducted daily by publishers is known as Setting The Printing. Here again, publishers do all they can to minimize the guesswork involved in determining the number of copies of any given book to be printed. The author's previous track record and the sales history of similar books on the publisher's list (as well as those on other publishers' lists) are among the key figures deliberated on by sales and production staffs.

Sales representatives solicit orders from buyers at bookstore and at bookstore-chain offices, and those orders furnish publishers with what is known as the "advance sale" numbers that enable them to fix a minimum print run. Worked into the calculations might be such pertinent information as movie, maga-zine, or foreign deals made on the book prior to publication, tie-ins of current events, the author's promotability, and other factors that promise to stimulate interest among potential consumers. Then some tricky number-crunching takes place. For instance, it is well known that the more copies printed in one print run, the cheaper is the cost per copy. Just as obviously, if a publisher prints too many copies, the losses from returns will usually outweigh the profits of a lower cost per copy. Usually, but not always. Publishers may sometimes "force" a large print-ing, gambling that the profit from a 150,000-copy printing that takes 50 percent returns will be higher than that from a 100,000 copy printing that takes only 40 percent returns.

Publishers gamble in quite a lot of other ways. They may try a daring cover concept or an unusual advertising campaign, offer an unusually high discount to lure stores to stock more copies of a book, or put an author on tour in the hope that the books sold on the strength of his charisma will make more money than what they would save if they did not put him on tour at all.

The real hotbed of gambling activity is literary agencies, how-ever. Perhaps because they are not heavily burdened by rigid organizational structures and procedures, and are responsible only to their clients, most agencies can maneuver faster than publishers and are more comfortable in an environment of risk.

On a typical day I am confronted with half a dozen situations that challenge my gambling acuity. Here are a few that I jug-gled the other day. What would you have done in my place?

• I did a multiple submission of a nonfiction book and set the closing date for bids for a Friday. On Friday, three publishers called turning the book down without making an offer. A fourth made an offer of $25,000, barely acceptable but up to that point the only offer in town. Then the last house checked in. The editor adored the book and was totally confident that she could top $25,000, indeed top it substantially. But her boss was out of town and unreachable and she could not make an offer until the following Monday. Could I extend my closing date to next week? I asked the $25,000 bidder if he would do so. He said no, and he would withdraw his offer at the end of Friday. Should I turn him down and wait to see what, if any-thing, happens next week?

• A publisher wanted to sign a fast-rising paperback author I represent to a long-term contract. The author's latest book had just been published and it figured to earn him about $10,000 in royalties above the $10,000 advance his publisher had paid him. The publisher's offer was $60,000 advance, or $20,000 per book. The royalties on the three book package were to be jointly accounted, meaning that even if any single book in the package earns more than $20,000, he will not be entitled to royalties until a total of $60,000 has been earned on the entire contract. the offer was attractive: The author is guaranteed twice the advance he currently receives. However, there is a strong possibility that if we contract for one book at a time, the value of the second or third book could be considerably higher than $20,000. Of course, it could also be considerably less. Should we go for the bird in the hand, or speculate on the two in the bush?

• A best-selling paperback novelist has ambitions to be published in hardcover, and I have entered into discussions with two publishers. One is a hardcover house that does not own its own paperback firm, the other a hardcover-softcover combination. The former is a very prestigious company, but because it is not in a position to guarantee paperback publication it can offer no more than $250,000 for the author's next novel. If the firm does well with it, however, a paperback auction might bring the author a headline-making $1 million paperback deal, and her 50 percent share of it would come to $500,000.

The hard-soft house is offering a $500,000 guarantee, and, as in all such deals, the author will receive a full paperback royalty instead of splitting it with her hardcover publisher, as she would have to do if she chooses the first option. The hard-soft house does not, however, possess the cachet of the hardcover-only house, nor does the deal have the publicity value of a paperback auction conducted by a hardcover-only house. But—what if, after we select the hardcover-only house, that firm conducts a paperback auction that turns out to be a flop?

How I handled these situations isn't important in this context; what is, is the difficulty of calculating the odds, and being responsible for the consequences of a wrong guess. Most agents I know discuss these options with their clients, so that the decision is as well informed as possible. Some agents make the decisions on their own, however, because they (and perhaps their clients as well) take the attitude that the agent knows best, otherwise why hire one? Early in my career I learned that that is not always the wisest course. I called a client who was making a good living writing paperbacks, and casually informed him I'd turned down a $2,500 offer for a quickie paperback. "You did *what*?" he snapped. It turns out he'd had some financial setbacks, had a couple of weeks of downtime, and would very much have appreciated the opportunity to make a few thousand relatively easy dollars, even though his going rate per book was closer to $20,000. Since then I've decided never to second-guess my client, even though I run the opposite risk of having a client say to me, "Why are you bothering me with these piddling offers?"

If I ever retire from publishing, I figure I will have received superb training for the career of bookmaker. But if I've learned anything, it's this: You can't possibly lose by betting that in the long run, publishers will make bigger profits on books than authors will.

I'm willing to lay ten to one on that.

CHAPTER 40

Lawyers (Groan!)

Whenever a client asks me if he should show a publishing contract to his attorney, I emit a noise not unlike that of a rutting moose whose girlfriend has just trotted into the woods with his rival. "Please," I beg, "anything but that. Take my firstborn. Take my co-op, even. But don't show your contract to a lawyer. He won't understand."

My attitude is by no means unique. Many publishing people consider lawyers to be humorless spoilsports placed on our planet to raise hypothetical questions about events that have only the remotest possibility of coming to pass. In response to our reassurances that "It will never happen" or "It doesn't work that way," they smugly cite *Gumbo v. Dittersdorf et al.* and send groaning agents back to the negotiating table to haggle over the nuances of such words as "book," "pay," and "publish." And whenever a breach of contract is imagined, these learned jurists are right there with their lawyer-letters, writs, petitions, and injunctions to hold the offending party to the explicit meaning of the contractual provision.

Most of the lawyers I know don't fit this caricature. They make serious efforts to understand the unique nature of publishing law; are reasonable, thoughtful, realistic, and no more venal than anyone else; and regard litigation as an extremely distasteful last resort. Nevertheless, by the very nature of their profession, lawyers tend to be extremely literal-minded about the language of contracts. And, sad to say, the literal language of publishing contracts is enough to induce cardiac infarction in even the most liberal of lawyers.

Lawyers ofttimes use legal precedents and forensic experiences that may be germane to coal mining, automobile manufacture, and real estate transactions, but are hardly applicable to publishing situations. Once an attorney is engaged, however, he has an obligation to show his client results for his fee. It is hard for me to believe that an attorney being paid $150 or $200 an hour will read a contract and hand it back to his client saying, "Looks okay to me," or, "I'd say your agent did everything that I would have done." It is far more likely that he will raise those hypothetical questions and will not be satisfied with an agent's breezy assurances that if This or That happens, "I'll take care of it." After all, most agents don't have law degrees, and while their experience must be respected, how can they predict with any certainty that This or That, or, even worse, The Other Thing, will not happen? Thus do agents frequently find themselves pushed by lawyers into composing contractual language applicable only to the red end of the spectrum of probability.

Many years ago, after negotiating with no fewer than five different parties, I got them all to agree on the terms of a diabolically complex book, movie, and merchandising package. I spent two days assembling a custom-built contract that reflected the special interests of all five, and on a Friday I convened a closing in a conference room. For an hour the various parties and their lawyers passed the contracts around. All confirmed that the papers reflected everything they'd agreed on. All but one, that is. A lawyer for one party spoke up. "What would happen," he asked, "if there were a walkout by the Key Grip and Best Boy Guild during the third week of preproduction?" (That wasn't the question, but it was something as mad as that.) "That's covered by Article V, Paragraph 2 (e) 8 (b) iii," I pointed out. "No, it's not," he said, "and unless it's in there I can't let my client sign this contract." "If you put it in," warned a lawyer across the table from him, "my client walks." The room broke into squabbling that grew louder and angrier until, an hour later, I watched the entire structure of this magnificent edifice collapse into a thousand fragments. I excused myself, went to the men's room, and cried. The odds against the lawyer's worry materializing were slightly longer than those that

Madagascar will become our fifty-first state. But the lawyer made it seem as likely as the sun rising tomorrow morning.

The involvement of lawyers in publishing contract negotiations often polarizes situations that might otherwise be settled through negotiation. Publishers hate lawsuits and with a few exceptions (described below) will do almost anything to avoid them. While litigation is certainly the ultimate weapon in a dispute, agents are adept at working out compromises that are scarcely different from settlements forged by lawyers after protracted litigation. The difference is that the agent performs gratis the same function that a lawyer may charge thousands of dollars for. Recently I worked out a compromise in a dispute between an author and his publisher, and when it was all over, my client said, "I showed the settlement to my lawyer."

"Oh? What did he say?"

"He said it was pretty good, but he probably could have squeezed another five thousand dollars out of them."

"Really? So why didn't you use him instead of me?"

"Because," my client replied, "he said he would have charged me ten thousand dollars."

In another recent incident, a client of mine wrote an exercise book illustrated by photos he himself had taken. When the book came out, I received a lawyer-letter. It said that the author had used photos of his client without her permission. The photos were of her behind and legs only, but he could produce witnesses proving beyond a shadow of a doubt that the leotard in which her rear was clad was *her* leotard. At first I laughed, but it became no laughing matter when he threatened to go to the publisher. The publisher would have frozen some tens of thousands of dollars in royalties while the claim was being reviewed or litigated. The author might never see another dime from the book. "I can't afford a lawyer," the author said to me. "Won't you try to work something out with the guy?"

I called the attorney, who told me he wanted fifty thousand dollars. I said, "You know, the publisher is part of a vast newspaper, television, and book publishing empire. It retains one of the most prestigious law firms in the country, a firm that will protract this action for five years. How much do you think your client is going to net out of that fifty thousand dollars after paying your legal fees?"

"I don't know," he said. "How much?"

"A thousand dollars if she's lucky."

The attorney thought for a minute. "Maybe not a thousand dollars," he finally said. "But maybe two thousand."

"Maybe fifteen hundred," I came back.

"Yes," he said, "maybe fifteen hundred."

"Send me the papers," I said, grinning.

Most authors hold the legal profession in the same awe in which they hold the medical one. I would recommend a healthy dose of skepticism and common sense when it comes to dealing with the former, however. Practitioners of the law are of woman born like the rest of us. Their actions are often dictated by their emotions, their convictions guided by who pays them and how much, and they make as many mistakes and misjudgments as surgeons, engineers, stockbrokers—or literary agents.

You should regard contracts the same way. Contracts are solemn undertakings, yes, but they are not sacred covenants written in fire by the Lord Almighty. Too many authors regard contracts as rigid structures of legal language constructed to thwart and constrain them. Actually they are flexible tools when used skillfully, and can liberate as well as restrict.

In the relations between publishers and authors or publishers and agents, a great many factors balance the literal language of contracts. Custom and tradition, market conditions, practicalities, and, above all, the power of the players, affect the way any given contractual provision gets implemented, ignored, or defied. Let's look at some examples.

Not all contracts provide for a grace period in case an author delivers a manuscript late. Yet I have seldom heard of a publisher canceling a contract at the stroke of midnight on the day a manuscript is due. For practical purposes, a manuscript that is days, weeks, even a month or two late, can still be published on time without undue strain on the editorial or production staffs of a publisher. Now, an attorney may insist on specifying a grace period in a client's contract. Publishers don't like grace periods because they give authors another reason to be late, and authors have too many such reasons already. A zealous attorney might feel that that's a deal-breaker. In practice, if your publisher says, "Try to meet your deadline, but don't sweat it if you're a few weeks late," you can rely on that assurance ninty-nine times out of a hundred.

Friendships between agents and publishers mitigate the stringent language of publishing contracts. Despite a strict option clause requiring an author to deliver his next book to his publisher, on the strength of a tight friendship and an appeal to the goodness of an editor's heart an agent can often arrange for a one-time waiver of the option clause in order for the author to take on a project for another publisher, as long as that project doesn't compete with the work the author is doing for his regular publisher. "Thanks, I owe you one" is a common phrase heard in our business, and when the time comes for the publisher to lean on an agent for the return of favors, the agent may have to twist his client's arm a little to tidy up the debits and credits in the ledgers of obligation. Try to explain this system to a lawyer!

A few years ago I made a deal for somebody, and this person decided that I hadn't done anything for him that he couldn't have done for himself. So, unknown to me, he eradicated the agency clause in the contract and made the money payable to himself. By the time I found out about it, the publisher had paid him and I was out a sizable commission. This character disappeared, making it impossible for me to recover my commission. I was furious and called the editor, who should have caught the error before paying this crook the money. I demanded a commission, but when the editor begged me not to do so, as she would have been fired, I accepted her offer to make it up to me as a favor one day. We never referred to it until five years later, when I reminded her that she owed me one. The favor she did was worth ten times the commission I was gypped out of.

The most important factor by far in tempering the rigidity of publishing contracts is power. Don't let anyone tell you that might does not make right. While the language of any contractual provision may be plain as day, enforcing it is quite another matter if you don't have the money, status, influence, or leverage to do so. A first novelist has very little influence over a rich, powerful publisher, and no matter what his contract may say it's going to be hard to compel his publisher to live up to every letter of his contract. If the author is a big name, however, the publisher's eager compliance may certainly be counted on. Indeed, a powerful author or agent can compel a publisher to do things that are *not* in the contract. For instance, few contracts grant approval of cover art or jacket and advertising copy to authors, even big-name writers. Yet those stars are routinely consulted about such things, and if they don't like them they may well be able to get them changed or thrown out.

When contractual disputes arise, the interpretation that prevails usually belongs to the party with the most power. Nine times out of ten that's the publisher. An individual author of no particular clout may be able to enhance his legal leverage if he is represented by a strong agent, however. The agent who has a large and important clientele in, say, romance fiction may be able to gain advantages for an author who otherwise would have little standing against a publisher and who cannot afford to hire a lawyer.

One of the most important things that experienced agents know is precisely which issues publishers are prepared to litigate and which ones they will back down on. Authors who owe refunds of advances to publishers because of undelivered or rejected manuscripts are often harassed but seldom sued because it's too expensive for the publisher, as well as bad public relations. If there is a lot of money involved, however, a publisher may well go to the mat to recover its advance, or to resist having to pay the balance due on acceptance. The publisher's motive isn't entirely financial. As I pointed out previously, such disputes focus on an important issue: Is an advance a loan recoverable by a publisher if the author fails to meet his obligation? Or is it instead a nonrecoverable investment?

Another issue that publishers are not afraid to go to court over is breaches of the author's contractual warranties, especially those for libel. With damages, settlements, legal and court costs, and insurance premiums reaching catastrophic heights, most publishers are, I would say, prepared to sue authors they perceive to have dealt with them in bad faith.

Finally, publishers tend to get rather cranky about authors

who play fast and loose with their option clauses, particularly big-money authors. The trend over the last decade or so has been for publishers to write more elaborate and tighter option clauses so that star authors cannot capriciously duck out of their obligations when another publisher waves a big check at them. I must say that option clauses are for agents what elaborate locks are for safecrackers. But even if you, your agent, or your lawyer discover a tiny loophole through which to escape from the necessity of submitting your next book to your publisher, there is nothing to guarantee that your publisher won't sue you anyway.

Other than breaching the acceptance, warranty, and option provisions of your contract, there aren't too many offenses you can commit that will land you in court, and even these may be worked out through negotiation most of the time. The same is true, perhaps even more so, for breaches or perceived breaches of contract by publishers. I can think of few so flagrant as to be worth an author's while to prosecute to the bitter end. The threat of a lawsuit, and its attendant bad publicity, may force a negotiated settlement that nets you as much as you would win in a full-blown lawsuit after you have paid legal costs. *If* you win, that is.

I say all this as a counterpoise to any boasts your lawyer may make that you have an open-and-shut case. Lawyers do their clients a disservice by encouraging them to think there is such a thing as an easy and inexpensive victory. Don't forget that it was an unagented writer, William Shakespeare, who wrote, "The first thing we do, let's kill all the lawyers."

CHAPTER 41

"Let's Run It Past Legal"

Having alienated the legal profession in the previous chapter, I hope to return to grace with some high praise for one branch of the species.

It may be hyperbolic to refer to the legal counsels of publishing companies as gray eminences, a term one usually assigns to the shadowy power brokers who manipulate the controls of vast corporate or political networks. But it would be no exaggeration to state that tremendous influence resides in the hands of the attorneys who counsel publishing executives on the legal aspects of their companies' operations. Few significant corporate decisions are made without clearance by a publisher's lawyers, and no book is published that has not somehow been affected by procedures originating in the firm's legal department. To the degree that the men and women of those departments are seldom colorful, their eminence may indeed be depicted as gray. But it must never be underestimated, because the power they wield over the fate of your book is both total and final. However headstrong the chief operating officer of a publishing company may be, he or she will almost never override a house counsel's advice.

Owing to the enormous number of legal affairs confronting every publisher, attorneys must be engaged to advise the firms' executives. Small houses with little money to spare for lawyers may hire a small firm or sole practitioner on an hourly or flat-fee basis to perform specific tasks such as drawing up incorporation papers, writing a lawyer-letter, or rendering an opinion about a specific situation. Larger publishers may engage an outside law firm for an annual retainer, which is adjusted if the time spent by the lawyers exceeds a prearranged ceiling. Fees and expenses of litigation are always a matter of separate arrangement, as they absorb extraordinary amounts of billable time.

The largest publishing companies maintain a salaried in-house legal counsel or staff to advise them on the countless matters arising out of the daily operation of the company. Or they may share the legal staff of the conglomerate of which the publisher is one component. In any event, some of the matters dealt with by the in-house counsel may be as minute as a single, but potentially actionable, provocative word in a manuscript; other matters may be as immense and complex as a corporate merger or a major litigation. The publisher's legal department is also in charge of contracts: not just publishing contracts, but those pertaining to everything from the office lease to a bank loan to a distribution deal to the acquisition of another publisher. If there is a notable increase in the time it takes for your book contract to be processed, as authors commonly assert these days, it may be attributable to the workload of the lawyer at the top. Although routine contracts or deals for sums below a certain figure may never end up on their desks, most of them run very tight ships and insist on reviewing everything contractual that is generated in their bailiwicks. And there is scarcely a corner of the publishing company that does not in some fashion fall in a general counsel's bailiwick. Indeed, his office is sometimes a convenient dumping ground for many of those corporate problems that executives cannot pigeonhole and thus cannot deal with. "You should see some of the stuff I have to handle," one attorney told me. But he handles it decisively. "A general counsel is often a general troubleshooter for the corporation, and we solve lots of problems that are very far afield from our job description. You name it—they'll run it past Legal."

Here are some items that might appear on a typical day's agenda of the house counsel for a large publisher.

• The directors are concerned that the company is vulnerable to a hostile takeover. There is a great deal of stock on the market and its price is temptingly low. A raider might be interested in adding a publishing jewel to his conglomerate crown. A decision must be reached about buying back the stock and funding the maneuver.

• A news magazine has managed to get hold of a set of proofs of a major autobiography that the publisher is bringing out six months from now. Under the guise of a "news story" the magazine has summarized the juiciest passages of the book. The potential for selling first serial rights has been damaged if not ruined. The general counsel is contemplating litigation and is reviewing the legal precedents.

• This publisher is also at the other end of a possible lawsuit. An author has threatened litigation because, he claims, the publisher rejected his book in bad faith. He'd been hired by the publisher to write a biography of a glamorous starlet. But just as he turned in the manuscript it was learned that she'd been arrested for cocaine possession. The publisher rejected the book on the grounds it was simply a poor job and wants back the large advance paid on signing the contract. The author not only doesn't want to repay the initial advance, but wants to compel the publisher to pay the money due on acceptance, too.

• A delegation of literary agents is scheduled for a meeting to discuss improvements in the publisher's royalty reporting system. The firm's management is loath to spend the large sum of money it will cost to revamp the computerized royalty statements for thousands of books. At the same time, management is anxious not to give offense to the agents and to the large number of authors they collectively represent. The house counsel must determine a negotiating position before going into that meeting.

• There are several high stacks of paper on his desk and coffee table requiring attention. One pile contains routine contracts and contract requisitions calling for his signature or initials. Another contains affidavits, depositions, briefs, and other court papers for him to review. Still another has corporate minutes and other company business for his comments, approval, or other action. And in yet another are some items demanding urgent attention: a subpoena to which a response must be made by Friday; a summary of the terms sought by an agent for a major book on which there is an auction closing at five this afternoon; and a memo from an editor containing the distressing news that a reader has pointed out a dozen passages in a book the company recently published that seem to have been lifted almost verbatim from a book published ten years ago.

• A staff attorney has completed a line-by-line reading of a recently delivered manuscript, a biography of the late great Senator Clemenceau Osterdonk. Osterdonk was allegedly a pederast, a sadomasochist, a drunk, a cokehead, an arsonist, an influence peddler, an ax murderer, and an embezzler with dandruff, halitosis, and athlete's foot—your typical politician, in other words. Although the laws of the land plainly state that one cannot libel a dead person, the senator's estate and its Rambo-type lawyer are ferociously protective of the hallowed reputation of their late lamented, and have threatened to nuke our publisher if he prints Word One of this scurrilous hatchet job. The book will, the lawyer contends, irreparably damage the family's business interests which are dependent on maintaining an image of the deceased as the closest thing to an angel that is to be found in this imperfect world.

The book was impeccably researched by a journalist of unassailable pedigree, then reviewed by his own attorney, who happens to be the world's authority on libel. Our publisher is not afraid to publish this insightful and entertaining book, but neither does it want to provoke a lawsuit it cannot successfully defend. So the publisher's counsel has a ton of questions, modifications, and requests for documentation to take up with the author, and on the corner of his desk rests this thousand-page manuscript to which yellow Post-its are affixed. On each of these mini-memos a question has been raised, and there are so many sticking out of the manuscript it looks like a forsythia in bloom. The author must either alter the text to satisfy the attorney's requests, answer his questions in a point-by-point letter of response, or furnish sufficient documentation to demonstrate beyond reasonable doubt that the items in question rest upon a concrete foundation of fact. Even after the author has complied with all of the lawyer's requests, our house counsel will comb the manuscript again and pick a few dozen more nits before declaring it judgment-proof and fit for public consumption.

It's worthwhile for us to tarry over this function of our in-house lawyer. Every "flag" fluttering along the margins of that manuscript represents a fear fluttering in the heart of any responsible attorney. If the threatened lawsuit does materialize, it might take only one poor choice of phrase, one unsupported allegation, one overenthusiastic innuendo, one unattributable quotation to pave the way for a judgment against the publisher. Old Rambo will be poised to pounce with claws and fangs bared, you may be certain. And not just Rambo, but the attorneys for anybody else mentioned in the book who may feel a victim of defamation, libel, or invasion of privacy.

The fact that the publisher holds a substantial insurance policy indemnifying it against adverse judgments in those areas is of no comfort to our attorney. In the first place, the policy calls for a sizable deductible, somewhere between $100,000 and $500,000, an unrecoverable expense that will make a painful dent in the publisher's profits. For another thing, if the insurance company believes that the publisher was negligent in its responsibility for purging the manuscript of assailable allegations, it may give the company a very hard time and may even cancel its insurance. "No publisher can afford to take that kind of hit," I was told by another attorney. Nor is it of great comfort that the publisher's contract with the author entitles it to recover some or all of its litigation costs and damages from authors' royalties. Rarely is there sufficient royalty revenue to balance the cost of an adverse judgment.

Our house counsel will therefore be forgiven if the queries he has raised in his review of the Osterdonk biography seem picayune. Let's look over his shoulder at a few of them:

> Page 15. How do we know O. abused his half-sister when she was four months old? And what, precisely, do you mean by "abused"?
>
> Page 26. Can you document that Uncle Floristan turned O. on to the kicks of Blue Nun administered intravenously?
>
> Page 36. Can you support the innuendo that O.'s German shepherd was "a lot more than his best friend"?
>
> Page 75. Were there any witnesses to O.'s "uncontrollable urge" to flagellate the family chauffeur?

Page 106. Re your statement that O. "bribed his way in one door of the Senate and bribed his way out the other." Was anyone actually standing at the doors taking bribes? Names?

Page 140. Any documentation to verify that O. and Hermann Goering were "considerably more than nodding acquaintances"?

Page 141. Same question for Joseph Stalin.

Page 142. Same question for Al Capone.

Page 155. For my own enlightenment, can you explicitly describe the sexual contortion alluded to in second paragraph?

Page 202. Did anyone actually observe O. picking his nose at the luncheon with President Eisenhower?

Page 261. Was O. actually divorced when he started his affair with Mister Ed?

Many such queries are exasperating for an author, particularly in cases where "everybody knows" that the subject of his biography slept with this or that person for years or publicly smacked his wife around on a regular basis. If all you have to go by is a photo in a movie magazine of the subject escorting his alleged mistress to the Academy Awards ceremonies, however, or if not a single soul can be located who actually witnessed the subject striking his wife (or is willing to testify to that effect), you may be required by a prudent lawyer to fudge your language or throw the dubious passages out entirely.

Your publisher's general counsel does have a degree of discretion about some of the statements made in your book. If, for instance, reference to an affair has been made in half a dozen previous biographies and the persons alluded to have never contested the references, the attorney may see fit to let your allegation pass, even though it does not rest on hard primary documentation. If he is a literary as well as a legal type, he may be reluctant to water a book down excessively because an overly "lawyered" book can be a ponderous bore. His recommendations may be challenged by publishing executives who feel he is being overly cautious.

You the author have few options if your publisher insists on legal changes. Most publishing contracts permit a publisher to declare a manuscript unacceptable if the author fails to comply with requests to modify a manuscript to satisfy legal objections. In such cases the author must refund the advance paid on signing the contract, exactly as if he had turned in a book that was editorially unacceptable. The author may then seek a publisher that doesn't have quite so many compunctions.

I would think twice about doing that, though. For one thing, the same objections raised by the original publisher will undoubtedly be raised by others. And, more important, your publisher's attorney seeks to protect you as well as his company. You may find the legal vetting of your book upsetting at first, but after you cool down you will probably be grateful to have this eagle-eyed gray eminence on your side.

CHAPTER 42

Sacred Honor

• An author under contract to write a book for a publisher delivers an awful, unpublishable, unrevisable manuscript, and his publisher demands a refund of the advance paid upon signing of the contract, as is the publisher's right. The author agrees to refund all of the money except his agent's commission, but feels that his agent ought to refund the commission. The agent refuses to do so, since it's not his fault the author screwed up. Who's right?

• Two authors collaborate on a book under contract to a publisher. Both signed the contract and both are therefore equally liable for the warranties in that contract. One author is responsible for furnishing the research, the other for writing the manuscript. After the book is published, somebody sues the publisher and authors for libel. It turns out that the researcher provided his coauthor with incorrect facts. Should the coauthor be equally liable with his partner for the costs and damages of the lawsuit?

• Same situation, except that this time the researcher has done an unimpeachable job. The writer, however, turns in a perfectly lousy manuscript, and the publisher demands his down payment back. Should the researcher be required to repay his share?

• Agent A sold an author's first book to a publisher. The author becomes dissatisfied with his agent and leaves him for another, and Agent B goes right back to the same publisher and sells the author's next book there. Agent A is very upset. After all, he established this author at the publishing company, and now Agent B is reaping profit from Agent A's labors. Is Agent A justified in feeling angry? And whom should he be angry at: the publisher, Agent B, or his former client?

• An agent sells a book to Publisher A, but before contracts have been signed, Publisher B hears about the deal. "If I'd known about this book, I'd have offered you twice as much money as Publisher A," says B. Should the agent try to get out of the deal? Should he tell Publisher A about Publisher B's remark and try to get Publisher A to match Publisher B's price? Was Publisher B out of line for saying something so provocative to the agent?

• A publisher signs a contract with an author to write a biography of the current, and currently popular, President of the United States. Before the book is finished, the President is embroiled in a scandal and his popularity plummets. The publisher then cancels the contract because it fears no one will buy the book under the new circumstances. But by that time the author has already delivered his manuscript. The publisher wants his down payment back. The author wants his acceptance check. Who's right?

The above are examples of disputes arising in the publishing business that can be said to fall as much into the category of ethics as they do of law. Although all of these cases could end up in court, they could all just as well be resolved by the application of business ethics. In fact, it may be said that they might not have arisen at all if the parties had considered their ethical positions when the problems began to develop.

The subject of business ethics makes front page headlines every day in one form or another. As I write this, the hot topic is the fortunes made by insiders trading on privileged information about corporate takeovers. But some other news stories of late, such as the trials of corrupt New York City officials and the Iranian arms scandal, also raise acute questions about business ethics.

Ethics is a code of behavior governed by morality on the one hand and the law on the other. It is based on a sense of right and wrong that is not necessarily dependent on what the law says one can or cannot get away with. The best definition of ethical behavior I've heard was furnished by *New York Times* columnist Russell Baker: It means, Baker said, that there are just some things that are not for sale at any price. Many people believe that ethical conviction has weakened in our time from what it once was, and fewer people ask themselves whether there is anything they hold so dear that they would not relinquish it at any price.

I can't speak for the world outside the little fishbowl that is publishing, but it does seem to me that people in our industry have held up better in the ethics department than corresponding workers in many other trades. I'm not talking about the ethical conduct of publishing corporations, but the behavior of the individuals who work for them. I would imagine this owes in some measure to the gentlemanly tradition of our industry, and to the creative nature of the product we deal with. Still, given the notably if not notoriously low pay scale for all but the very top publishing personnel, it's a wonder that one seldom hears of any instances of dishonesty in our trade. Years ago an acquaintance who worked in the ladies' garment business expressed amazement to me that the publishing industry operated so successfully without the payoffs and kickbacks that are prevalent in the garment business: "You can't drive a truck from Thirty-fifth to Thirty-sixth Street without shmearing somebody," he said, using the Yiddish slang for "bribe." Although there are opportunities or at least conditions for corruption, I know of no literary agents or editors who have ever done anything much more corrupt than using the company stamp machine to mail personal letters. Compared to our sister industry, the movie business, publishing is like a white-gloves tea party.

And, unlike so many other lines of business where a deal is not a deal until contracts have been signed and money has changed hands, in publishing a handshake is usually firm enough to create a binding commitment from which one backs out only at the peril of losing the other party's trust forever. Whatever nightmarish problems may ensue once contracts have been signed, it can at least be taken for granted that the intent of the parties was and is honorable. And to me, that means a lot.

"Honor" is a word seldom heard in discussions of modern ethical values, though the time when men fought duels over it and women took their lives defending it existed less than a century ago. Honor in business dealings means, I suppose, taking responsibility for one's commitments, particularly when those commitments turn out unprofitably. If we look at them that way, it's easy to understand why honor in our business has become so difficult to maintain. The goal of the corporation, profit, is usually at odds with the sympathies of the editors. And the evolution of publishing into a highly complex corporate endeavor has meant the dispersal of responsibility to the point where, when one tries to assess blame for a mistake, one is left with a handful of mist.

It's easy to find people in charge at publishing companies, but not always easy to find people who will accept responsibility. The men and women who work in our trade are decent individuals, but the companies they work for seldom appreciate or reward employees for having moral scruples about corporate policies. Of course, agents are also responsible to a higher authority, namely their clients, so the challenge of Doing The Honorable Thing is by no means restricted to publishing executives. But I wonder if we've forgotten that there may be An Even Higher Authority. You know which one I mean.

Unfortunately, my qualifications for preaching about ethical conduct are less than impeccable. Although I happen to believe that I am morally above reproach, sound of mind and body, spiritually chaste, and extraordinarily humble, the only other person who thinks I'm a saint is my seven-year-old, and even he's beginning to show signs of wising up.

Nevertheless, I do feel that honor in business dealings is an ideal worth striving for, if for no other reason than that it is good business. The agent who delivers on a promise will be trusted by a publisher the next time; the editor who stands by his or her word knows that an author or agent will accept that word the next time around. And although accepting responsibility can prove very costly—you can lose a job, a customer, a client, a lawsuit for it—I respect those who own up to commitments or mistakes far more than I do those who try to duck responsibility or pass the buck. And I prefer doing business with them, because I always know where they stand and know I can count on them to do the honorable thing in a crunch. When the mistake is mine and I own up to it, I respect myself more,

too. And maybe self-respect is the only thing worth taking with you to the Great Beyond on Judgment Day.

When you examine in this light some of the hypothetical situations I offered at the beginning of this article, you can see that if the parties in any given dispute were to stand by their ethical responsibilities, the outcomes might be far less costly and bitter than if everyone looked to save his own skin. In fact, it might even create the kind of good will that binds people tighter than ever before. "It's my responsibility," says one party; "No, it's mine," says the other; and perhaps they have paved the way for splitting the difference or reaching some other kind of compromise that will generate mutual respect

Honorable behavior calls for no small degree of courage, for it means making sacrifices and disdaining easy ways out. For an author to take responsibility for blowing an assignment, for a publisher to take responsibility for the failure of a book, for an agent to take responsibility for messing up a deal, a tremendous amount of honesty and fortitude are required.

And that's just honor. I haven't even gotten to *sacred* honor yet! But here I have to laugh. Show me the agent who, in the hypothetical case above, would not think long and hard when Publisher B says "I'll pay twice the price if you can break your deal with Publisher A," and I'll show you a zombie.

CHAPTER 43

Scruples

We all know that literary agents are supposed to determine whether books can be published. But should they decide as well whether some books *ought* to be published? Should publishers be passing moral as well as literary judgment on books being considered for publication? Do film and television producers have a responsibility to audiences to turn down projects that glorify criminals? I've been thinking about these questions a lot lately, and so, it seems, have many publishing people even as they prepare their bids for the memoirs of this month's slasher, traitor, or Wall Street robber baron.

Virtually hours after Robert E. Chambers was charged with the sex-related murder of Jennifer Dawn Levin, Chambers' attorney was inundated by phone calls from authors, literary and film agents, movie producers, TV docudrama producers, book publishers and packagers, playwrights and screenwriters. More than one hundred bids were made, according to an article in *The New York Times* by columnist William E. Geist. One agent raved about how excited she was by what was quickly dubbed "The Preppie Murder" by the media. "It has money, sex, a defendant who is movie-star handsome, a lovely girl and kids who seemingly had everything." Another agent said, "This is an upscale crime." And still another agent was quoted by Geist as saying, "To be completely venal about it, the people involved in this crime fit the demographics that TV is shooting for."

Not everyone could be completely venal about it, however. Another agent said, "It's like personal injury lawyers flocking

to a car accident, but more ghoulish." And former Alfred A. Knopf editor-in-chief Robert Gottlieb used a similar metaphor. "I find something deplorable about people pouncing on what are horrible human situations," he commented. "It's a little like ambulance chasing."

When a literary agent evaluates a manuscript for representation, he applies many criteria: Is it well written? Is it well organized? Is it dramatic? Is it entertaining? Is there an audience for it? Is it commercial?

Sometimes, however, a question arises of whether we feel the material ought to see the light of day at all, of whether it is "good" for the public to witness the reenactment of an unspeakably brutal murder, an anguishing kidnapping, or the machinations of a swindler who left countless trusting investors ruined. Almost every agent can recount how he or she has been approached by the perpetrator, or attorneys for the perpetrator, of some heinous crime or another. This alleged or convicted killer, gangster, traitor, spy, fraud, drug runner, madam, wants to write a book: Would we be interested in handling it? Our commercial instincts immediately tell us the property could be a hot one. But is that all there is to it? Or are we obliged to consult our consciences as well as our mercantile sense when we formulate an opinion of a work's publishability?

Unfortunately, we can expect little help from publishers while we ruminate about the propriety of enriching felons with gains from the sale of their stories. With few exceptions, the first, second, and last impulse of most publishers is to stampede to sign up the recollections of a celebrated wrongdoer. One colleague tells me she had an opportunity to represent a convicted serial killer who wanted to tell his story. She called an editor to solicit interest in the book. "If they were entertaining murders we'd be interested," the editor replied, "but if they all sound the same, we'll pass." His only criterion, one which I can vouch is shared by many other editors, is, Will these murders move books?

It's easy for an agent to rationalize the handling of a criminal's story on the grounds that publishers are all but shoveling money at him to acquire it from him. "If I turn the book down," we reason, "one of my competitors will grab it and make those commissions. So it might as well be me."

Because the world in which criminals operate is often a dangerous and even violent one, I know of some agents who have declined to offer them representation out of fear that they, the agents, will come to harm. While I don't believe I've ever rejected a client for that reason, I would be less than candid if I claimed I hadn't spent some sleepless nights wondering whether one day a dark limousine would not pull up beside me as I strolled down the street, and several pairs of muscular arms would hustle me inside and a voice would direct the driver to proceed to the East River.

I overcame these paranoiac terrors by reasoning that nobody is very interested in harming agents, authors, or publishers to whom privileged information has been imparted by people with dark pasts. At least, I've never heard of anything more disturbing than a visit from an agent of the Internal Revenue Service (which can be horribly frightening, by the way).

So, while I can't blame an agent for turning down a client out of fear of reprisal, those grounds only beg the question of whether agents and publishers have a moral obligation to society to refuse to do business with malefactors.

The publishing industry is extremely sensitive to censorship of every kind, and what we are talking about here would seem to involve a form of censorship: self-policing. Ours is a liberal tradition stemming directly from the First Amendment of our Constitution: We abhor any attempt to suppress literature, however condoning or provocative of antisocial behavior that literature may be. The authors of our Bill of Rights did recognize, however, that the First Amendment could be taken advantage of by those who might see it as a license to publish whatever they wanted to without any regard for the good of the people. Over the centuries, numerous tests of the First Amendment have created a body of laws that curtail unrestricted use of the press. But—if the people themselves demand to read the first-person account of David Berkowitz, who randomly ambushed and killed six people during the mid-1970s, or Jean Harris, who murdered her lover, Dr. Herman Tarnower, or R. Foster Winans, who traded insider secrets on Wall Street, or

Claus von Bulow, accused of attempting to murder his wealthy socialite wife, or Mayflower Madam Sydney Biddle Barrows or alleged Preppie Murderer Robert Chambers or Bernhard Goetz or Jack Abbott, isn't it a little sanctimonious for a literary agent to tell these potential clients to take their business somewhere else?

And there's something more. Suppose their books aren't exploitive, but in fact shed some important light on criminal behavior that might help "the people" curb those antisocial impulses and prevent recurrences of certain crimes? If a book helps us understand what makes David Berkowitz tick, what compelled Charles Manson to stage his Los Angeles bloodbath, what caused convicted spy John A. Walker, Jr., to betray his country, doesn't that justify our involvement in it?

Fortunately, a number of state governments have relieved the publishing community of much of the burden of sorting these questions out. Spearheaded by the New York State legislature's revulsion at the prospect that David Berkowitz, who called himself Son of Sam, might sign a book deal and thus profit from his appalling crimes, New York and a number of other states passed laws requiring that the proceeds from such deals be diverted from the criminals to the victims. These statutes have come, generically, to be known as Son of Sam laws. There are variations on the basic principle. In some cases, the proceeds of book and film deals go to the victims and the next-of-kin of those victims; in others, the money goes into a general victims' fund that many municipal and state governments use at their discretion to pay victims of any crime committed in their precincts. Some Son of Sam statutes narrowly define the types of crime applicable, others are broader and include or have argued to include such things as "victimless crime" (pimping, prostitution, illegal gambling for instance), espionage (in which it may be said that the nation itself is the victim), and similarly ambiguous situations. Some interpretations embrace or attempt to embrace not just the author-criminal but the coauthor, the publisher, and yes, the agent as well, meaning that their shares of revenue generated by the criminal's story are subject to forfeiture. How much easier it will be for us to be righteous, now that there's no longer any profit in agenting the memoirs of a miscreant!

As I have stated more than once, I'm no saint. I have handled my share of books by authors whose hands could scarcely be described as clean. I was the agent for several books by a man I knew only as "Joey," who declared himself to be a free-lance hitman for the Mafia, claiming dozens of assassinations of Mob members who had broken the rigid code of that organization. In considering whether I should represent him, I weighed the fear factor, the profit motive, and my conscience, and managed to forge a delicate treaty with myself that enabled me to conduct my client's business in a state of relative guiltlessness. In the first place, I insisted that he never tell me his real name, address, or phone number, and indeed I never learned any of these until his death many years later. In the second place, I refused to let him tell me the real names of any victim, partner, or associate. In the third place, I refused to let him name names in his books. As a result, as far as I knew, Joey could well have been a complete imposter and every word he wrote a total fabrication. (He was never convicted of any of the murders he supposedly committed, though the federal government finally nailed him for tax evasion.) If publishers believed his story and the public enjoyed his books and paid good money for them, that was fine, but I acquitted myself of any responsibility for the truth of Joey's identity or the terrible nature of his deeds. Even if everything he claimed was true, I was sufficiently distanced from his victims to feel no pang of guilt by association or any sense of being an accessory after the fact.

That (plus some nice commissions) was enough to get me through that test of conscience without excessive anguish. Joey himself was in his own way a charming, funny, Runyonesque character with a conscience of his own ("I never torture my victims, I never rob them, and I never kill them in front of their families," he boasted), a man who made the task of living with myself even easier. I was young and hungry for business, and it was all something of a lark.

I'm not sure whether the times have become more cynical since then, or I've become more thoughtful, but I don't know if

I would, could, accept Joey as a client if he walked through my door again. I've stood before too many graves ever to think again of murder as a lark, even the murder of other murderers, which was Joey's stock in trade. And something happened to me that made it impossible for me ever again to see things the same way. Interestingly, it was a book.

Around ten o'clock on the evening of September 13, 1980, Eric Kaminsky, a promising twenty-two-year-old pianist, walked onto the downtown platform of the Eighth Avenue subway at 181st Street in New York City. He was attacked by two young assailants who robbed him, stole his wallet, stabbed him, and hurled his body onto the tracks. He was pulled back to the platform by witnesses, but by that time he had bled to death.

A few years later, his mother Alice contacted me. She had written a book about her son's murder and the subsequent trial of his assailants, and she wanted me to represent her. I read the manuscript the same night she sent it to me, and in a single sitting. My emotions were all but overwhelmed by the impact of her book. Unlike other books I had read written by the loved ones of victims, in which the authors eventually reconcile themselves to their loss, or forgive or even come to love the murderer himself, Alice Kaminsky's book was a volcanic outpouring of inconsolable grief and unmitigated anger untempered by the passage of time.

The following morning, still dazed by Mrs. Kaminsky's wrathful, righteous, biblical fulmination, I phoned her to pledge my commitment to her and to her book, and to the memory of her son. She had called it *The Victim's Song*, a deliberately ironic twist on Norman Mailer's *The Executioner's Song*, a book recounting the life, deeds, and death of murderer Gary Gilmore, and indeed the penultimate chapter was called "Literature and Murder (Norman Mailer)." In that chapter she excoriated Mailer and other writers and indicted the publishing industry for glorifying murderers and romanticizing murder while ignoring or glossing over the tragedy of the victims and the enduring suffering of the victims' survivors. "Many writers are like scavengers who run like wild dogs to the garbage cans of sensational murders and who try to extract perfume from what is essentially foul," Mrs. Kaminsky charged. Until her son's death, she had been a member of the vast audience that finds murder, and books about murder, fascinating. "But murder takes on sinister significance when it occurs to 'me,' not to the 'other,' and then what might have seemed like a harmless pastime takes on the stench of what Geoffrey Gorer calls 'the pornography of death.' "

I ran off several copies of Mrs. Kaminsky's manuscript, and it was difficult to keep the emotion out of my voice as I pitched the book to the half-dozen editors I'd selected for the first round of submission. On the strength of my impassioned appeal, many of those editors read the book overnight and reported the next morning with voices similarly aquiver with powerful feeling. They were not only deeply affected by the book but also felt, as I did, that they could never quite look at things the same way again.

I was positive I would have a sale, possibly even an auction, on the strength of those first reactions. But days and weeks passed, and at length the manuscripts began drifting back with the most abjectly apologetic notes I have ever received on a rejected book. What these notes said in effect was that although that particular editor has been tremendously moved by the book, the editorial board had raised some practical marketing considerations that made *The Victim's Song* a longshot. I was devastated, and launched a new round of submissions with practically religious zeal. The result was the same. Everybody was touched. Nobody bought the book.

It went to some twenty-five New York publishers. None of them made an offer for it. During that time, however, the publishing industry went into frenzies over a number of books by and about mad-dog killers, hoodlums, turncoats, flesh peddlers, and other culprits. Ultimately I had to report to Mrs. Kaminsky that I could not find a publisher for her book. On her own she took it to an out-of-town publisher who did bring it out. It received stunning reviews. One reviewer said the book is impossible to read without crying.

Not everyone will draw a moral from this story, but I did, and I think you know what it is.

I have too much to atone for to preach that agents should be holier than anyone else. But agents are the primary interface between the real world and the world of literature, and we are therefore not without responsibility for what does and does not get published. Neither are you, the writer, nor you, the editor. As the publishing industry evolves from one peopled by individual men and women whose convictions informed the selection of books they published to a collection of corporate entities dominated by the profit motive, questions of what is morally right and wrong to publish come up less and less often, or when they do the answer is usually a foregone conclusion. Whether the process can be reversed, I don't know. I would imagine that any editor who consistently votes down potentially profitable books on moral grounds will eventually find himself out on his righteous behind with instructions to take his scruples to a religious publisher where they belong. But a vote of conscience at an editorial board meeting is a vote nonetheless, and who knows how long and how far it will reverberate? For me, Mrs. Kaminsky's book still disturbs my complacency, and when those attorneys call to pitch to me the memoirs of their criminal clients, the memory of Eric Kaminsky's lifeless body sprawled across the subway tracks flashes into my mind and I grope for the courage to say, "Sorry, I'll pass."

Section Six

✿ ✿

Publishing and Perishing

Many conscientious editors, when changing jobs, do try to bring along with them some or all of their list, for they know what fate is in store for the books left behind. But much depends on the extent to which the old publisher is willing to part with the books, and how much the new one wants them brought over. If the option to leave them where they are or to send them to a new home belongs to the author, perhaps the book will have a fighting chance.

Why doesn't every contract have an editor's clause? One reason is, publishers don't like them very much, for such provisions make it easy for a valued editor to leave a firm. Another reason is the diminution of attachment between authors and editors. With all the musical chairs being played in the editorial job market, few editors stick around long enough for such strong ties to develop. So authors don't ask for editor's clauses in their contract, knowing that so many editors are here today, gone tomorrow. Still, an editor's clause would furnish some degree of comfort and flexibility for many authors, and they should try to work one into their contracts at the time of negotiation.

Supposing you don't have these contractual defenses to call on, or are unwilling or unable to exercise them (because, say, your book is already printed and it's too late to pull it out), there are, nevertheless, tactics available to you to try to rescue your book from oblivion.

If your editor has left the company (or the company has left your editor) and your book is still at a fairly early stage, when an editor's enthusiasm can make a difference, then you or your agent should contact the new editor and reintroduce the book and its author. Even though the new editor may already have been briefed about it, your personal contact may enable him to form an attachment to it that could make a difference when the book is entering the rapids of publication.

If the book is beyond the stage where an editor can help, you can try to go higher, to the head of the company, to petition him to familiarize himself with the book, get excited about it, push the salespeople, spend a little money on ads or promotion. You might introduce yourself to a few key people at your company—the sales manager, marketing director, head of advertising and publicity—and point out some ways they can boost the book.

Obviously, you may have to take matters into your own hands. In *How to Be Your Own Literary Agent*, I made some suggestions as to how authors could create their own promotional tours, buy ad space, and otherwise publicize their books. This calls for no small degree of determination, nerve and money, but rescue missions have always done so. Sadly and ironically, publishers don't always appreciate an author's independent activities on behalf of his or her book, and a few have been downright obstructionist. Recently, for example, an author I know decided to undertake her own campaign for a book for which the publisher had done nothing, a book that looked, in the author's words, "as if it was about to be tubed." She visited every bookstore in her city's phone book, romancing the owners and hyping her book. What did she get for it? A phone call from her publisher saying, "We wish you wouldn't do that—we get into trouble when an author promotes a book and then people can't find it in the stores."

The tragedy of an orphaned book can in no way be compared to that of an orphaned child, except perhaps for the amount of time it takes to bring both into the world. Yet, for those of us who have invested our love in writing a book, agenting it, acquiring or editing or manufacturing it, surely there must be more to be done than presiding over its remaindering with a shrug. Someone loved that book once; someone thought other people would love it too. That's why it was written, bought, and published. Can't we try harder to save the orphans?

CHAPTER 45

Belly-up

Agents don't like to admit that there are events beyond their control, and I suspect that is why I have never written more than superficially about such contractual matters as *Force Majeure*—acts of God—and bankruptcy. Such events serve only to reaffirm our human frailty and fallibility, our total helplessness before the awful natural and business convulsions that occasionally devastate the microcosmic world of book publishing. How easy it is to deny that they could ever happen or that there is anything we could do about them anyway. I am able to rationalize my omission of these subjects by telling myself that in the course of my career in the book business I have never seen a publisher invoke fire, flood, strike, hurricane, insurrection, or war as an excuse for screwing up a book, nor until recently had I or my clients even been burned by the bankruptcy of a publishing house.

Yet, anybody who works in this business long enough knows that sooner or later Murphy's law will clutch us by the throat, and whatever terrible things can happen will, perforce, happen. These tired old eyes have seen booming markets dry up overnight, seemingly omnipotent chief executive officers of great publishing houses fired ignominiously, and corporate acquisitions, mergers, and divestitures undertaken as casually as cards tossed in a low-stakes poker game.

For instance, some years ago, at the very apogee of the gothic novel boom, Avon, the leading publisher of the genre, announced that it was terminating its gothics program. Snap! Just like that. Writers, agents, and Avon's competitors were floored. It was not as if the market had begun to decline. Anybody who wanted to make a small fortune in those days had but to take anything vaguely resembling a gothic formula story and slap on it a cover of a filmily clad girl looking apprehensively over her shoulder at a fog-shrouded mansion with a light burning in one window. We were all the more baffled because it was said that the head of Avon at that time killed the program simply because gothics bored him, which was like the secretary of the treasury announcing that he is bored with the presses that mint money. But that's what happened, and it left the paperback market in chaos and countless writers and agents floundering around on the wilder shores wondering where their livings were going to come from.

Or, take what happened after Harcourt Brace, the trade and textbook publishing giant, acquired Pyramid Books, an independent and minor paperback house that had suddenly found itself on the map with the huge success of John Jakes's Kent Family Chronicles. Harcourt changed Pyramid's name to Jove, replaced most of its staff, and poured millions and millions of dollars into acquisitions and self-promotion in a bid to make it the number one paperback company in the industry. Then one Monday the editor-in-chief and a number of other key editors were given until the end of the day to collect their personal effects and leave the building, and not long afterward Jove was unloaded on the MCA-Putnam-Berkley entertainment complex. The upheavals created by these transactions were so immense that few of us had the experience of dealing with anything remotely like it, and the toll on writers, agents, and the industry at large was incalculable. And I can think of scarcely anything an agent might have done to predict or control the situation so that he or she and his or hers would not be adversely affected.

In recent years we have witnessed similarly seismic events. In the space of six or seven months in 1985, for example, the publisher of Bantam replaced the publisher of Pocket Books, then hired the publisher of Berkley, who quit a couple of months later and presently replaced the publisher of Avon, whereupon the editor-in-chief of Avon left and was replaced by the editor-in-chief of Pinnacle. The turmoil caused by these churnings cannot be described. Nor can the harm done to authors be mitigated by the efforts of even the most powerful agents in the business. You just stand there, mouth agape, and watch the majestic unfolding of events. Then you come in when the dust has settled and do what you can to pick up the pieces.

And then, also in 1985, we witnessed the collapse of a paperback publisher.

For many years, Pinnacle Books was a marginal paperback house publishing routine genre books. It was then acquired by an investment group and the old management and editorial staff replaced by a smart and enthusiastic team that expanded the firm's editorial vision, spent money to aquire better authors and properties, and marketed its books shrewdly and aggressively. Within a year or so the results were dramatic. Sales began to soar and Pinnacle was the hot shop in the industry, a genuine major league contender. But there were serious problems underlying the successes. The company had expanded so explosively that its cash flow couldn't keep up with demand. Furthermore, as was alleged to me by people close to the situation, Pinnacle's parent company had to "borrow" some of Pinnacle's working capital to cover deficits or corporate acquisitions elsewhere in the conglomerate.

For many of us the first crack in the structure appeared at the end of 1984 when a number of Pinnacle's checks bounced. As restitution was made shortly thereafter and cash started to flow again, most of us who'd been touched by that chilly wind accepted Pinnacle's reassurances that the situation was temporary and order would soon be restored. In mid-summer, however, agents and authors demanding overdue payments were told that there just wasn't any money. By August the crisis had deepened. Key employees quit or were let go. Inquiries yielded a sketchy but frightening picture of Pinnacle's parent company allegedly using the publisher's accounts receivable to pay off corporate obligations that had nothing to do with Pinnacle. By the end of August the disaster was all but complete: Matters were turned over to the firm's attorneys and the last of Pinnacle's staff was forced to abandon ship.

This was a tragic event. When a paperback publisher goes out of business there is none to replace it, for mass market publishers are simply too expensive to create easily from scratch. The loss of a competitor is bad for publishing and worse for authors: The fewer publishers there are, the less flexibility in prices and terms is available to writers. As if they didn't have it bad enough.

The possibility of an actual bankruptcy sent agents and authors scurrying to their contract files to examine the pertinent provisions of their agreements with Pinnacle. Almost all book contracts contain language to the effect that if a publisher goes or is forced into bankruptcy, takes advantage of any bankruptcy statutes, or assigns its assets for the benefit of creditors, the author is entitled to get his rights back automatically. Examination of the boilerplate of Pinnacle's contract confirmed the existence of such a provision. Specifically, Pinnacle's contract stated that:

> If (i) a petition in bankruptcy is filed by Publisher or (ii) a petition is filed against Publisher and is finally sustained or (iii) a petition for Arrangement or Reorganization is filed by or against Publisher and an order is entered directing the liquidation of Publisher in bankruptcy, or (iv) if Publisher shall make an assignment for the benefit of creditors, then Author may, at Author's option, terminate this Agreement by written notice and, thereupon, all rights granted herein shall revert to Author.

Well, that was a relief. Although we still weren't sure what would become of any royalties Pinnacle might owe, at least there was no question about the procedure for getting our rights back. All we had to do was wait for an announcement that Pinnacle had filed for bankruptcy (or find out for ourselves by sending a lawyer to federal bankruptcy court, where bankruptcy petitions must be filed). Then we send a notice terminating the contract. Right?

Imagine our shock when we learned that *the bankruptcy provisions of publishing contracts are, essentially, unenforceable.*

I consulted with a lawyer friend of mine, Michael A. Gerber, professor of law at Brooklyn Law School, who has published a book about bankruptcy, and he cited provisions in the Federal

Bankruptcy Code that invalidate the bankruptcy termination clauses of contracts. It turns out that book contracts are regarded by Congress as assets comparable to the furniture, typewriters, and light fixtures of a publisher. Section 365(e) (1) of the Code stipulates that an executory contract (that's what you have) may not be terminated just because your publisher goes into bankruptcy.

The reason the law takes that position is that if a company is trying to reorganize in order to work things out with its creditors, as it may do in some bankruptcy cases, its rehabilitation may be hampered if you yank your contracts away. Those contracts are, after all, a key source of potential revenue for a company trying to get back on its feet. Even if a company is not attempting merely to reorganize but is completely liquidating, the law still regards the earning potential of your contracts as an asset to which all creditors have some claim. Thus, you may not get your rights back if the company elects to assume the benefits and obligations called for in your contract. There is some saving grace in all this in that the company cannot keep you dangling interminably. In a liquidation case the company must decide whether to assume or abandon the contract within sixty days of filing. In a Chapter 11 (reorganization) case, there is no hard and fast deadline, but the bankruptcy court at your request might impose one.

So, contrary to the black-and-white language of your publishing contract, if your publisher chooses to take advantage of this provision of the Bankruptcy Code, you're up the creek, pal, at least for a while.

Fortunately, few publishers who get into financial trouble go bankrupt, because there is usually another publisher waiting in the wings to take it over. A publisher's backlist may continue generating income for anybody who takes it over, and because most creditors of a publishing company (such as a banks, printers, distributors, the landlord, etc.) are incapable of generating income from the publishing of books, sooner or later they will conclude that it makes good financial sense to turn over to a publisher the contracts the creditors control. That is precisely what happened in Pinnacle's case. Electing not to file for bankruptcy, Pinnacle sent a notice to all interested parties stating that it had signed an agreement in principle with Norfolk Publishing, publishers of Zebra Books, to take over the imprint. This meant that Zebra would be able to publish certain Pinnacle books under contract or on the Pinnacle backlist.

Back to their contract files scurried the authors and agents, where they confirmed that Pinnacle, like every other publisher, has provisions in its contract permitting it to assign that contract to anyone of its choosing without the author's permission. Some agents and authors are able to modify that clause in negotiations so that a publisher cannot assign the rights without the author's express permission, but most publishers resist that modification, for the freedom to assign is an extremely important one to them, more important at least than it is to authors, for whom it is seldom a deal-breaker. Even if your contract prohibits your publisher from assigning your rights without your permission, however, in a bankruptcy situation that prohibition would be invalid under the Bankruptcy Code, according to Professor Gerber.

Actually, the assignment of your contract to another publisher might be the best thing that can happen to you if you are worried that your books may be tied up for years in bankruptcy litigation or seized by some creditor who doesn't know a copyright from a coffin nail. For one thing, before a publisher can assume or assign a contract, it must pay you any royalties it owes you or at least provide you with assurances that they will be paid. Moreover, if your contract is assigned, at least there is someone you can talk to, someone who will keep your book in print and generate some income for you.

That, however, might not necessarily have been the case if Zebra's original plan for taking Pinnacle over had gone through, for the notice Pinnacle sent out stated that the money Zebra generated for Pinnacle would not be paid directly to authors, but rather would go into an escrow account controlled by Pinnacle and its "secured creditor." A secured creditor is someone who has extended credit that is secured by some kind of collateral. In this case that secured creditor appears to be the bank to which Pinnacle's owners allegedly pledged the publisher's accounts receivable. Authors are not secured creditors. If a secured creditor intercepts revenue that otherwise would have flowed to the company and eventually to you the author, that secured creditor is under no obligation to satisfy the claims of the unsecured ones. Of course, a judge might be most sympathetic to your plea for return of your rights and royalties, for it is clear that an author is a lot more helpless in situations like this than is a bank or a printer. But a judge is under no legal compulsion to grant an author's plea.

At length, no longer capable of fending off its creditors, Pinnacle filed for bankruptcy under the Chapter 11 provisions of the federal bankruptcy law, meaning it was seeking protection by the federal government while it could reorganize and formulate a plan to repay its debts and restore business. It took almost two years, from autumn of 1985 through summer of 1987, for the company to get its act together. It did make a deal with Zebra, which at this writing is reviewing the entire Pinnacle list to decide which unpublished manuscripts it will bring out, which backlist books it will reissue, and which properties it will release to the original copyright owners and under what terms it will do so. Any royalties generated by publication of these titles by Zebra from this point on shall earn royalties in the usual way, but as for royalties generated before Pinnacle filed for bankruptcy, the chances for their recovery are, as they say in the underworld, two: slim and none.

As I said at the outset, agents don't like to admit that there are things they are powerless to control, but I must tell you that bankruptcy appears to be one area where little an agent does by way of negotiating contractual language is going to help if your publisher goes belly-up; and once it does, little that an author, agent, or lawyer does will help if the bankrupt firm and its creditors don't want to cooperate with you. My best advice is, first, to move like lightning once you or your agent get the feeling your publisher is in serious trouble, demanding a reversion of your rights and/or settlement of whatever financial obligations the publisher has to you. Put short deadlines on your demands and send official letters stating that owing to failure of your publisher to comply with the terms of his contract with you, you consider that contract canceled. Second, make a horrid pest of yourself in the hope that your publisher will decide life is too short to do combat tooth and nail with a crazy author.

One author did just that in the Pinnacle case and did win his rights back, but at a terrible cost because of the onerous terms of his settlement and the cost of hiring a lawyer.

And you *will* need a lawyer. But if there isn't that much value in your books to begin with, the cost of hiring a lawyer to rescue them may not be justifiable. It's frustrating as hell, maddening in fact, but there you are.

And that's just bankruptcy. I haven't even mentioned how helpless we are before acts of God. But I think I'll wait until a tidal wave demolishes Harper and Row, Random House, or Simon and Schuster before attempting to write about that.

Given Murphy's law, you may be reading my remarks about that sooner that you think.*

---

*Murphy, or Someone Else Up There, must have read this, for about a month after I wrote it, an earthquake measuring 4.0 on the Richter scale struck the New York metropolitan area.

CHAPTER 46

�֍ �֍

Outrageous Fortune

I often ponder the role played by luck in the fates of books and authors. Are some authors luckier than others? Are there lucky breaks for writers, the literary equivalent of the understudy who replaces a lead actor in a show and becomes a star over- night? Do we make our own luck? Can good luck be bought or manipulated? Can bad luck be avoided? Are some of us, to use the poignant Yiddish word, simply *shlimazls*, those hapless folks who always seem to be standing under the flower pot when it falls from a windowsill?

Our natural egotism rejects the notion that our successes or failures are the products of random and indiscriminate acci- dents. This may be particularly true for writers, not (just) because they possess an excessive supply of egotism, but be- cause as intellectuals it is their task to rationalize their world, and the only way to do that is to start with some assumptions about human beings' control over their destinies. What after all is fiction but the depiction of human heroes and heroines em- ploying their wit, skill, strength, and other resources to defeat antagonists and overcome adversity? What would become of our fiction if the protagonists' achievements were portrayed as nothing more than lucky?

As we know, the road to publication is mined with perils. It takes intelligence, determination, and fortitude to avoid or conquer them. Yet, in my experience, there is no guarantee that these virtues will prevail in the writing game. Indeed, there's no guarantee that the most important asset of all, talent, will emerge victorious, at least not without a little assistance

313

from good fortune. For while writing is certainly a solitary occupation, publishing is a social enterprise involving scores of critical processes performed by numerous individuals, many of whom feel considerably less enthusiasm for the product than the author does. And beyond the mechanics of publication and distribution are processes of a magnitude and complexity impossible to reckon, including trends and fads that are no more predictable than the course of a cyclone. Any attempt to grasp this leaves us wondering how any books at all ever manage to succeed with so many hostile factors militating against them. Indeed, though I have handled many successful books in my career, I can recall only a handful that behaved in a way that might be described as An Agent's Dream, that is, were textbook case histories of books that performed precisely the way they were supposed to if everybody did his or her job. For me, the perfect publishing experience is a unicorn, glimpsed in my fantasies but never captured.

There was the Vietnam War novel that I sold to the perfect editor at the perfect publisher, which went on to do a great job of publication, eliciting dream reviews and sensational sales. At every step of the way I rubbed my eyes with astonishment and kept wondering when something would go wrong. Fortunately, it was not to be. The book went on to become not just a best-seller, but a backlist staple that continues to earn solid royalties to this day.

I am of course happy to take my share of the credit for the success of this book, and I'm sure that that success was created in some measure by my enthusiasm, commitment, and effort. But, looking back, I realize that Lady Luck influenced that book's destiny far more than I did, for there were numerous moments when disaster could have struck but was averted as if the book were defended by an invisible shield. For example, some months before publication, the three principal editors who had acquired and sponsored the novel quit or were fired, leaving the book in danger of having no champion at the publisher to guide it through the hazards of publication. Providence intervened, however, in the form of a key executive in the sales department who happened to be a veteran of Vietnam and stepped into the role of protector. Similar threats arose to imperil the book after that, yet it seemed to be under a star. Perhaps the same star that brought it to me in the first place, for I have speculated on what fate might have befallen it had it been offered to an agent who didn't love it as much as I did, or if I had submitted it to a less suitable publisher.

In another instance, a writer submitted a police thriller to our agency. The format was awful: he had typed his book single-spaced on canary yellow paper, then bound the manuscript so tightly you needed a crowbar to read the left side of every page. In addition, the writer had not queried us before sending his book in, but simply submitted his big fat manuscript unsolicited. The book seemed to be begging for rejection. But the first page or two arrested the attention of the assistant who took it out of its mailer, and he showed it to me. I was predisposed to dislike it, particularly the single-spaced aspect, for an agent's eyes are his most precious tool and this manuscript would have triggered a migraine headache by the third chapter. But I too liked the first few pages. "If he wants to retype the whole damn thing double-spaced, I'll look at it," I grumbled at my young colleague. I figured it would be three months before I saw the book again, if ever.

It showed up on my desk two days later. I hadn't reckoned on word processors.

It turned out to be a marvelous read, and I sold it for quite a lot of money to a hardcover publisher, which sold it for twice that much to a reprinter. Foreign and movie deals followed in quick order. But I wonder what would have happened if my assistant hadn't persisted. The book may well never have seen the light of day.

If a book is the bearer of bad karma, even the most hardworking author, enthusiastic agent, and committed publisher may not be able to overcome what appear to be the machinations of evil spirits. Editors leave their companies, abandoning books at critical moments; publishers are sold or acquired, playing havoc with books making their way toward the light of day; competitive books pop up out of nowhere to steal the limelight from what was expected to be a surefire best-seller; production snafus create fatal delays, putting books in stores too late to sell when they were intended to; trends veer off in unexpected directions, leaving great books stranded on the caprices of popular taste.

We are not talking about bad publishing, or wrong decision making, or poor judgment. We're simply talking about fate, the things that can happen to books when all of the gods watching over them happen to be named Murphy.

A few years ago my agency handled a business book by one of America's most prominent moguls. It had everything going for it and I'd have bet the store that nothing could stand in the way of this baby hitting the best-seller list and staying there a good long time. Another baron of industry had brought out a book of his own a short while before my guy's, however. That man's name was Lee Iacocca, and his autobiography was nothing short of the biggest hardcover best-seller in publishing history, a book whose sales, heaven help the author, challenged those of the Bible itself. And although our book performed respectably by ordinary standards, it was utterly eclipsed by *Iacocca*.

You might think that bad luck can be warded off by the expenditure of a lot of money, by researching the competition, by taking every precaution to produce the book competently, position it shrewdly, promote it vigorously, and sell it enthusiastically. It just isn't so. Fickle Fortune's Finger taps any book, any author its whims designate. Even one superstar author, it was rumored, became upset when she learned her latest blockbuster was pitted in the same month against another author's latest blockbuster, threatening that guaranteed Number One best-seller position she had come to assume was her right. And who can blame her for making that assumption, considering the millions spent on acquiring and publishing her books? Yet, all that money couldn't control another publisher's schedule.

I've had similarly sad experiences with a few books. A beauty book by a leading figure in the cosmetics world should have had it made, with a committed publisher, a strong advertising and promotion campaign, the whole bit. But it was published at the tail end of a beauty book trend in which the laurels had all been awarded to the likes of Jane Fonda, Victoria Principal, and Adrienne Arpel. The buyers were just not there, and there was nothing anybody could do about it. In another instance, a publisher paid a ton of money for a medical book we were handling. A little while later, that publisher acquired another author whose popular books on medical subjects almost invariably went to the top of the best-seller lists. There was clearly a conflict of interest here, and when it became clear that my client's book was going to be on the losing end of that conflict, I protested and pulled his book from the publisher. It was obvious that the publisher was prepared to sacrifice all that money paid to my client in order to land an even bigger author.

And I remember the show business client of mine who had written a beautiful novel. After I sold it, the publisher invited him in to chat about promotion. At the meeting the author boasted he could furnish plugs from just about any celebrity they could name. The promotion people's eyes lit up. "Great!" they gasped. And, true to his word, he brought in a sheaf of star endorsements an inch thick. There was scarcely enough room in the ads to fit them all in.

And how did his book fare?

Don't ask.

It's one thing for a single book to flop because of bad luck. Most of us pick ourselves up, dismiss the experience philosophically, contemptuously, humorously, and get on with our lives. It's quite another matter when one's entire career comes to grief, when unforeseen calamities befall book after book, crushing the author under the burden of misfortune. We know that there are winners and losers in the writing game as there are in every other, but it is impossible to be philosophical or good humored when, over a stretch of time and a string of good books, everything goes wrong and goes wrong consistently. I know of more than one author who can identify with the one who has had seven or eight books published and on not a single one did the editor who'd acquired it remain at the company long enough to see it published.

And there is more than one soul staggering around shell-shocked after seeing his first book crushed by a corporate takeover, his second sucked into the maelstrom of its publisher's bankruptcy, a third shut out of the stores in the Christmas sales season because a production snafu delayed publication by two months; and a fourth, fifth, and sixth orphaned after their editors quit their jobs or got the sack. Fires and floods in the warehouse, presidential assassinations, newspaper strikes—you name it, it's befallen these unfortunate souls.

Literary agents exist to even the odds against malevolent providence. We cannot of course prevent those calamities, but we may be able to help our clients avoid them, or rescue them before it's too late. If I've heard a rumor that a publisher may be up for sale, I am certainly not going to submit anything there until the situation stabilizes. And, on a more routine level, we try to locate the editor who will do best by a book, to push for promotional campaigns, to make sure our clients' books are scheduled for the most appropriate season, to reintroduce books to editors who have replaced those who originally acquired the properties. In short, we can maneuver our authors into the best possible positions to take advantage of good luck and evade bad.

We are certainly not deities, however, and ourselves are dependent to a goodly degree on luck. Years ago I launched an author's career when I sold her book to an editor who was so compatible with her that it seemed he had been put on earth specifically to minister to her work. One December day, just before the holidays, she visited my office and presented me with a bottle of champagne. "This," she declared, "is for your brilliance in selecting the perfect editor for me." Modestly I lowered my eyes. How would she feel, I wondered, if she knew the truth: that on the day I'd sold her first novel, I had called six or eight editors I thought were more appropriate. They were all on vacation, ill, or too busy to come to the phone. The "perfect" editor I had so presciently selected had actually been way down toward the bottom of my list!

I decided not to tell my client. A magician never reveals his secrets, and besides, I like champagne.

I could tell countless more stories about agents who just happened to be in the right place at the right time. The point is simply that success isn't everything we crack it up to be. Good luck plays a tremendous part, and though the most successful business people are those who are best prepared to deal with fortunate coincidences, and who place themselves in the best position for lucky breaks to happen to them, nobody has the advantage over anybody else in making luck happen.

But it's a strange thing about luck. The lucky look back and see one or two incredibly fortunate accidents, godsends as it were. The unlucky look back and see a conspiracy of evil forces that seemed to stalk them deliberately and maliciously. And perhaps that is how those who have lost in this nasty game may console themselves. There are so many good writers who have not made it, talented and industrious people whose careers don't deserve to perish, who have done everything necessary to win, yet still they fail. Perhaps, instead of blaming themselves or immolating themselves in guilt, they can hold their heads up and say, "I had some hard luck."

CHAPTER 47

Endangered Species

We often refer to the publishing world as an environment, and recently, as I discussed with a colleague the state of the industry, I realized how apt the metaphor is. Why is it, I asked, that some types of literature flourish while others fade or perish? The answer seems to be that the healthiest genres spring out of the richest and least-spoiled breeding grounds.

Breeding grounds are not particularly glamorous places: marshy wetlands, dank rain forests, remote and dusty plains. Yet they produce some of the most vigorous and beautiful of earth's species. By the same token, the places where literature is incubated are often dark, humble, and homely, far from the chic world of blockbusters and spectacular seven-figure publishing deals. And most authors who achieve stardom do not spring there fully formed; they emerge only after a long, slow, and often painful gestation in that netherworld of penny-a-word pulps, esoteric magazines, or even pornography.

I entered the publishing field at a time when there were still many fecund habitats for authors to develop. By far the most important of these was the magazine field. Countless publications, ranging from avant-garde to highbrow to slick to pulpy, published fiction of every kind. Agents did not turn their noses up at short stories as most of them do today, and although commissions on them seldom made up a large part of an agent's income, they did make an agreeable contribution to the rent. There were ten or fifteen markets or more for any story taken on by an agent, so if you couldn't place it for big money with *Saturday Evening Post* or *Good Housekeeping*, you could hope to sell it eventually to the *Detroit Athletic Club News* or *Chatelaine* for $250 or $500.

Western, mystery, adventure, horror, science fiction, confession, romance, and other genre magazine abounded, offering writers a plethora of outlets for their budding talents. More sophisticated, "slick" magazines such as *Saturday Evening Post, Look, Redbook*, and *McCall's* devoted substantial space to fiction for men, women, and the general reader, and these publications commonly serialized novels. Somewhat elevated ones like *The New Yorker* and *Harper's* provided a haven to authors with literary ambitions, and there was an abundance of experimental and "little" magazines that could afford to pay their contributors only with subscriptions. Yet, a host of splendid authors apprenticed in such magazines, and the demise of those publications did incalculable damage to the development of new talent in subsequent years.

Another fertile hatchery for authors was paperback originals. In the 1950s and 1960s this was largely a male phenomenon, and it was a booming one. The markets for western, crime, science fiction, war, and action-adventure paperbacks were accessible to any starting writer with talent, persistence, and fast fingers. The rates paid for this material put a premium on speed and the skill to turn out publishable copy in a single draft.

One genre in particular could be likened to a kind of salmon spawning ground, and that was soft pornography or, as they were called then, sex novels. Sex novels were designed to string together the maximum number of sex scenes on the skimpiest thread of a story. Owing to obscenity laws that still carried some weight at that time, sex novels gingerly treaded a euphemism-strewn path between the Scylla of clinical anatomical terms and the Charybdis of vulgar ones.

At its peak in the early 1960s, the market for sex novels was insatiable, with some publishers turning out ten or twelve of them every month. The demand for writers was stupendous, and publishers generously rewarded any who could produce on a rigid assembly-line schedule. Some turned out three or four a month, and if a regular collapsed in the traces leaving his publisher with an open slot that month, one of his colleagues might find himself called upon to turn a book out over a weekend.

You would probably be shocked to learn the names of some of today's leading novelists who got their start in sex books, producing dozens and even hundreds of them under pseudonyms before ever creating anything on which they wanted to put their own names. When they did at length turn their hands to other kinds of fiction, however, it was with fully realized capabilities, thanks to the opportunity afforded them by that very lowly genre, pornography.

The most important incubator of all is the literary first novel. Only a very short time ago, most trade publishers believed it was their responsibility if not their duty to reinvest some of the profit from successful books in the work of new authors. It was assumed that the initial output of those authors would lose money or at best break even before rewarding its patrons with a profit and eventually a best-seller. At the time I was learning the book trade some twenty-five years ago, that attitude was still an important factor in the decision-making process at most hardcover publishers. But that was a time when a publisher could break even on a five thousand-copy sale, and a burgeoning paperback reprint market could actually make a profitable venture out of what we today call, opprobriously, a midlist book

Toward the end of the 1960s, a number of turbulent economic, cultural, and business trends placed these ecosystems in serious jeopardy. Many magazines got into trouble because both advertisers and subscribers were turning to television, and by the 1970s the market had been decimated. Those publications that survived cut back radically on fiction, conceding the field to television sitcoms, western series, cop shows, and other types of programming that did not call for deeper investments of time and imagination than reading did. Whatever fiction magazines did still demand was from established, popular authors. New writers found themselves on the losing end of a struggle to recapture the kind of access they had enjoyed in the previous decades. A star system was beginning to emerge, and it was not to be limited to the magazine field.

Another major upheaval was a sort of Ice Age that descended on the male paperback market in the 1970s as female readers (and, some say, female editors) created a boom in mass market paperback fiction for women that is still the dominant factor in original paperback publishing today. It started with gothic novels, which then gave way to formula historical and contemporary romance consumed by avid readers by the boxcar load.

Although many male writers tried to shift their skills to these genres, and some succeeded, paperback editors usually insisted on women writers for women's fiction on the grounds that men weren't sufficiently sensitive to the romantic emotions that stirred in the female bosom. Thus did a new and vast breeding ground open up on the publishing landscape, creating conditions for women writers very similar to those of what might be called the Golden Age of male paperbacks: a seemingly infinite base of readers, an assembly-line approach to formula storytelling, accessibility of editors, and a sellers' market for young talent.

The romance boom contained the seeds of its own recession as every paperback publisher jumped in and in due time glutted the market. Of late we have seen a softening of the women's paperback fiction category and the shutting down or curtailing of a number of struggling formula romance lines. The survivors of these cutbacks are a superb breed of women novelists who have advanced into leading positions in paperback, moved up to hardcover, or even broken out into serious mainstream endeavors. But with the tightening of the market comes a reduced demand for fresh female talent.

Once writers are driven from the market, it's very hard to get them back, and once again the comparison to a biosystem seems apposite, for when the population of certain species dwindles below a certain number, extinction becomes a foregone conclusion. It happened to an extent in the area of male-oriented fiction. During the 1970s, as women's fiction was rising to the fore, most of the male genres shrank to a fraction of what they once had been. Science fiction, mysteries, westerns, and male action-adventure did go on selling, but in sharply reduced quantities issued by secondary publishers like Pinnacle, Ace, Tower, and the then-fledgling Zebra. The larger and more powerful paperback houses, chasing after female readers, ignored the male. Except for a few stars like James Michener and John Jakes in historical, Stephen King in horror, Louis L'Amour in westerns, Robert Ludlum in international adventure, and a handful of science fiction greats, it was hard to discover who spoke for, or to, male readers. A lot of male writers turned to nonfiction; a lot more went and did something else for a living.

Male fiction was regarded as a minor industry throughout much of the 1970s until some recessionary economic trends forced the big paperback houses to take another look at it. They realized that the market was vaster than they'd thought, and these companies thus began male fiction lines or acquired publishers of male fiction. As a result, there was an upswing in that market during the 1980s that has lasted to this day. But a toll had been exacted. During the darker age of the seventies, a combination of poor management and intensified competition drove out of business the weaker paperback houses which, schlocky as they might have been, provided a great market for new writers.

Hardest hit of all have been the breeding grounds for serious fiction. A series of recessionary cycles over the past few decades forced publishers to concentrate more and more on immediate, frontlist successes. Those houses unable to keep up have been forced to make one of a number of unpleasant choices: merge with other publishers, be acquired by nonpublishing conglomerates, or abandon their traditional commitment to quality in favor of the instant best-seller. Whichever they chose, it meant the rejection of a fundamental principle, namely, that talent requires time to mature.

The rise to dominance of paperback publishers exacerbated the problem, because paperback is an even more frontlist kind of publishing than hardcover. Paperbacks that don't prove themselves in a week are usually doomed; they seldom are afforded the luxury of remaining in a store for months, available to browsers, the way hardcovers are (or used to be). The establishment of all-powerful chain stores with their emphasis on fast-moving best-sellers, and the elimination of publishers' slush piles as a source of new talent, have dumped more and more landfill into the breeding grounds. As we've seen, a great deal of the responsibility for discovering and nurturing new authors has fallen on the literary agents, but agents are not in a position to support authors with money, nor does their enthusiasm raise their clients' public recognition by one iota. All that agents can do is get an author's work onto an editor's desk; from that point on, the manuscript is at the mercy of a process that is essentially hostile to unperfected talent.

When we survey the current publishing scene we see that the healthiest markets are those that continue to tap the wellsprings of new talent, much the way that successful major league baseball teams draw from a deep farm system to replace aging stars. Science fiction, for example, thrives and will continue to thrive because of the abundance of magazines, the accessibility of editors, the frequent conventions around the country giving hopeful young authors exposure to their literary heroes and heroines, and slush piles that are still actively combed by editors for interesting work. Male action-adventure, romance, and westerns are also doing well because they still have something of a support system, even though it is no longer what it used to be. In the area of serious literature, *The New Yorker* is far and away the most significant incubator for exciting talent, which is why the recent change in editorial management sent such terrific tremors through the world of letters. *The New Yorker* is a landmark: Its integrity must be preserved at any cost.

As I was writing these words, it was announced that a takeover war was in progress for the assets of Harper and Row. The reason that would-be acquirers gave for coveting Harper is its rich backlist. A good backlist is a tremendous asset, as it generates steady income for a publisher without intensive investment of capital. But when you think about it, what is a backlist but a file drawer full of old contracts? Or, if we extend the metaphor of the environment one last time, we realize that a backlist is a sort of museum of natural history depicting the kind of world we had when the breeding grounds were turbulent with life. If we do not find ways to generate tomorrow's backlist, to reopen or restock the breeding grounds, we may well awaken one day to the literary equivalent of a silent spring.

CHAPTER 48

Editors: The New Disenfranchised

I've always liked editors, but I never felt sorry for them until the acquisition of Doubleday was announced.

Until then, whenever I heard that a publisher had been acquired by some sprawling conglomerate, or merged with another publisher, or had simply given up the ghost and shut its doors, my first thought had always been, This is bad for authors. The displacement, the disruption, the disarray caused by these corporate earthquakes have been nothing short of calamitous. The publishing landscape of the past twenty-five years is littered with ruined books beyond counting and haunted by the shades of authors whose careers have been maimed and prematurely terminated.

But in the tumultuous last week of September 1986, when deals were concluded for the acquisition of Doubleday and New American Library, my first thought was, How terrible this all must be for editors. I spoke to a great many editors after the deals were announced, and I can assure you that few were not anxious and disturbed if not downright scared. It has finally dawned on editors everywhere that there is no longer any such thing as job security at a publishing company. Doubleday in particular had symbolized, for as long as most publishing people could remember, bedrock stability, a fortress impervious to the corporate wars that left almost none of her sister-houses unaltered. If anything, Doubleday had bolstered its foundations some years ago with the acquisition of the Dell Publishing Company, a major paperback house. But now, the shadow of change has darkened the desks of everyone who works in publishing, and anxiety lurks in every corridor. "Every time my boss buzzes," one editor told me, "I say to myself, 'That's it. They're letting my department go.' " This constant knot in the stomach doesn't belong exclusively to editors, either. The threat exists for workers in every area of publishing: sales, marketing, accounting, publicity, art, bookkeeping.

That the deals were good for the buyers and sellers, few observers question, although there are some aspects that could tarnish the splendor of the prizes. Doubleday's book division had been losing money for some years, owing in good measure (in my opinion at least) to its failure to adjust to the revolutionary change in the nature of our business that has made the so-called hard-soft publishers the predominant beasts in the jungle. Indeed, one of the few divisions of Doubleday that was operating in the black, other than the New York Mets baseball team, was Delacorte Press, which always acquires hardcover and paperback rights together. Doubleday seldom if ever acquired books for its Dell paperback line. Nor did it bend in its rigid refusal to give authors a greater share of paperback reprint revenue than the traditional fifty-fifty split, something that other hardcover houses had yielded to in order to gain competitive parity when bidding for properties against hard-soft houses.

The German publishing group that acquired Doubleday also owns Bantam Books, which controls the largest share of the paperback market of any American publisher. The addition of Dell potentially eliminates one competitor from the already shrunken list of paperback firms, and swells Bantam's market share to a size that may one day attract the attention of Justice Department trustbusters. And as nice a plum as Delacorte may be, its hard-soft existence may eventually become redundant now that it is part of the same company that owns the Bantam hard-soft line. "Something's got to give," one Dell editor said to me. "I've got my resumes out. When the other shoe drops, I'll be ready."

If you can stand back and simply admire the deal, Viking-Penguin's acquisition of New American Library is an excellent one all around. A few years ago, Viking united with England's paperback giant Penguin in order to give both companies stronger hard-soft capability in the United States. But Penguin lacks

entry into the critical wholesale paperback market. And so New American Library, which had been bought by an investment group a few years back, was seen as a perfect place for Penguin to enter that market. And now Viking will be able to play hard-soft ball in the major leagues.

Job anxiety had infected the thinking of editors throughout the history of postwar publishing. But because many of you may be too young to have lived through the turmoil of acquisitions, mergers, overhaulings, phasings-out, reorganizations, disassemblies, and absorptions, or for those in the publishing business who are too close to daily affairs to step back and see the carnage through a panoramic lens, let me recite a partial roll call of companies that are no more, or are now just divisions or imprints of the companies that consumed them.

> Appleton-Century-Crofts (a division of Prentice-Hall)
> Prentice-Hall (acquired by Simon and Schuster)
> Simon and Schuster (a division of Gulf and Western)
> Atheneum (acquired by Charles Scribner)
> Charles Scribner (acquired by Macmillan)
> Atlantic Monthly Press (acquired by Little, Brown)
> Little, Brown (a division of Time Inc.)
> Avon Books (a division of the Hearst Corporation)
> William Morrow (a division of the Hearst Corporation)
> Arbor House (a division of the Hearst Corporation)
> Fawcett Books (an imprint of Ballantine Books)
> Ballantine Books (an imprint of Random House)
> Times Books (acquired by Random House)
> Pantheon Press (a division of Random House)
> Alfred A. Knopf (a division of Random House)
> Random House (acquired from RCA by the Newhouse organization)
> Bantam Books (acquired by the Bertelsmann Group)
> Doubleday (acquired by the Bertelsmann Group)
> Dell Books (a division of Doubleday)
> Basic Books (a division of Harper and Row)
> Crowell (a division of Harper and Row)
> Abelard-Schuman (a division of Harper and Row)
> Playboy Press (acquired by Berkley Books)
> Ace Books (acquired by Grosset and Dunlap)

Grosset and Dunlap (acquired by Berkley Books)
Berkley Books (acquired by G. P. Putnam's)
G. P. Putnam's (acquired by MCA)
Pyramid Books (acquired by Harcourt Brace, renamed Jove)
Jove (acquired by Berkley)
Coward-McCann-Geoghegan (acquired by Putnam, then dissolved)
Dial Press (acquired by Dell, sold to Dutton)
Dutton (acquired by Elsevier, sold to JSD, sold to NAL)
NAL (sold by Times-Mirror to Odyssey Group, resold to Viking)
Viking (merged with Penguin Books)
Harper and Row (acquired by Collins, a division of News-America, owned by Rupert Murdoch)
Rawson, Wade (a division of Macmillan)
Silhouette Books (acquired by Harlequin)
Popular Library (acquired by Warner)
Hill and Wang (a division of Farrar, Straus, and Giroux)
Lippincott (a division of Harper and Row)
Congdon and Weed (acquired by Contemporary Books)

This partial list is drawn from a thumb-through of *Literary Market Place,* the publishing industry's directory, and I could certainly go on and on. Taken as a whole, this list represents a pattern of seismic instability so severe that if I were an editor today I would strap myself into my chair just to get some work done.

Publishing is a social enterprise that calls for a large degree of organization, hierarchy, and interdependency, and so by the very nature of what they do, editors are corporate creatures. It stands to reason, then, that the more attention an editor must devote to matters corporate instead of editorial, the weaker will be his or her attachment to books and authors. The emergence of the super-publisher in our century, a corporate entity whose goals only incidentally have anything to do with the quality of literature and the well-being of authors, has impinged to a greater and greater extent on the time, energy, thought, and care that editors are able to give over to books and those who write them, and as you will infer from the list above, the last couple of decades have raised the level of distraction to critical mass.

The most obvious, as well as detrimental, manifestation of this shift of editors' attention is job-hopping. As their love of books and authors is battered by all the firings and hirings, reorganizations, streamlinings, office politics, shuffling of responsibilities, and the buying and selling of the companies they work for, editors feel fewer compunctions about accepting job offers from other publishers. It's hard to feel company loyalty when corporate logos change with the frequency of automobile styles. Low wages have always prevailed in the editorial profession, but higher pay is not in itself a compelling lure for an editor contemplating a move to another company, unless it is coupled with a promise of greater job satisfaction. But if an editor is not getting such satisfaction, he's going to think a lot about his salary. It behooves us to think about how a fifteen thousand dollar a year editor must feel when he listens to the complaints of authors making many times that amount. "Few of my authors make less money than I do," an editor told me, "and none makes less than my assistant."

The vicious cycle is accelerated as more and more editors, looking out for number one, jump to other publishers or leave publishing altogether for more lucrative, satisfying, and stable jobs. Even those remaining in publishing find themselves burdened with corporate responsibilities that take them away from what they love most dearly to do, acquire and edit books. Thus the industry eventually becomes bereft of dedicated editors, and the vacuum is too often filled by people who are more adept at playing corporate games than at developing writers.

In turn, such people place more and more emphasis on buying winners instead of breeding them: acquisition without cultivation. Less and less attention is paid to developing writers; instead, everyone asks how much it will cost to buy and sell them. The publisher that proves itself most capable of acquiring will become the most successful. But the price is dear: When authors are deprived of the time to grow, creativity will be snuffed out. It's as true of literature as it is of agriculture or forestry.

The cycle spins yet faster and higher as other publishers try to emulate the successful ones. Abandoning the philosophy, the tradition, the taste and judgment, and the people that got them where they were, these houses join the chase to try to capture frontlist hits. Even when they snag them, however, they lose a little bit more of their character if not their soul.

The soul of a publishing company is its editors, and when a publishing company alters its fundamental attitudes about books and authors, the sensibilities of its editors must of necessity change as well. With promotions and increased corporate responsibilities comes loss of contact with the sacred places in an author's heart where literature is born.

The rest of the editorial staff, as well as the staffs of the other departments that fuel publishing companies, carry on as best they can in the midst of this furious turbulence, but they do so in a constant state of apprehension. How difficult it must be to concentrate, to plan, to pay attention to the work at hand, when upheaval is only one announcement (or even one rumor) away.

Editors today have more in common with authors than they do with the publishing companies that employ them. Both are disenfranchised, both have become fodder for the relentless march of Takeover.

CHAPTER 49

Must Youth Be Served?

Owing to some caprice of providence, I happen to have been born on the very same day and in the very same year as Charles Brown, publisher of *Locus,* the trade magazine of the science fiction field, in which most of the material in this book first appeared. Recently, as he and I celebrated one of those depressing landmark birthdays with a zero suffix, I muttered some cliches, as old men are wont to do, about how baseball players and policemen suddenly seemed to be mere children and not the imposing adults that we once looked up to. Brown's response was, "Editors, too."

He was right. I don't know whether it's statistically verifiable, but the trade book business *appears*, at least, to have become populated largely by the young, many of whom serve in critically important executive positions. Despite recent expressions of concern in trade journals about the industry's failure to attract the young, I haven't noticed any diminution of college graduates flowing into publishing, and I'm not terribly worried about it. What I am terribly worried about is the flow of senior editors and executives and other mature publishing personnel out of the business as a result of mergers, takeovers, reorganizations, conglomeratizations, and internationalizations. There are few more disturbing manifestations of this turbulent era of consolidation than the departures from our scene of older men and women who have been fired, forced out, or made unwelcome by management. Luckily, I am my own boss, and my prospects for tenure are therefore excellent. But I'm thinking about my many friends in the industry who are not—or were not—as fortunate, and I would like to speak up about the potentially detrimental effects of this trend. I'm not just worried about decent people losing jobs, but about the threat to the publishing business and the very quality of our literature itself.

Publishing has always been attractive to youth. It is not a rigidly organized or forbiddingly hierarchical industry. It has no effective union on the editorial level, no demanding apprenticeships, and the windows of opportunity at the entry and junior levels are pretty much wide open, requiring only a reasonable degree of literacy and office skills. Tasks, at least on the editorial side of things, are not strictly defined, so anyone with a normal measure of ambition and enthusiasm can learn a variety of disciplines, find the right niche, advance to a middle or even senior editorial level in a matter of a few years. The pay is not great, but the person who sticks with it will find himself or herself in a position of responsibility if not authority while still young. Publishing offers young people a chance to apply their ideals to the creation and dissemination of literature. And even after many of those ideals have perished in the crucible of business reality, there remain some compelling attractions for young people: Publishing is glamorous, and it's fun.

Publishers like to employ the young, too. They like their enthusiasm and energy, their sensitivity to new trends and fresh ideas. And it doesn't hurt that young people are a source of relatively cheap labor.

Unlike what happens to workers in many other types of business and industry, the maturation of publishing people is seldom attended by stagnation or decline of vigor, skill, or initiative. Quite the opposite. As they get older, they usually become wiser and more skillful, and their experience becomes a significant factor in the formulation of critical publishing decisions.

One way to define experience is efficiency of performance. A task that takes hours or days or weeks for an inexperienced person to perform may be achieved in a fraction of the time by someone who has been there often and understands the procedures without having to invest a lot of energy into them. In some undertakings, like the appreciation of literature, the task becomes easier and easier with experience. A senior editor told me, "About once a month a young editor comes running into my office having 'discovered' a fresh story, and I have to tell him that it didn't work in 1955, it didn't work in 1966, it didn't work in 1974, and it didn't work in 1981, and I don't think it's going to work in 1988, either."

From what I have learned about the history of our industry, the founders of the great publishing companies started their careers at very tender ages, but worked far into their twilight years with no diminishment of intellectual potency. E. P. Dutton died in the traces at the age of ninety-two after seventy-one years in business life. Moses Dodd died at eighty-six, Henry Houghton at seventy-two, James Harper at seventy-four, and so on, and their children and grandchildren also lived to relatively ripe ages while extending the power and glory of their predecessors' companies until they became the institutions of today. Of course, living to ripe old age is not a virtue in itself, but these founders did assemble teams that ran their firms for long, long stretches of time, establishing a tradition of staff continuity that gave each firm a distinct identity. Today, among the many publishers I deal with, I've discovered that those whose staffs have worked together for the longest time are often the most efficient, effective, and responsive to the needs of authors. But such teams are becoming harder and harder to find.

The takeover trends of the last few decades have reversed the industry's reverence for its elder citizens. Coming from orientations very far afield from the publishing business, the acquirers of publishing houses see nothing untoward about mandatory retirement at fixed ages. Examining ways to reduce the overhead of acquired or merged companies, their eyes focus all too quickly on the relatively higher salaries of editors with seniority. Thus, when the axe falls, it falls first on older employees, with little regard for past performance, ability, experience, or any of the other intangible and unquantifiable values such as wisdom and dignity that enhance the life of a publishing house, inspire young editors, and make authors feel at home.

Perhaps the worst by-product of all is the loss of corporate memory that accompanies the dismissal of senior staff members of publishing companies. No matter how much data is storable in computer memories today, the knowledge of how to do things, of what works and what doesn't, of house history and tradition, of where skeletons are buried and dirty linen stored—all this knowledge and more resides in the hearts and hands, minds and souls of employees who have worked for publishers for a long time. From the smallest details of spelling and grammatical usage to the broadest applications of insight into human nature, the memories of mature employees provide untold aid to those who would otherwise have to grope in the dark, often in vain, for the right word, the right information, the right way.

The shunting aside of such people can deal a serious blow to a company's memory the way a blow to an individual's head can cause amnesia. One can reconstruct events from files (if they are still accessible, complete, or accurate), but that can take considerable time, Even then, the recollections that are so vital in formulating a completely textured picture of what happened five or ten years ago cannot ever be conjured out of dead files.

And if, as has been widely asserted, there has been over the last few decades a decline in line-editing and proofreading skills, resulting in an increase in the number of poorly edited books, it may well be attributable to the loss of mature editors and the tradition of professional pride they brought to their work. "I would become physically sick to discover an overlooked typo or grammatical gaffe in a book for which I was responsible," I was told by one retired editor. She went on to say, "Editors today are almost all hired to acquire books, not to edit them. And the books show it. The new breed of editors is undisciplined and uneducated."

The same may be said of the decline in the manufacturing arts and skills; the memory and knowledge of how books are made, and made sturdily and beautifully, dies a little bit more with every older publishing person who leaves the field. Diana Klemins, a senior editor at Doubleday, stated it succinctly when she told me, "They just don't treat books like newborn babies anymore."

Even more tragically, this disregard for the value and values of older people may actually be affecting the kind and quality of literature published today. The impatience that is usually associated with youth corresponds to the impatience of today's publishers to make quick profits as opposed to the more time-consuming nurturing of talent until it develops into a force capable of producing work of lasting significance and loveliness.

The emphasis on youth parallels the emphasis on frontlist publishing, on "new product," on best-sellers. The young editor of today has been raised in an environment dominated by movies, television, and similar technologies whose impact is ephemeral. He or she may therefore be more favorably disposed toward books that offer the quick jolt rather than the delicious lingering immersion into a work of complexity and subtlety, one that challenges the intellect and demands an investment of time. I have seen this vividly illustrated, for example, in the changing nature of humor books, which have shifted from full-length, elegant satires to highly visual quickies, very much akin to comic books or television cartoons.

The seemingly perpetual state of corporate upheaval that characterizes modern publishing has all but fatally undermined, the virtue of company loyalty among editors, just as it has among authors and agents. This means that the editor who acquires a book will not necessarily be with the same company when that book is published. The result is a widespread attitude that publishers exist to publish *books* rather than authors, that authors are only as good as their most recent success or failure, and that a cumulative body of good work does not count for as much as the single breakthrough blockbuster.

This attitude is definitely held by many young editors, who almost cannot comprehend the idea of longevity in an era of musical editorial chairs and even musical publishing companies. Indeed, you don't have to be a toothless crone to realize the extent to which our business has been vanquished by a children's army. One editor complained to me, "My God, I'm thirty-one, my boss is thirty-four, and he's responsible to a twenty-eight-year-old corporate officer. I've been here eighteen months and no one's been here longer. It's kind of scary!"

The accelerated superannuation of editors threatens to destroy the delicate tradition of honesty, integrity, pride, and manners that has always characterized the publishing profession. And perhaps it is this legacy above all that senior publishing people stand to bestow on the younger generation. While there is much to be said for youth's perpetual reassessment of tradition, the maintenance of the old ways still lies at the heart of the relationship between publisher and author.

CHAPTER 50

Down on the Levy

As if it weren't hard enough for writers to make a living, another menace has been growing, subtly and insidiously, to rob them of the fruits of their labors. I'm referring to the taxes imposed on money paid to American authors by foreign publishers. The time has come to blow the whistle on foreign governments that are taking shameless advantage of our authors to the tune of 10, 20, or 30 percent or more of the money to which they are entitled. And lest American publishers feel that this isn't their problem, let me stress at the outset that they are every bit as much victims as are the authors, for the very same imposts laid on American authors are exacted on money going to American publishers.

The problem has its origins in the reciprocal arrangements most western nations have concerning the imposition of income taxes. To put it simply, if you are an American citizen or company paying United States income taxes, then you are not required to pay taxes to a foreign government on income you earn from the licensing of foreign rights to your literary properties. Until not long ago, many foreign governments did not even bother to ascertain whether the American authors receiving money from publishers in those countries were American citizens. Those that did try to verify citizenship required a minimum of paperwork, usually the signing of an affidavit before a notary or a declaration by the Internal Revenue Service that the author was a tax-paying United States citizen or resident.

In the last few years, however, a number of foreign governments have come to view book deals as a potentially lucrative source of revenue, and have levied taxes on money going to American authors and publishers that are not recoverable. And those governments that do eventually release or refund withheld taxes have made the requirements so complex and time-consuming that months, and sometimes a year or more, may pass before the author gets relief.

I am not talking about countries like Turkey or Bulgaria or Hungary where a certain degree of civil service obstructionism is to be expected. I'm talking about such countries as France, Germany, and Spain. I'm talking in particular about England, which has not given Americans tax headaches of this size since the Stamp Act of 1765.

With the assistance of Elizabeth Waxse, director of my agency's foreign rights department, I've assembled a country by country rundown of the tax situation as it affects American authors and publishers.

GERMANY: Although the German government has not yet gotten tough about taxes, authors are strongly advised to fill out a form furnishing their Social Security number and the address of their local IRS office. Payments owing to American authors could be held up if this information is not provided.

SPAIN: There is no exemption from double taxation in Spain, which imposes a nonrefundable 20 percent tax on advances and royalties paid to American authors and publishers.

FRANCE: American authors and publishers must file an exemption form to avoid paying a 33 percent tax on advances and royalties paid on licenses of literary material to French publishers. Unlike some other governments that require only a one-time procedure, French authorities require you to refile for exemption *every year*!

ITALY: Italy's setup is similar to that of France, except that the tax is 21 percent instead of 33 percent. Authors and publishers anticipating revenue in any given year must file an exemption form even though they originally filed one for that literary property the year before, or two or three or four years ago.

JAPAN: The Japanese impose a 20 percent tax on money earmarked for American authors and publishers, but Japanese publishers apparently file a document that automatically cuts the 20 percent tax in half. Nevertheless, a 10 percent tax is imposed on money going to American authors and publishers, and it is not refundable.

ENGLAND: It may come as a surprise to readers familiar with the dreadful bureaucracies of some European and Asian nations, but at this writing the prize for red tape unquestionably goes to the English government. The procedure for exempting American payees from English tax has always been tedious, but recently the country's Inland Revenue Bureau added some wrinkles that lead one to wonder whether it is deliberately making it hard for authors to get their money, in order to earn for the Exchequer interest on withheld taxes.

In order for us to help a client avoid a 29 percent tax on money owed him by a British publisher, we have to go through the following procedure:

1. As soon as we make a deal for the author, we fill out a British tax exemption form detailing the names and addresses of the British publisher and agent, the date of the contract, the information about the advance and royalty rate. We then mail the form to the author.

2. The author fills in name and address and answers nine questions ascertaining citizenship, residency, travel history, business activities, etc., signs a declaration, and mails the form to a regional Internal Revenue Service center. The author must follow this procedure for every British publisher to whom he sells a book. The exemption is good for five years.

3. At the IRS center, an official certifies that "the last United States tax return filed by the claimant was made as a citizen or resident of the United States." The IRS official is then supposed to mail the certified form to England's Inspector of Foreign Dividends (a Branch of Inland Revenue), and to send a notification to the author that certification is on its way to England. Whether the certification is airmailed or sent in the cargo hold of a tramp steamer, I am not sure. Given the amount of time it will take for the Inspector of Foreign Dividends to process the certification, it really doesn't make that much difference.

4. When the Inspector of Foreign Dividends receives the

certification from the IRS, it processes the form and issues the author or his British agent a tax exemption number. If the Inspector receives your certification in the spring, the trees will probably be bare by the time you are notified that your tax exemption has come through. If your British publisher pays the advance after the tax exemption number has been issued, you will not have any tax withheld from your advance. If, however, the tax exemption has *not* come through at the time the publisher pays the advance, the 29 percent tax must be withheld and remitted to the Inland Revenue Bureau. You must then fill out another form when your advance does finally arrive, petitioning the Inland Revenue people to release the tax to you.

At length—and I mean *Length*—Inland Revenue will release your money. In pounds sterling, requiring you to put the check (or, more accurately, cheque) through for collection at your American bank and wait several more months for the funds to clear, a process usually attended by an exorbitant charge for the conversion of foreign currency.

This, then, is what you have to go through in England. It makes me wonder why we are exporting our technology, giving them our McDonald's franchises, and shielding them beneath our nuclear umbrella.

Besides the immense nuisance of trying to recover one's own money, the foreign tax problem has imposed unnecessary strains between authors and their publishers or agents, whom they accuse or suspect of keeping their money or being too casual about collecting it. Agents have also been placed in a quandary over the proper deduction of commissions on taxed foreign remittances. Should an agency base its commission on the $1,000 deal it made in Japan for its client? Or on the $900 it actually collected after deduction of the Japanese tax? Should it take its commission off the £5,000 a British publisher remitted for a client's book, even though 29 percent of that money was withheld pending certification of the author's tax exemption application? Or should the agency commission only the 71 percent collected, then wait for the rest of its commission until the withheld tax is released? Each agency approaches the problem differently, but one thing is clear: Either the agency will lose money, or it will lose good will, over a dilemma that is not of its own making.

Nobody to my knowledge has, until now, examined the issue of foreign taxes or revealed how extensive it is. But you can see that with up to one-third of the sums owing to American authors and publishers being seized or held hostage to the vagaries of foreign bureaucracies, it is high time for all the organizations representing American authors, agents, and publishers to raise their voices in protest.

Either that or give Americans a voice in those foreign governments. It would do well for us to remind them that No Taxation Without Representation is a cornerstone of American democracy. We fought a war over it. And we won.

Section Seven

***

Let's Work It Out

CHAPTER 51

✦ ✦

The Two Worlds of Literature

About once a decade some member of the intelligentsia launches an attack on one literary genre or another, setting off vitriolic debate about the legitimacy of popular fiction. Perhaps the most famous of these outbursts was critic Edmund Wilson's assault on mystery literature, "Who Cares Who Killed Roger Ackroyd?" In October 1985, the conflict fulminated again with a particularly nasty broadside aimed at science fiction and published in *Harper's* magazine. The writer termed the genre "detritus" and "the domain of hobbyists and hacks," and argued that "science fiction has become a dead zone useful for dumping space travel, extraterrestrials, weird inventions, time warps, extrasensory perception, biological mutations, the morals of intelligent machines and anything else that would be of genuine scientific interest were it not fictional."

This sally provoked a firestorm of retaliatory letters from practitioners of the genre, and, as far as I am concerned, these consigned the essay to the garbage heap it so aptly deserved. My own revenge is to invoke journalistic privilege by declining to utter here the name of the perpetrator. But the episode did stimulate some thoughts about the age-old war between the intellectual establishment and the world of popular literature, and I would like to express them.

When I went into the publishing business after graduating from college, I discovered a literary culture so vastly different from the ones I had studied that I could scarcely find any common ground between them. This world was populated by romance, science fiction and fantasy, and male action-adventure

345

writers, by pulpsters, pornographers, and countless others who earn their living producing genre books.

Since then I have become a citizen of that world, both as a writer and as a literary agent representing other writers of category fiction. I have come to know and respect, to admire and even love this world and its denizens and have had the privilege of attending the birth of some works that have come to be regarded as masterpieces of their genres. During this period of twenty-five years, I have become increasingly concerned about how little is known about this world by the writers and critics who dominate the world of serious literature. And I've concluded that we are all a little poorer for these gaps in awareness, appreciation, and communication.

The belletristic establishment regards the world of popular literature as a subculture, but one could seriously argue that it is really the other way around. Very few "serious" writers make enough money from their writing to support themselves without having to moonlight. Their audiences are often modest in size and elitist in taste. Their work is frequently inaccessible, intellectual, experimental, and sometimes incomprehensible. Literary authors are often isolated from their fellow writers both physically and artistically, so that they have little sense of community or opportunities for intellectual cross-pollination.

Now look at the world of genre literature. Its purveyors are professional authors most of whom earn a comfortable living and many of whom earn a substantial one, all without having to rely on nonwriting jobs to supplement their incomes. These authors reach a wide audience: Because many write original paperbacks, they can count on a minimum readership numbering in the hundreds of thousands and even millions. Their prose style and craftsmanship range from competent (they must at least be competent to sell their work to publishers) to superb; I will stake my career on the assertion that the craftsmanship and prose to be found in the best genre books matches or exceeds that found in the work of many so-called literary stars.

Professional writers enjoy a strong sense of cohesiveness and mutual support that is lacking in the world of belles-lettres. Professional science fiction, western, romance, and mystery writers belong to guildlike organizations that publish newsletters, hold conventions, and lobby for improvement of terms and conditions for their constituent authors. Taken altogether, these factors suggest that the life of the professional writer is far better integrated into the social fabric than that of the literary author. Genre writers might be likened to the guild artisans of medieval times, with the exception that the medieval craftsmen had the respect of their peers and patrons and were completely integrated into the community.

I have frequently pondered what it is that separates these two worlds of literary endeavor, and can think of a number of elements. One is ideas. The world of serious literature stresses the primacy of ideas, and the format of serious literature is designed to express those ideas. Another critical element is viewpoint: the serious author's viewpoint, or vision, is what makes those ideas fresh and special. And then there is style, the unique garb in which the author's ideas are dressed. The most interesting authors are able to identify themselves after a page or two because of what they have to say and how they say it. All too often, however, that format is not accessible to the mass reader because it doesn't follow the universal verities that, as Aristotle contended, humankind supposedly responds to. It is sometimes remote, dislocated, overly stylized, tedious, or just plain badly constructed and expressed. But the author, and presumably his audience, doesn't necessarily care as long as the essential idea is conveyed in a stimulating way.

Few professional authors approach their work this way; not, at least, if they want to stay in business. In the value system of the professional author the most important element is story, for stories are what pros are paid to write, and the ones who are paid the most are those who write the best stories and write stories best. Ideas may be articulated, certainly, but only insofar as they help delineate the viewpoint of the characters themselves. The professional author never allows his own ideas or viewpoint to override those of the characters who people his books, and the idea of calling attention to himself through unique stylistic techniques is totally alien to him. Indeed, if a professional novelist slows the pace of his book to express some personal viewpoint, or distracts the reader's involvement with his story by employing stylistic gimmicks, he can expect his editor to come down very hard on the offending passage with a blue pencil. Totally unlike serious literature, it is often impossible, upon reading a popular novel, to guess who the author is, so well disguised is he or she behind the excellence of the tale itself. And that is the way that they, their publishers, and their readers, like it.

The lives of professional genre writers differ in many significant ways from those of their more literary brothers and sisters, and indeed from the romantic image so many people have of the way writers are supposed to live. They are, for example, extremely businesslike, or at least extremely concerned with the business of writing. They study the provisions of their publishing contracts carefully and actively consult with their agents in the negotiating dialogues with publishers. They know the market value of their work before they sell it, sometimes within $500 or $1,000, and in fact most of them sell their work before they write it, lining up contracts (often for more than one book at a time) in advance. They approach the work at hand in a businesslike fashion as well. Because genre book lines have specific word-length requirements to fit them into the publishers' rigid price and marketing structures, genre writers have to design their manuscripts to those lengths and to pace the development and dramatic flow of their books so that all is resolved within 60,000, 75,000, or 100,000 words.

Which leads us to another quality of the professional writer: discipline. Inspiration as it is commonly understood plays little part in the life of the genre author, for, as we have seen, ideas are subordinate to story in his value system. Having selected a milieu or location, outlined a story, and sketched the cast of characters, the writer then tackles the job the way a skilled carpenter might approach the building of a piece of furniture, day by day, piece by piece. Of paramount importance is the outline. The synopses of genre books are often highly detailed and broken down chapter by chapter or even scene by scene, so that every day, when the writer sits down at his desk, he knows precisely what work is cut out for him. It is here, in the daily task of writing the book itself, that inspiration plays a role. As the author follows his outline, the nuances of character, the details of time and place, the fine points of story and complica-

tions of plot flow endlessly onto the page from a source that is wondrous and mystifying. Characters take on lives and wills of their own, struggling with the author for control of the work (and sometimes, to his astonishment, winning). This day-to-day grind with its little pleasures, epiphanies, and triumphs may not be as romantic as the Big Bang variety of inspiration we usually associate with art, but it does enable professional writers to get their work done no matter how ill, rotten, depressed, exhausted, or bereft of spirit they may feel on any given day: "You turn it on," they will tell you, "and out it comes." Writer's block is therefore seldom a problem for professional authors, and besides, it's a luxury they cannot afford.

These writers know pretty much to the word how much they can write daily before growing fatigued: two thousand words, say, or twenty manuscript pages, or three chapters, whatever it may be, of work that is consistently good, often good enough to be acceptable in a single draft. They can therefore predict almost to the day when they will be turning their manuscripts in to their publishers. This is critically important both from an author's own viewpoint—so that he can project his income flow—and from the publisher's, for the firm must be able to count on reliable production in order to schedule books far in advance with relative confidence. Because covers and monthly catalogues are produced by paperback publishers before manuscripts are actually in hand and salespeople solicit orders months before publication, the failure of an author to deliver a book on schedule is a nightmare that haunts paperback editors. Reliability therefore becomes the prime virtue of professional writers.

Unlike so many literary authors, professional writers are intensely attuned to the demands of the literary marketplace, because their lives and livings depend on its fluctuations. Genres go in and out of style, and heaven help the author who doesn't adapt to a trend. As I write, science fiction is booming, westerns are holding steady, horror is on an up cycle, mysteries are making a strong comeback, and the market for formula romances is soft. Authors working in these fields are expected to know about these cycles, indeed to know about nuances within the cycles: that within the science fiction genre, fantasy is doing well except for the subspecies known as sword-and-sorcery; that

in the romance genre historicals are still sought after, romantic mystery is in demand, and sexy contemporaries are still salable.

Like professionals in other fields of endeavor, professional writers exchange information with each other about the state of their fields. They belong to organizations devoted specifically to their genres, such as the Science Fiction Writers of America, Mystery Writers of America, Western Writers of America, and Romance Writers of America. These organizations regularly publish newsletters profiling leading writers in their fields, offering market reports about which publishers are buying what material, how much they're paying, and whom to contact. Annual national conventions (and frequent regional ones as well) are held; there, organization members exchange information, conduct seminars, meet agents and editors, and honor their own for achievements in various categories. These meetings are usually well attended by representatives of the publishing industry and offer writers and editors an opportunity to conduct business on a less formal basis than is customary.

While I realize I've painted a black and white picture, discussions I've had with countless numbers of writers in all fields strongly suggest that the polarity of admiration and emulation runs from genre writers to mainstream ones but not vice versa. Oh, from time to time a mainstream author will confess a secret passion for genre fiction that can be likened to a craving for junk food; and on occasion a mainstream author will cross over into genre fiction by writing a science fiction or mystery novel, a sort of literary equivalent of slumming. But these are exceptions that play up the rule that most literary authors don't feel genre writers have anything to say to them. That this is arrant snobbery goes without saying. I also happen to feel it is bad thinking.

The time has come for serious writers to pay far more attention to their genre colleagues than they have done up to now. The increasingly monolithic publishing industry now concentrates such power that the livelihoods and freedom of expression of writers of every kind are seriously threatened. As publishers focus more intently each year on producing blockbuster best-sellers to carry their bottom lines, the time and space in which writers can develop shrinks, meaning they are

being forced to mature far too early. As the spawning grounds for writers get squeezed harder and harder by economic exigencies, the pressure on tenderly budding talents to turn out commercial successes becomes more and more intense. This disease has spread from giant bookstore chains to publishing conglomerates and has now infected the thinking of authors of every stripe, who feel their only choices are to hit the pot of gold on the first shot, or become computer programmers or insurance salesmen. When I entered the publishing business in 1959, a writer could still cherish—and achieve—the fantasy of a quiet life of literary accomplishment, a life in which one could be content with a modest living and the admiration of a small but dedicated audience. Today, this notion is so laughably out of date that I cannot imagine anyone seriously harboring it. More to the point is that if anybody did, it would be impossible to achieve it. And I believe there is worse ahead: As the conglomeratization of the publishing industry continues, it is possible that literature will no longer be a place in which writers achieve any dreams at all save that of getting rich writing stuff they don't give a damn about. If this vision seems excessively dark, you have only to listen to the complaints of television writers in order to foresee the future.

It is vital for the writing establishment to realize that literature is far more than a ladder with junk at the bottom and art at the top. Rather, it is an ecosystem in which the esoteric and the popular commingle, fertilize one another, and interdepend. Principally, if it were not for the immense revenues generated by science fiction, romance, male action-adventure, and other types of popular fiction at which so many literary authors and critics look down their noses, there would be no money for publishers to risk on first novels, experimental fiction, and other types of serious but commercially marginal literary enterprises. Furthermore, from the aspect of the writing craft itself, there are many extremely important lessons for literati to learn from their genre comrades in arms, if only the former would take the trouble to study them. Although serious writers tend to reject formula plotting, for instance, they sooner or later realize that if they wish to reach any kind of audience at all, they will have to construct at least a minimum of formula skeleton for their works. When they do realize it, they have but to visit the popular-literature departments of their local bookstores to discover a trove of skillfully fashioned works to teach them about creating sympathetic heroes and heroines, daunting conflicts and antagonists, masterful pacing, and the building of dramatic tension to a thrilling climax and a satisfying ending.

And there is more: pride and professionalism, skill and discipline, reliability, attention to the business aspects of the writer's trade, a healthy respect for publishers and for the vast audiences that publishers speak for—these are among the lessons waiting to be learned by those on the other side of the gulf that separates the two worlds. Above all, serious writers stand to discover that they by no means have a monopoly on integrity. And because the integrity of all writers is now in jeopardy, it is incumbent on those of both worlds to talk and listen to each other, to read each other, and, above all, to respect each other.

CHAPTER 52

✦ ✦

Toward Reform

The publishing industry is critically ailing, and no one, from the creator of the written word to the consumer, is untouched. The signs are everywhere, some statistically demonstrable, others less tangible but still manifest to anyone who has been in the business long enough to watch it evolve. Some of the more commonly voiced ones are:

- The conglomeratization of trade and paperback book publishing
- The bureaucratization of editorial decision-making
- The "blockbuster mentality" and the increased dependence of publishers on big-name authors
- The insecurity and instability caused by the buying and selling of publishing companies
- The growth of bookstore chains, with their emphasis on current best-sellers
- The narrowing of publishers' profit margins
- The high prices of both hardcover and paperback books
- The diminution of new and experimental literature
- The soaring rate of books returned unsold to publishers
- The drop in advances and royalties paid to most authors
- The increasing delays on settlement of advances and royalties with authors
- The decline of professional standards of line editing
- The failure of publishing to keep dedicated editors
- The influx of business administrators into publishing, and their influence on editorial policies

• The assertion by authors and agents that publishers are cheating them out of royalties

Obviously, there is no single comprehensive explanation of what has gone wrong, nor any all-embracing solution. Still, it is surprising that authors, agents, publishers, booksellers, and other book people, highly intelligent individuals all, should continue applying patches and poultices to the symptoms when it is clear that the dimensions of the problem call for a thorough reevaluation of the way things are done in the publishing industry.

Although I would not be so vain as to suggest I have a panacea, I would like to focus on what I feel is the essence of the matter: the way books are merchandised. And I will be so bold as to propose a plan for restoring health to the industry. It is a radical plan that calls for a new way of looking at how we do business and for cooperation among all the elements of the book community, from authors to booksellers. Whether my observations are on the mark or not, the issues they touch on are of tremendous importance and urgency to everyone in the publishing community, and like it or not we will have to address them if that community and its magnificent tradition are to be preserved.

Book publishing may be big business in some ways, but its system of distribution is a ridiculously antiquated one. Unlike most other forms of manufacturing, the product, books, is sold on consignment. That is to say, the books are in effect loaned to wholesalers and retailers, and though they do pay publishers for their merchandise, they can get their money back (or at least credit) if the consumers don't buy the books. At best this system is grossly inefficient, wasteful, costly, and risky. In its worst manifestations, however, it is pernicious and very close to fraudulent. Unsold books, under a consignment system, are a form of currency, and like any other form of currency are subject to manipulation. It is well to keep this point in mind as we examine how business is conducted in publishing.

In times gone by when money was looser and the book business was booming, consignment merchandising of books worked well enough in its dinosaur fashion. The publishing community shrugged resignedly and concluded that that's the way things have always been done and it would be too much trouble to change them. In the last few years, however, both the economy and the publishing industry have experienced severe downturns from which no robust or permanent recovery is on the immediate horizon. Battered by high costs that have driven book prices to the limits of consumer toleration, assailed by such tough competitors for discretionary dollars as movies and television, video games and arcades, both publishers and bookstores have seen volume sales and profit margins erode year after year. In their increased eagerness to maintain cash flow they have taken greater and greater advantage of the opportunities inherent in the old consignment system to bolster their financial positions.

The source of cash flow for the publishing industry is of course the book consumer. But whereas a few years ago the consumer thought little of spending $10.00 for a hardcover book or scooping up two or three $1.75 paperbacks at the airport newsstand, today with prices drifting toward $20.00 for routine hardcovers and $5.00 for routine paperbacks the consumer has become cautious, selective, and resistant, and he or she spends money only on blockbuster best-sellers, familiar big-name authors, or highly promoted titles. With cash receipts diminishing, bookstores frantically seek ways to generate capital and hold what capital they generate. Many prolong settlements with distributors and publishers and, as we shall see, use the currency of returns to buy new merchandise. Publishers in turn stretch out settlements with authors or with other publishers (as in the case of paperback reprinters who owe money to hardcover publishers), and they often yield to the temptation to manipulate returns to generate funds. At every step of the way from book buyer to book creator, cash is held as long as possible to earn interest or simply to settle the most urgent obligations.

There is nothing new about businesses holding money as long as they can in hard times. What does seem to be of recent vintage, however, is the use of the old consignment system as the principal source of cash. To put it simply, the returnability and refundability of books has become the chief means for publishers and booksellers to raise, keep, and earn interest on money. This is possible because returns have risen steadily over the last few years and are now at all-time highs. Let's look at some tricks of the consignment trade and see exactly how it has become corrupted.

As I have demonstrated in the past, publishers are the prime beneficiaries of a system that requires unsold books to be returned for full credit. Because they presumably cannot predict what percentage of their books will be sold and what percentage returned, they establish a reserve fund when they collect money from booksellers; this fund is supposedly used to pay the booksellers for returned copies. Although the reserve is supposed, by virtue of the publisher's contract with the author, to be "reasonable," and the publisher usually has a good idea of what percentage of returns can be expected on any particular book or genre of books, publishers invariably hold far in excess of that reasonable figure. Not only do they hold too much money, they hold it far longer than they ought to, for although a book's sales picture usually emerges sharply after one year (indeed, the actual shelf life of most trade books and paperbacks can be measured in weeks), many publishers hold their reserves for years, releasing royalties at an unjustifiably slow rate. They often are able to accomplish such manipulations undetected because, with few exceptions, publishers' royalty statements do not stipulate the number of copies printed, distributed, or held as a reserve against returns, making it impossible for the recipient of statements to understand let alone argue with them. ("If royalty statements were manuscripts," one editor confided to me, "I'd reject them.")

Unfortunately, many authors and agents don't understand publishing accounting practices and therefore don't even know what questions to ask; those who do are often fearful of reprisal. Hardcover publishers tend to be lax in demanding accountings from paperback publishers out of fear that the tables will be turned on them—many hardcover publishers now are tied corporately to paperback publishers. So many hardcover publishers aggravate the hostility of authors and agents by never including in their own royalty statements copies of statements they receive from paperback reprinters, book clubs, or other sources of subsidiary revenue such as foreign publishers.

Although it is hard to sympathize with publishers, they happen to be victims of creative bookkeeping as well as perpetrators. Bookstores suffering cash flow problems, for instance, have been known to manipulate the ordering, holding, and returning of books in such a way as to maximize their own cash position. Finding itself short of cash to buy a forthcoming blockbuster, for example, a bookstore might ship back to publishers unopened boxes of books the store considers marginal; or it might decide that now is the time to return some backlist books that haven't moved fast enough. Returns being a form of currency, the publishers must take these books back and give the stores the credit they need to buy that hot new bestseller. These practices only intensify the scramble for best-sellers and the concomitant drop of interest in new, experimental, and other less-than-commercial literature—what publishers derogatorily call midlist books—that have characterized book merchandising in the last twenty years.

Then there is the problem of overordering. Stores and chains frequently order unrealistically large numbers of copies of books they believe to be big hits—a practice encouraged of course by the publishers' salespeople. If a book *is* a big hit, the store has the stock to fill the demand. If not, the store can return the books for credit. Although publishers do try to make it as hard as possible for stores to do so, it's still very little skin off the bookseller's nose to overorder in this no-lose situation. But for a publisher to print a large number of copies on the strength of heavy orders, then to suffer huge losses when the stores return their overstock in massive quantities, is both outrageously unprofitable and tragically wasteful.

Needless to say, the tensions, resentments, and suspicions created by these practices and subterfuges are terribly destructive to harmony among authors, publishers, and booksellers at a time when the spirit of cooperation has never been more desperately needed. Isn't it clear that the source of these antagonisms, the acid rain that is poisoning the delicate ecology of the publishing environment, is the system by which books may be returned for credit? Isn't it clear even from this general survey of the problems that the entire system is hopelessly antiquated and urgently in need of reform?

Over the last few years publishers have talked about merchandising books on a nonreturnable basis, and a few have done something about it. Some of the bolder experiments, such as one attempted by Harcourt Brace Jovanovich, failed, though the latter was by no means a debacle. Generally speaking, the efforts failed for lack of cooperation among all the sectors of the publishing community. Specifically, they failed, first, because bookstores do not particularly like getting stuck with unsalable merchandise, and, second, because the discounts offered by publishers to induce booksellers to buy on a nonreturnable basis weren't high enough. If, however, publishers could raise their discounts substantially, perhaps the stores would feel less resistant to accepting merchandise now considered marginal, such as first novels, midlist books, experimental fiction, and slower-moving backlist books—literature that is now being frozen out of the marketplace by the blockbuster mentality.

But, how can publishers possibly raise their discounts any higher than they already are without cutting even further into slim profit margins? With printing, paper, editorial and production, postage, and other costs sky-high, there doesn't seem to be anything left to trim. Or has something been overlooked?

As a matter of fact, something has. It happens to be authors' royalties. I believe they should be cut. Perhaps by as much as 50 percent.

Now, as that's the kind of statement that can get an agent strung up by his heels in the public square by a rabble of maddened authors, let me hasten to state the rest of the proposition: Publishers should stop paying royalties on the number of copies sold and start paying them on the number of copies printed. In other words, an author who now earns a 10 or 12 percent royalty on his books would earn 5 or 6 percent under the new arrangement, but instead of waiting for years (maybe forever) for his publishers to release reserved royalties to him, he would collect royalties on the date of printing. On publication date the publisher would simply furnish a copy of the printer's affidavit stating the number of copies printed, and pay the author 5 or 6 percent of the list price based on that number, less whatever sum the publisher advanced to him at the time the contract was signed. If the book did well and the publisher went back to press for a new printing, the publisher would simply send the author another check when the copies came off press. Publishers would then pass the savings along to booksellers in the form of deeper discounts—on the condition that books they buy are not returnable.

Although this plan must sound totally alien to authors and publishers alike, there are precedents for it both past and present. A number of foreign publishers structure deals this way today, and the arrangement has proven satisfactory to all parties. More significant, perhaps, is that until ten or fifteen years ago, a major paperback publisher, Fawcett, offered this kind of deal, and I don't know of a single author who didn't grab it. When negotiating with authors or agents for books in its line of original paperbacks, Fawcett frequently proposed two alternatives to them: The first was a royalty of, say, 6 percent on the first 150,000 copies sold and 8 percent thereafter, to be calculated on the traditional basis of copies *sold*; the other, a lower royalty of 4 and 6 percent, was calculated on the number of copies *printed*. The authors who chose the latter were usually satisfied with it on all counts: Payments were prompt and dependable, the bookkeeping was elementary, and, because proof of the number of copies printed was furnished with royalty checks, any suspicion that the publishers were cheating was completely allayed.

Eventually Fawcett discontinued this arrangement. One reason, I suspect, is that authors and agents got greedy and decided that since 6 and 8 percent is more than 4 and 6 percent, they would eschew the printing-based royalty in favor of the sales-based royalty. At that time, when return rates were much lower than they are today, that must have made sense. But as return rates soared to the 50 and 60 percent levels at which they are today, authors and agents realized they were no better off than they had been under the old setup, and in fact they were worse off because rising return rates enabled publishers to justify holding enormous reserve royalties as a hedge against returns. One reason Fawcett may have been all too agreeable to doing away with printing-based royalty accounting is that they, like all other publishers, recognized how much money was to be made on the "float," as bankers call it—the time it takes

- Wasteful overordering or overshipping would be reduced.
- All expenses connected with returning books would be eliminated.
- Unsold hardcover books would be more easily remaindered; instead of being returned to publishers and in turn sold back to remainder jobbers, these books would remain in the stores and be placed on sale.
- Hostility between booksellers and publishers would be reduced.

And from the consumer's viewpoint:

- More books would be available at discounted prices, and more at remainder prices as well.
- Good backlist books would remain in stores, available to readers, for longer periods, helping to reverse the blockbuster mentality that now tends to sweep everything out of stores except current best-sellers.
- Availability of heavily marked-down books (books that are now returned or stripped of their covers and pulped) would give lower-income consumers access to them, helping to raise literacy levels.

When I first conceived this plan I issued a challenge to all publishers to try this experiment, and I did get one taker for what was dubbed the Curtis Plan. Tor Books made a deal with me for *Artifact*, a novel by Gregory Benford. Unfortunately, the results were inconclusive because the success of my scheme requires it to be adopted by a publisher across the board, and not just for one book. Indeed, it really requires adoption by the industry, a new way of thinking, marketing, distributing.

I'm certainly not going to hold my breath waiting for it to happen. But my challenge is still on the table.

CHAPTER 53

Union Now?

One autumn day, one of my clients phoned, boiling mad at his publisher, so mad that if he'd bitten his editor at that moment she'd have needed rabies shots. He had delivered his contracted manuscript to her two months earlier, precisely on deadline, and she'd accepted it two weeks later. But the company was taking an interminable time to draw his check, and our best efforts to collect it had led us into a quagmire of buckpassing, bureauspeak, and indifference. This had happened to him twice before, not counting the chronically late and undecipherable royalty statements the firm issued semiannually, and, well, he'd had it up to *here*. I was able to calm him down by promising to short-circuit protocol and complain directly to the head of the company. Agents are loath to use up their precious currency of phone calls to heads of companies with dunning calls, but this time I had no choice. I secured the check the following afternoon.

During my client's homicidal diatribe he said he was going to organize his fellow writers with a view to boycotting his publisher and others who delayed payment beyond the limits of reasonable expectation. Later, however, he called me back in a far more subdued tone. He'd just consulted with his lawyer, who'd warned him he could go to jail for organizing a boycott. Was this true? he asked, and if so, what recourse, if any, was open to writers desirous of taking collective action in their dealings with individual publishers or the publishing industry at large?

I've thought a great deal about his questions, and would like to offer some reflections about them here.

Agitation to unionize writers waxes and wanes in intensity like the cycles of some pulsing star. Anger and frustration build and at last boil over. An organization is formed, rage is vented, principles declared, action demanded, radical emotions rallied. Then cooler heads propose reason and moderation. The fires of revolution are banked. Conservatism, common sense, fear, and legal and economic realities take over. The complexion of the organization transforms, and you are left with two dozen writers sitting around bitching over wine and cheese. Disgust and apathy set in. The writers eventually throw down their weapons and return to their hearths. And the cycle begins anew.

The time has come for writers and literary agents to break the cycle. In many ways, things have never been worse for writers, and there is little prospect of their getting better as consolidation tightens publishers' control over authors' fates with each passing year. Before they can take meaningful and effective action, however, they have to understand a few things about human and corporate nature, about writers, about publishers, and about the law.

The first thing we should realize is that we don't need any more organizations. There are plenty as it is. There's the Authors Guild. There's the National Writers Union. There's the American Society of Journalists and Authors. There's the Science Fiction Writers of America, the Western Writers of America, the Horror Writers of America, the Mystery Writers of America, the Romance Writers of America. There's the Council of Writers Organizations, a coalition of yet more groups. There are countless local and regional writers' clubs. There are two literary agents' organizations, the Society of Authors Representatives and the Independent Literary Agents Association. God knows there are more than enough organizations to do whatever the job may be.

Some of the organizations are better organized, more outspoken or aggressive, more effective and influential than others. They have managed to establish minimum prices for their members' work, set standards for working conditions, take harmonious and effective action to protect members' interest. Others have contented themselves with communicating to members current market trends, changes in publishers' editorial staffs, industry news and gossip. Their activism is restricted to predictable grumbles and calls to arms in the letters to the editor columns of their newsletters.

But if the goal of these organizations is to coerce publishers through collective action or the threat of it, they must be judged sadly wanting. One has only to look at the Writers Guild of America, the trade organization of theatrical and television writers, to realize how far the rest of us have to go. The Guild has established rules, standards, guidelines, suggested minimums, and sanctions for just about every aspect of its members' endeavors. Its "Basic Agreement" with producers and studios is a book hundreds of pages long that prescribes regulations for everything its members do short of tying their shoelaces. Definitions run on for pages. Minimum compensations are set forth in exquisite detail. Grievance and arbitration procedures, the proper accord of credit, pension and health care, all come under one heading or another of the WGA Basic Agreement. When the Guild strikes, as it did in 1977, 1981, and again in 1988, the movie and television industries stagger.

The second thing we have to come to grips with is the fact that writers don't really want to be organized. Oh, they do, but they don't. Two important psychological factors tend to undermine their impulse to act collectively. The first of these is individualism. Except for collaborations and special team projects, book writers are individual craftspeople who take pride in their independence and consider it the source of their strength and creativity. The idea of being likened to teamsters or auto workers is thoroughly alien to them; organized militant action and the social discipline required to conduct it take most writers disorientingly far from the comfortable private battlefield where artists struggle with blank paper. The notion of picketing Random House or Doubleday or Simon and Schuster, of blocking UPS trucks from delivering parcels to Dell or Ballantine, of putting the covers on their typewriters in the cause of brotherhood and unity, is ridiculous to most of them.

While this individualism is a source of creative strength, it makes authors completely vulnerable to exploitation by publishers. Understanding full well how dependent authors are on them, publishers use divide-and-conquer tactics to keep them that way, and not even the intercession of powerful literary agents can convince most writers that in any test of wills, publishers would not be the victors. This is true even of some of the biggest of big-name writers, who have a tendency to become conservative and loath to rock the gravy boat. These fears are reinforced by writers' convictions that publishers are well organized. To a degree this is true. The Publishers Association is a powerful trade organization with extensive resources at its disposal. But the idea that it is a despotic monolith capable of blacklisting troublemakers and crushing organized resistance is absurd.

Like so many other trade organizations, the Publishers Association is composed of companies that are in competition with each other. Although its members may talk about many things, there are many more they can't or won't discuss. I haven't attended a Publishers Association meeting, but I'd give long odds that they don't spend a great deal of time talking about which authors are cooperative and which are not. An author would have to be so thoroughly and pervasively awful as to alienate every publisher in the business before he could expect some sort of organized reprisal—and even then, he would not get it. I have represented some pretty thoroughly and pervasively awful people (you know who you are), authors who have made colossal pains of themselves, authors who have ranted and cursed at publishers, insulted and humiliated them, even tried to slug them. Yet if they had commercial talent there was always a publisher out there willing to buck that author's bad reputation and buy his work because he thought he could make a profit on it.

A more genuine and serious threat to organized action by authors is antitrust legislation, a body of law designed to prevent unfair restriction of free and unfettered trade. The boycott, an organized abstention from trade with a company or industry, is obviously the most effect potential weapon writers

and agents have to use against publishers, yet they are specifically enjoined from employing it.

It is undoubtedly this prohibition that has hamstrung most
serious efforts by writer and agent organizations to take meaningful action against publishers. I remember attending the organizational meeting of the Independent Literary Agents
Association some ten years ago. At that meeting an attorney
briefing the founders warned strenuously of publisher reprisals
and suggested that antitrust statutes would surely be invoked.
The tremors of fear that his speech caused were so great that
they unquestionably set the conservative tone that was to dominate the organization's activities for years afterward. And although I have maintained that those fears are excessive, they
are not entirely unrealistic. A few years later, the federal government took action against the Society of Authors Representatives on this very issue of restraint of trade, though not in the
area of collective action against publishers. It seems that one
point of the SAR's code of ethics stated that members were to
charge only a 10 percent commission. The Justice Department
maintained that if member-agents wanted to charge more than
10 percent (as a number of agents do these days), they shouldn't
be restricted from doing so. The SAR was forced to back down
and eliminate the fixed commission from its code.

With all the injustice that exists in the publishing industry,
the government's action against the SAR was one of the more
shameful examples of misguided government zeal in the application of antitrust legislation. But the taste of the whip served
to remind agents that Big Brother was watching them, and it
reinforced the cautious approach they take in dealing with
unfair publishing practices. Today, the prevailing strategy among
most agent and writer organizations, if they have any at all, is
merely to discuss the problems at meetings and leave it to the
individual members to act on what they learn, so that there is
no suggestion of conspiracy. In recent years, representatives of
the agent organizations have sat down with individual publishers to air complaints, and these activities have sometimes yielded
positive results. But such approaches fall far short of the vision
of locked-arms militancy that most of us imagine when we
conjure a vision of collective action.

Are we to believe, then, that a central, powerful writers union is doomed to die stillborn?

It would be tempting to draw that conclusion, were it not for the inspiring example of the Writers Guild of America, which has defied both the powerful motion picture industry and the government to become as powerful a union as any writer dare dream of.

The Guild, with permanent offices both in California and New York, is the exclusive collective bargaining agent for all writers earning, or seriously interested in earning, their living writing for American motion pictures or television. And because a sufficient number of important producers has signed the Guild's Basic Agreement over the years, the Guild's clout is now hefty enough to cripple the movie and television industry whenever a strike is called.

The contrast between the Guild's achievements and those of other writers' organizations is so immense that after you examine the WGA's Basic Agreement you want to cry. The Agreement is a book of more than 350 pages, and from time to time supplements are issued with updated pay scales, rules, and other information. I urge every writer, whether interested in screenwriting or not, to acquire these documents, which are available for a small charge. The addresses are: WGA West, 8955 Beverly Boulevard, Los Angeles, CA 90048; WGA East, 555 West 57th Street, New York, NY 10019. You need not belong to the Guild to buy this material.

At the front of the book you'll find a long list of producer-signatories to the Basic Agreement, all members of the Association of Motion Picture and Television Producers. Although the list is by no means comprehensive, it is large enough so that even writers who are not members of the WGA and producers who are not signatories to the Basic Agreement follow Guild minimums and other guidelines when they make screenplay deals. The Guild's influence thus extends far beyond its membership.

By signing the Agreement, producers recognize the Guild as the exclusive representative of all writers in the motion picture industry for the purpose of collective bargaining. This does not,

of course, mean that Guild members can't have agents as well. Many if not most of them do, and one of the functions of those agents is to secure terms for writer-clients that exceed the Guild's minimums. But for the purpose of *collective* bargaining, the Guild's representation of authors is exclusive.

The first section of the Basic Agreement is devoted to defining terms. To most of us, a writer is a writer and a movie is a movie. But in the movie and television business, a great deal of money, influence, power, and glory ride on explicit definitions. A "story" is different from a "treatment," and the pay scales are accordingly different. A "final draft" is different from a "polish," and again the distinction is reflected in the compensation. "Writers" are differentiated from "professional writers" (the former are *employed by* producers, the latter *license their work to* producers), and there is writing and there is *writing:* You could cut a screenplay, write bridge material in cut scripts, write changes in technical or stage directions, assign lines to other characters occasioned by cast changes, make changes necessitated by unforeseen contingencies such as accidents to performers, and make a lot of other writing alterations on a screenplay—yet not necessarily be entitled to call yourself a "writer" by Guild definitions.

If this matter of definitions does not seem germane to the conditions of other kinds of writers, think of the frequent and often bitter misunderstandings that arise between authors and publishers over such vaguely defined terms as "outline," "portion," "editorial changes," and that perennial favorite, "acceptable in form and content." Defining some of the terms of a publishing contract would be the first step to quantifying its elements and then establishing prices and rules for each one.

Dozens of pages of the Basic Agreement are devoted to minimum compensation scales to writers for employment by producers, and these are set forth with a precision that takes one's breath away. For example (I'm going by the latest available Basic Agreement, 1985), the Guild distinguishes between high-budget theatrical films ($2.5 million budget or higher) and low-budget ones (below $2.5 million), then stipulates the minimums payable for every step of the writing of a screenplay from

story to treatment to first draft to final draft to polish. The current minimum for a high-budget completed screenplay including treatment is $47,865; the minimum for a high-budget two-hour teleplay including story is $21,612. If a producer engaged you to polish a fifteen-minute teleplay for a high-budget program, he'd have to pay you $712; if that teleplay were sixteen minutes long, however, he'd owe you $1,185. If the programs were low-budget, on the other hand, the scales would be $519 and $889 respectively.

Another feature of the WGA's Basic Agreement, and one that will make every free-lance writer drool, is the provision concerning waiting time for decisions and payment. For screenplay work, for instance, producers must pay writers within forty-eight hours of delivery of a completed story, treatment, first draft, or final draft screenplay. Payment is not, repeat *not,* repeat NOT, contingent upon acceptance or approval of the material by the producer. Furthermore, if the producer fails to pay the author on time, he must pay the author interest computed at the rate of 1½ percent per month. Producers are required to file agreements with the Guild and report all compensation, as well as—hold on to your pacemakers—to make a contribution to the members' pension and health plans.

There are many, many other provisions of the WGA Basic Agreement that, taken as a whole, make us wonder whether the rest of us are living in some sort of aboriginal society at the farthest reaches of the civilized world. Perhaps the one that inspires the most envy is the Guild's procedures for handling members' grievances with producers. There is both grievance and arbitration machinery established for resolving claims arising out of the provisions of the Basic Agreement. The disputing parties are first required to try settling their differences through an informal conference between a representative of the producer and one of the Guild. Failing that, the parties go to Grievance. A hearing must be held within thirty days of receipt of notice by the Guild. A committee of six, three chosen by the complainant and three by the respondent, then hears the case and votes on its merits. A majority finding in favor of one party or the other is final and binding. Although that finding cannot

be appealed, the matter can go to arbitration if there is a tie vote of the committee members, or if the parties waive the grievance committee procedures. A mutually acceptable arbitrator is then chosen by the disputants: either a disinterested party acceptable to both, or one from a list of authorized arbitrators furnished by the Guild. Hearings are usually held in Los Angeles or New York. The arbitrator has the power to award damages or order any other reasonable relief he deems appropriate.

This system does not preclude court proceedings, but as you can see, with such a refined system for settling disputes, the number of differences settled short of legal action is substantial. Though the decisions may not always fall in favor of the writer, the emotional and financial savings alone make the grievance and arbitration procedure worth going to jail for.

How has the Writers Guild of America managed to achieve all this in the teeth of the same sort of opposition from business and government that confronts other writer and agent groups today? I have spoken to WGA members, to lawyers, and to movie and television executives, and heard many answers that make the matter seem more complex than it is. But in essence the answer is the same one you'll hear about any other union success story: anger, solidarity, and guts. The WGA prevailed because its founders were tired of being exploited, they held their ranks, and they were not afraid to sacrifice their security to realize their dream.

These qualities can be found among some of our writers' organizations. The staunchest unity exists among the genre-writer organizations, and if and when the Revolution starts, the first bricks will be thrown by genre authors. They are among the most professional practitioners of the writing craft, as I've pointed out; they are the best informed, the best organized, the most aggressive. Genre literature is most easily quantified for contractual purposes. It's hard to set a value on a noncategory book; it will fetch as much or as little as the market will bear. But most category authors can tell you within five hundred dollars what the value of a Harlequin or DAW or Del Rey advance is; the difference between a brief outline and a detailed

synopsis; the length of time to the day that it should take to turn in a sixty-thousand-word book.

The publishing industry, particularly the prosperous paperback branch, depends heavily on reliable delivery of genre material. I would guess that at least half of every paperback publisher's monthly list consists of romances, science fiction, thrillers, male adventures, westerns, horror, occult novels, and the like. Most of these books are contracted for on the basis of outlines, and schedules are established in the expectation that manuscripts will be delivered on time and will not require a lot of editorial work. Covers are printed, commitments made to printers, shipping dates guaranteed to distributors. A hitch of even one month in this smooth-running machinery could prove catastrophic to the paperback industry. Does this not suggest that genre writers have incredible leverage?

Admittedly, as effective as an action aimed at the paperback industry might be, it is too radical to contemplate seriously. And what is more important, many of the same goals can be achieved in a far simpler and more restrained fashion. The tactic is called bad publicity.

While large corporations (such as publishers) must seem impregnable to most individuals (such as authors), the truth is that corporations are, after all, little more than highly structured social organizations employing individuals who are insecure about their jobs. They take their strength from the seemingly monolithic structure of their companies, the awesome power they wield, and their capacity for dispersing responsibility for mistakes. Corporations spend a great deal of effort on publicity to project this image of invincibility on the outside world, and indeed internally as well so that employees may feel protected and safe.

Bad publicity is a glaring light that reveals the vulnerability of the corporate individual. All at once, in the midst of that seamless structure, that effortless process, that relentless power, someone is being asked to take responsibility for something that went wrong. Bad publicity punctures the monolithic image that the company strives to foster and focuses light on the insecurities and inadequacies of its individual employees. And if the problem is of any magnitude, the effects of publicizing it can be dramatic as those implicated hasten to cover their tracks, cover their positions—cover their asses, as the saying is.

Unless the problem is of the dimension of a scandal, it isn't likely that adverse publicity will hurt a publisher's stock value to its investors. For one thing, many publishers no longer have stock on public offer because they are owned by larger companies. You can't buy stock in Simon and Schuster, because it's owned by Gulf and Western; you can't buy stock in Putnam because it's owned by MCA Corporation.

But if bad publicity is seldom serious enough to hurt a company's stock value, it certainly can injure the firm's "stock" with authors and agents. If even a few of them choose a different house because of something they heard or read, the loss of prestige—and perhaps of revenue as well—can be considerable.

Unlike strikes or boycotts or other collective actions by authors, it takes very little time, energy, money, or courage to exert leverage over publishers by means of publicity. For instance, if a publisher habitually renders royalty statements two months late, a writers' organization might choose to publish this fact in its organizational newsletter. Nothing need be stated about members not doing business with that company; it is implicit that members will be more inclined to offer their work to a firm that renders statements on time. Many editors subscribe to those newsletters and are extremely sensitive and responsive to criticism published about their company's practices.

The most effective use of publicity I can think of is for writers' organizations to survey their members about their publishers' business practices, then to publish the results of the survey in their newsletters. "How long after you sign contracts does it take your publisher to pay your advance?" "How long after you deliver a completed manuscript does it take your publisher to give you its editorial response?" "How long after the due date of royalty statements does your publisher actually issue them?" "How long after you request clarification of your royalty statement from your publisher do you get an answer? And is it satisfactory?"

The tabulated results accompanied by a best-and-worst rating would then be issued in the organization newsletter. Although some publishers may pretend to be indifferent to the results, I can almost guarantee that the firms that show up best in such lists would feel pride and those that show up worst would feel embarrassment; both reactions would reflect in their dealings with authors. All other things being equal, who would not prefer to be published by the company that boasts a thirty-day payout rather than by one that averages sixty?

CHAPTER 54

Then and Now

Nearly a decade has passed since I began writing about the publishing industry, and, as middle-aged people are wont to do, I recently browsed through my pile of tearsheets and wondered where the time had gone. Nostalgia is a sweet but essentially useless emotion, so, after dabbing the mist from my eyes, I took a harder look at the body of this work and began to ruminate on the changes that have occurred in the industry since 1981.

Our tradition-bound field evolves very slowly, but with the perspective of time one can see definite trends—some good, some ominous.

The advance of the publishing business toward monolithic consolidation continues inexorably, leaving almost no independent companies of large dimension operating today. The result is the emergence of a system for producing literature that might best be likened to dairy farming, with authors forced into the role of domesticated cattle resignedly allowing themselves to be milked to satisfy the thirst of a mass market. That the product will inevitably become homogenized goes without saying. Most distressing is the extension of these conditions to the book distribution system itself.

From my viewpoint, the most significant change in publishing in the last few years has been the tightening of the control exerted by bookstore chains over the creation of literature. Because purchasing decisions are made by a handful of buyers operating out of the chains' central headquarters, the leveraged influence of these buyers over decisions made by consumers, publishers, and ultimately writers has become immense. And because such decisions are usually reached by the calculation of the lowest common denominator, the selection process annually becomes more and more best-seller oriented. Aided by computerized sales information, the buyers tend to order in significant quantity only books by authors with proven track records, pushing publishers further and further into frontlist, bottom-line, star-author, hit-book thinking, and putting increasing pressure on authors to truncate their apprenticeships, attempt blockbusters every time they sit down at their typewriters, and follow or repeat formulas. As this process evolves, our criteria for evaluating writers have begun to homogenize too, until we are left with only one: Is he or she a winner or a loser?

The winners become richer and the losers poorer. While star authors are now getting million-dollar advances for their books, the starting pay for new authors and for writers working in genre fiction is pretty much what it was ten or fifteen years ago, somewhere between $1,500 and $5,000, and of course if you adjust those figures for inflation you will see that struggling authors are horrendously worse off than they were in the 1960s and '70s.

Although the rise of bookstore chains has improved the efficency with which books are marketed to consumers, authors have not been the beneficiaries of any profits created by that efficiency. For one thing, the returns problem has become colossal, meaning that while more copies of any given book may be getting into the stores, a higher percentage than ever before is being returned, and as we know, no royalty is paid on returned books. Higher return patterns also cause publishers to fix reserves against returns at higher figures, meaning lower and slower royalties.

For another thing, the bookstore chains, with their growing stranglehold over publishers, are demanding and winning higher discounts, and because authors' royalty rates ride on discount schedules, many authors are waking to discover disappointing if not shocking royalty statements even though their books shipped in large quantities. In fact, their royalty statements are disappointing *because* their books shipped in large quantities!

The level of interest in book discounting expressed by most

authors is on a par with their interest in Manichaeism in fourth-century Persia, and although I can't blame them, it must be stated that their apathy is costing them dearly. Hardcover and paperback publishing contracts provide for a gradual or sudden reduction in royalty rate when the discount offered by the publisher to retail store or wholesale distributor exceeds a certain percentage. In some contracts the royalty is reduced by, say, half a point for every point by which the discount is increased. In others, the royalty is cut in half when the discount reaches a high level.

There is nothing inherently wrong with offering high discounts to induce buyers to order large quantities of merchandise. Nor is there anything wrong with tying authors' royalties to the discount rate. After all, the publisher is receiving less money for each unit sold, and it is only fair to ask the author to share in the reduced profit. Both publisher and author are compensated, however, by the high volume of sales. At least, both should be. In practice, however, authors lose out because most publishing contracts call for the same slashes in royalties today that existed ten or twenty years ago, before deep discounting became commonplace. For instance, your paperback royalty may, by contract, go from 8 percent to 4 percent if your publisher sells your book at a discount higher than 50 percent. In the 1970s that discount was not given often; today it is commonly exceeded. Yet, no one has told the authors, and even agents have been slow to realize the significance of the change. Late in 1985, three authors brought suit against Addison-Wesley, claiming that the publisher's interpretation of the discount clause had resulted in the loss of more than $100,000 in royalties. Although the authors were supposed to get a royalty of 15 percent of the list price per copy, the contract called for a drop in royalty to 10 percent of the publisher's net receipts (after discount) for copies sold at half the list price or less. The publisher invoked that adjusted royalty on a large quantity of copies sold. The case was settled, but it pointed up the necessity for authors and agents to recognize, and to build into contracts, the realities of modern book marketing. Many publishers are negotiable when it comes to adjusting the relationship in authors' contracts between discount and royalty. But they're not going to give you more favorable treatment on a silver platter. You'll have to educate yourself about book discounting.

Another disturbing development of the last half decade is the adoption by many publishers of an exceedingly restrictive option clause. Until the late 1970s, the option language in the boilerplate of most publishing contracts was fairly weak, giving the publisher little more than the right to see the author's next work before anybody else, and to negotiate in good faith for it. If publisher and author couldn't reach agreement, the author was free to seek a deal with another publisher.

This loose option made it easy for authors to leave their publishers, but with the stakes getting higher and higher, such freedom of movement becomes an alarming threat to publishers. Their legal counsels therefore started to build more restrictive language into their option clauses, until today the tight option is more the rule than the exception. (Paradoxically, the same language that enables a publisher to keep his sheep in the fold makes it harder for him to acquire sheep trying to leave his neighbor's. He who lives by the option perishes by the option.)

Under the terms of the new option clauses, a publisher is granted a first look at the author's next work, as before, and the right to negotiate with the author. In the event negotiations break down, however, the publisher has the right to match the best offer that the author may secure from other publishers. Now, this is all well and good for the author who seeks only to get the very best price for his book. If, however, he is dissatisfied with his publisher and doesn't want to be published by that firm at any price, he's out of luck.

In my experience, an author's dissatisfaction is seldom restricted to money, and an author who is aggrieved with his publisher will not feel compensated by a raise in pay. The way options are designed today, however, the only legitimate way to escape from your publisher is to get another publisher to make a bid for your book that is so high your original publisher can't match it. One cannot guarantee that will happen. Furthermore, the sophisticated language of some of the new options implies that you are in effect indentured to your publisher forever, as long as he continues matching the highest price you obtain in the marketplace. And, while I doubt that this interpretation would hold up in court, one publisher did recently attempt to invoke this interpretation to keep an author against her will. Only on threat of a lawsuit did the publisher decide, out of the goodness of his heart, to release the unhappy author from her contract.

As I've said before, agents like to boast that there isn't an option they cannot break, but the new phraseology is starting to spoil some perfect records.

Another significant change in contractual language has to do with so-called electronic rights, specifically audio- and video-tape cassettes. The last five years have witnessed explosive growth in consumption of videocassette recorders, Walkman-type tape players, and automobile audiotape cassette players, and the appetite for suitable programming has become ravenous.

Until recently, such rights were either reserved to authors as part of their motion picture and television rights, or if they were granted to publishers the publishers did not exploit them very aggressively because the market was so weak. Now, however, talking books, instructional tapes, and the like have become a source of intense contention between publishers and authors, and many publishers are quietly infiltrating contracts with language reserving those rights to themselves or granting themselves the right of first refusal to acquire those rights in the event that an outside company makes an offer for them to the author.

Not all of the changes manifest in contracts over the last few years have been for the worse. At the time I started writing my column, "Agent's Corner," the only way that authors could secure insurance against the costs and judgments of libel and related lawsuits was to buy it themselves at exceedingly high premiums. Then a few publishers offered to include authors under the umbrella of their company's libel insurance policy, free of charge. Many, but by no means all, publishers followed suit. In a typical contractual provision for libel insurance, the author is responsible for a deductible sum, usually in the tens of thousands of dollars. Thereafter, his expenses and damages if any are absorbed by the publisher—at least as long as the author has not flagrantly abused the warranties in his contract.

Although a libel suit would still be costly to an author because of the high deductible, at least his liability is limited in the case of a catastrophically expensive lawsuit.

This was and still is a generous gesture on the part of publishers. But the soaring costs of libel insurance premiums may force publishers to drop authors from their coverage.

Even more gratifying is some progress toward truth in royalty reporting. Six or seven years ago I asserted that many publishers, particularly paperback, issued deceptive royalty statements disguising the withholding of excessive reserves against returns. I have a sense that the raising of authors' and agents' consciousness has started to yield greater candor among publishers. Growing numbers now reveal in statements the total copies shipped, returned, and reserved against returns, while other publishers have installed provisions in their contracts agreeing to furnish such vital information at the author's request. This is most commendable, and wherever these practices have been instituted, I am told, authors have felt increased trust in their publishers. To the extent that this observer has had anything to do with promoting harmony between authors and publishers, I am more than happy to take the credit. Lord knows, some people were happy to give me the abuse.

One reason for increased candor on the part of publishers is that the returns problem has become chronic and severe, and publishers want authors and agents to understand that the withholding of large reserves is justified by the extremely high return rates prevalent in the industry today. Many publishers believe the returns problem has reached crisis proportions in the last year or two, and book trade publications have reported creative schemes aimed at combating returns. Unfortunately, much of that creativity is at the authors' expense. I am skeptical that many such plans will work without the cooperation of authors and agents: The correlation between the way books are discounted and the way authors are paid points to further exploitation of writers.

I have tried in this book to raise the collective consciousness of writers in the hope of equalizing the lopsided advantage publishers have over them, even over those who have literary agents. I don't believe that anything important will be achieved in this respect until writers enter the realm of collective action. No single author or agent, however powerful, can compel publishers to establish a decent minimum advance and royalty, to pay out money due to authors within a reasonable period of time, to issue comprehensible, timely royalty statements, and to respond positively to reasonable grievances expressed by writers' and agents' organizations. Such improvements in the fundamental rights and conditions of authors will be conceded only under pressure applied by a unified author and agent community. The wherewithal to apply it exists now. No more courage is required than what it takes to raise your hand over your head when the vote is taken.

Surely we can find that much, can't we?